Mastering

APA Style

Mastering

APA Style

Instructor's Resource Guide

Harold Gelfand, Charles J. Walker, &
the American Psychological Association

American Psychological Association • *Washington, DC*

First Printing — Oct. 2001
Second Printing — Dec. 2001
Third Printing — Aug. 2002

Published by
American Psychological Association
750 First Street, NE
Washington, DC 20002-4242
www.apa.org

Copies may be ordered from
APA Order Department
P.O. Box 92984
Washington, DC 20090-2984

Tel: (800) 374-2721, Direct: (202) 336-5510
Fax: (202) 336-5502, TDD/TTY: (202) 336-6123
Online: www.apa.org/books/
Email: order@apa.org

In the United Kingdom, Europe, Africa, and the Middle East, copies may be ordered from
American Psychological Association
3 Henrietta Street
Covent Garden, London
WC2E 8LU England

Typeset in Minion Display Regular and Memphis by EPS Group Inc., Easton, MD
Printer: Goodway Graphics, Springeld, VA
Cover Designer: Naylor Design, Washington, DC
Technical/Production Editor: Catherine Hudson

Library of Congress Cataloging-in-Publication Data
Gelfand, Harold.
    Mastering APA style : student's workbook and training guide / Harold
Gelfand, Charles J. Walker, & the American Psychological Association.
        p. cm.
    ISBN 1-55798-891-9 (acid-free paper)—ISBN 1-55798-890-0 (instructor's
guide)
    1. Psychology—Authorship—Study and teaching.   2. Social sciences—Authorship—
Study and teaching.   3. Psychological literature—Publishing—Study and teaching.
4. Social science literature—Publishing—Study and teaching.   I. Walker, Charles J.,
1947–   II. Title.
    BF76.8 .G452 2001
    808 .06615—dc21
                                                                                    2001053555

Mastering APA Style is the only instructional module prepared under the guidance of the American Psychological Association and designed to conform in every way with the style components set out in the fifth edition of the *Publication Manual of the American Psychological Association*.

Printed in the United States of America

Contents

Foreword

The *Publication Manual of the American Psychological Association* is used not only by psychologists but also by anthropologists, sociologists, nurses, criminologists, and numerous other professionals in scientific and nonscientific fields as a guide to structuring their writing. The style elements described in the *Publication Manual*, which have come to be called "APA style," are used increasingly as a standard format for writing student papers, laboratory reports, and journal articles, among others. It is estimated that hundreds of scholarly journals and magazines in the United States and other countries require authors to use APA style and that professional editors who copyedit those articles edit according to its standards. Scholarly presses and commercial book publishers alike use APA style.

Like all teachers who are dedicated to teaching students to understand and use the knowledge in a particular field, the authors have discovered that many of the tasks they have to perform do not necessarily seem to be related, at least at first glance, to their chosen field of psychology. Teaching students the stylistic conventions set forth in the fifth edition of the *Publication Manual of the American Psychological Association*—how to format a reference, create a table, or use italics—can be an onerous and time-consuming task.

Until now, the only means of learning APA style was to memorize the *Publication Manual* and, by trial and error and with a little help from those who were more experienced in its use, learn to use it. Teachers and others responsible for training people to use APA style have relied on their own ingenuity to develop materials to use in teaching it. The development of such materials was inconsistent and incomplete, and understandably so given their typically lower priority than the tasks required to teach the substantive matter of a course.

Mastering APA Style is the American Psychological Association's answer to the expressed need of both instructors and those who need to learn APA style. Over the years, the authors have developed a system for teaching their psychology students how to write using APA style. *Mastering APA Style* is the result of their efforts and those of the staff of the Communications Office of the APA; it is also a by-product of input from colleagues in psychology (authors, journal editors, teachers), students, and instructors in other fields in which APA style is used.

Developed especially for the American Psychological Association, *Mastering APA Style* is the only official instructional tool of the APA for teaching and learning APA style. The exercises and tests in *Mastering APA Style* have been developed over more than a decade and have been tested where it counts—in the classroom. The authors and staff in the APA Publications and Communications Office have reviewed and corrected this material time and time again; however, should you note something we have missed, please let us know, and we will make the appropriate corrections in the next printing. We provide a "Request for Comments" form at the end of this manual. Your constructive criticism about the structure of the module and how we explain its use is vital in the process of refining this training tool.

The value of this module has been demonstrated in the classroom. *All* of the students who participated in field tests of the module achieved mastery. They were able to identify and remediate their own deficiencies more effectively than students who did not use the module. In time, the students made an important discovery: that *Mastering APA Style* made it easy for them to learn APA style, good writing skills, and other course requirements effectively and simultaneously. The quality of the students' writing improved with the use of *Mastering APA Style*. By using the feedback from the exercises and tests in the module, instructors were able to identify problems that *all* students were having and to devote a minimal amount of class time to remediate the problem, or they could more easily assign relevant parts of the *Student's Workbook and Training Guide* for review. Most important, because instructors had to spend less time providing line-by-line feedback about style to individual students, they had more time to give productive feedback about the organization and content of students' papers.

I am certain that your students will learn more efficiently and effectively from *Mastering APA Style* and that you, the instructor, at last will be able to enjoy "teaching" APA style.

Gary R. VandenBos, PhD
Executive Director
APA Office of Communications and Publications

A Note to Trainers Not in an Academic Setting

In reviewing the contents of *Mastering APA Style*, trainers who are not teaching in an academic setting will note that this module has been developed for teaching individuals who are inexperienced writers how to use APA style. The exercises in the *Student's Workbook and Training Guide* have been structured to both teach style and provide examples of good writing through individual sentences and larger selections of text. The examples are drawn from psychological literature because that is the field we know best.

Regardless of the setting in which you wish to use the module, its contents and instructional procedures can be used effectively. It may be necessary to modify some of the techniques we recommend. For example, you may wish to use the module to train copy editors to use APA style. Copy editors *must* know APA style thoroughly. It is their function to correct others' use of it and to support the author's efforts to communicate with his or her audience. Both inexperienced and experienced writers depend on the copy editor to identify and fix writers' errors.

In training copy editors, the major differences in using the module are that a different kind of orientation may be necessary and the trainer may want to monitor performance more directly, which is often possible because the training is more individualized and the goal is of higher priority than in the academic setting. For example, orientation should probably include information on why APA style is used on the publication that will be edited, exceptions to and special applications of APA style required in the text that is edited, and similar information. Keeping in mind that copy editors edit the written work of professionals who may not know APA style thoroughly, the mastery that copy editors must have is likely to be even greater than that attained by an accomplished writer. The copy editor must have mastery of all aspects of style. To ensure that the trainee learns as effectively and accurately as possible, the trainer will probably want to review all exercises and practice tests and to administer and score at least two forms of mastery tests. The trainer may also wish to develop additional tests and to review the trainee's copyediting of actual manuscripts over a period of weeks or months. Further guidance on APA style can be found at www.apastyle.org.

What's new in APA Style?
Visit the APA *Publication Manual*
Web site:
www.apastyle.org

Acknowledgments

Mastering APA Style has followed its own developmental path. From its inception about 4 years before the publication of the third edition of the *Publication Manual of the American Psychological Association*, our project has grown, matured, and become more complex. Over the years, many people contributed in small and large ways to the development of the current form of *Mastering APA Style*.

It was Charles Walker who first recognized the need for materials that would help students learn APA style and began by developing mastery test materials suited to the task. After Harold Gelfand used the materials for a lab course, the two of us agreed to improve and refine the materials and pursue some outlet for sharing them with our colleagues.

Gary R. VandenBos, the Executive Director of the APA Office of Communications and Publications, contacted us after hearing a presentation on the topic at an APA convention. His support was a major factor in bringing this product to fruition. Regular liaison on the project was the responsibility of Brenda K. Bryant. Without her prodding, encouragement, and overall stewardship, the package would have been fixated at early adolescence and might not even have been allowed to see the light of day. It was through her stimulation that the package took on a new identity, shifting from a collection of testing materials to a full workbook with exercises. It was also in this phase of development that the concept of "student as editor" was developed. Although those ideas were incorporated into the package by Harold, it was Brenda who provided structure for the project, kept us focused on deadlines, and served as our editor to keep our audience in mind at each stage of our writing.

In the final days of the original project, staff at APA again played a crucial role in moving the project toward adulthood and independence. We are especially grateful for the work of Julia Frank-McNeil, Director of APA Books Magination Press, and Deanna D'Errico. Deanna rewrote the student workbook instructions and revised the instructor handbook instructions. Julia tactfully managed the conflicts that tend to appear when people experience the stress of deadlines. Donna Stewart, past Manager of APA Books, and Christine P. Landry, Technical/Production Editor, also must be applauded for performing an exhaustive and exhausting technical edit of the final and earlier drafts of a huge body of material. Their task was complicated by the near obsession displayed by all of us involved with the project for strict adherence to APA style. It would hardly do to have errors in APA style sprinkled throughout, except where designated as part of the student's task (and it was ever so tempting to correct those) in materials that are designed to teach APA style! Donna and Chris worked efficiently and effectively in giving our materials a physical form while catering to our idiosyncratic preferences and styles. In this latest revision, Kathryn Hyde Loomis and Christina Davis updated the information to conform to the fifth edition of the *Publication Manual*.

In addition to the people at APA, numerous people closer to home were also instrumental in enabling our project to come of age. We are particularly grateful to the teaching assistants who helped Chuck instruct students in APA style between 1979 and 1983. April Clements, Thomas Brinthaupt, Linda Schummer, and Deborah Hansen submitted drafts of test questions and diplomatically managed student feedback when the testing materials were in a younger and rougher form. Since then, new materials have been added, tested, and refined.

During the middle age of the project, many other people assisted our efforts in significant ways. John Watson, Vice President for Academic Affairs at St. Bonaventure University, allocated funds to support the project. Kim Murray helped us tame computers, Catherine Panzarella wrote some new test items, Ed Stevens processed extraordinarily large files of computer materials and assembled them in a much more manageable form, and Elaine Gelfand and Patsy O'Brien did the same with the files containing exercises or other materials. Field testing was extremely useful. We are indebted to the experimental social psychology students of 1987 and 1989 for their insightful and honest feedback and to all our students for making clear what their needs were and for inspiring us to take on this project as a way of satisfying those needs.

Successful development requires a supportive home environment, for the authors if not the project materials. It goes without saying that projects such as this one take their toll on family life.

Chuck is thankful for the support of his spouse, Etta, and the understanding of his children, Courtney and Lindsay, without whom he could not have worked the long, odd hours he did to bring this project to completion. Chuck also thanks Harold for work he did above and beyond what one would expect of a coauthor. Beyond any particular contributions to the project, Harold earns Chuck's highest gratitude for his heroic work while preparing for and recovering from triple bypass surgery. Despite the obvious distractions major heart surgery would cause most people, Harold somehow continued to work on the project.

Harold takes full responsibility for all of the lifestyle factors that led up to the need for that surgery, and he is grateful for the support of friends and colleagues who helped him through surgery. Harold reserves final thanks for his spouse, Janice, and daughters, Cheryl and Elaine, who not only tolerated and adjusted to (as usual) the temporal and cognitive demands of the project, but who provided the environment that enabled Harold to approach surgery and flourish thereafter. Most important, they contributed substantively to the project with ideas and examples for some of the exercises, through service as Harold's small but high-quality sample for field testing new material, and when his own resources failed, through service as Harold's personal editors.

Harold Gelfand
Charles J. Walker

CHAPTER 1

The Purpose of *Mastering APA Style*

1

What Is APA Style?

Learning effective means of communicating ideas and information is a prerequisite to being able to share ideas with and learn from others. As professionals who are responsible for teaching students, we are partly responsible for teaching these communicative skills, as well as teaching the facts and processes of our fields of expertise. One of the ways we do this is to have our students submit written assignments as part of the requirements for successfully completing a course.

To adequately prepare these writing assignments, students have to develop a writing style. For most students, it is easier to adopt a style developed and perfected by others than to develop their own.

Style encompasses uniform standards and formats for capitalization, punctuation, spelling, word division, use of terms, and so forth. The elements that compose a style of treatment in a language can vary from one language to another and even from one group to another using the same language. For example, the style used for writing an analysis of English novels takes one form, whereas the style used to report on a chemistry project takes another. Commonalities are established in a particular style of writing because the function of style is to facilitate communication by providing a common ground for understanding among members of a particular scientific or professional community.

If students want to advance professionally in subsequent courses, graduate work, and a career, they must adopt the language of their professional community. Because our community is psychology, we start our students on the path to professionalism by requiring that their writing use the style acceptable to psychologists, namely APA style.

The formalization of APA style began in 1928, when a group of editors and business managers of anthropological and psychological journals met to discuss the form of journal manuscripts and how to write instructions for their preparation. Over the years, the components of style accepted by psychologists and other behavioral scientists were refined, and several articles about style were published in the *Psychological Bulletin*. Finally, in 1952, a 60-page supplement to the *Bulletin* was published. That supplement was the first publication to carry the title *Publication Manual of the American Psychological Association* and marked the beginning of recognized APA style.

The *Publication Manual* is a compendium of the guidelines known as APA style. The *Publication Manual* is a reference book; it was neither designed nor intended to be a textbook or how-to manual. As with any reference work, there is an art to using the *Publication Manual*. Dictionaries, for example, offer much more than the definition and pronunciation of words. There is a wealth of information in a dictionary, including information on the origin of words, nuances of meaning, word division, where major cities are located, and so forth. However, one needs to be familiar with the dictionary and to practice using it to be aware of all of the kinds of information it offers and to use it expediently. Books and articles on how to use various reference materials abound, but until 1990 none existed that dealt exclusively with using the *Publication Manual*. We wrote *Mastering APA Style* to fill that void, and it has been updated to reflect changes made in the fifth edition.

The Challenges Faced by Those Who Teach APA Style

Teaching—and learning—should be rewarding experiences for both instructors and students. Ideally, courses should generate in students some enthusiasm that sparks their own excitement about the field of study and should lead students to be actively involved in the scientific process, even if only a few of those students go on to become professionals in that field. Unfortunately, the requirement that students know and apply APA style to complete their writing assignments can hamper the educational process. Much time may be spent correcting papers and giving feedback about technical matters of form and style, time that could otherwise be devoted to the paper's substance and the conceptual and methodological issues relevant to the course. The benefits of using APA style are probably not immediately apparent to students; your insistence that they use it may cause them to feel that you place more emphasis on form than on content, a feeling you may share.

Let's be honest: The motivation for requiring students to use APA style in preparing the papers they submit is also somewhat selfish. Future uses aside, as instructors, we want our students to use APA style now, in our courses, so that we and our students can reap the very benefits that APA style is intended to provide: to improve our comprehension and evaluation of their work and enhance the learning value of the feedback we give them.

When students do attain mastery of APA style, the rewards are apparent to us and to them. The difficulty, and the challenge, is getting them to that point, and we understand why it is so difficult. Up to the time most students enter fields of study that require the use of APA style, they have been required to write using stylistic conventions that probably differ from those used in APA style (or, in many cases, their instructors were lax in requiring adherence to any stylistic convention). When they enter a course in which APA style is required, not only are they required to learn and use a style that is new and different, but they must use one that has been developed on the basis of a more scientific and precise approach to writing, a form that is typically foreign to them. Thus, the requirement that written assignments be prepared in and conform to APA style poses a challenging learning task, in addition to the other challenges that the course already offers.

The responsibility for teaching APA style has never been clearly defined, but traditionally it has fallen on the instructor of the first laboratory or research methods course. One approach that instructors have taken has been to give the students the entire responsibility for learning APA style. Students are instructed to buy a copy of the *Publication Manual* and to use it to write their papers. The result, as you might expect, is seldom satisfactory. Students struggle with learning the conventions by their own means, they interpret and apply the guidelines in different ways, and they turn in papers that are riddled with mechanical errors and inconsistencies. Often they have spent so much time worrying about the mechanical details that they have had little time to evaluate and refine the content. Instructors have then been faced with the time-consuming task of providing corrective feedback; both you and students are likely to resent having to spend time on stylistic issues at the expense of subject matter.

Many instructors assume some or all of the responsibility for teaching APA style and have used a variety of techniques to do so in effective and efficient ways. Some instructors supply students with written models (e.g., sample articles or papers that use APA style correctly). Some instructors actually guide students through the *Publication Manual* and point out those sections that have particular relevance for them, or they give students lists of other resources that will help them learn APA style. Some instructors spend much time giving written feedback on papers, perhaps by correcting stylistic errors or by citing the section of the *Publication Manual* to which the errors pertain. The fact is, however, that regardless of how involved you become in teaching APA style, the process is time consuming, disruptive to the teaching of substantive content, fraught with frustration for both instructor and students, and too often only marginally successful.

The challenges that you face when you take on the task of teaching APA style may be summarized as follows:

- Students will have different levels of expertise in using various writing styles: Some will be familiar with another style, whereas others will have no experience using any style guide. Thus, you may have to tailor your curriculum to address students' different skill levels.
- Students who come to their first course to focus on the subject matter of their chosen course of study may be overwhelmed by also having to learn a set of style rules. You are faced with the difficulty of successfully integrating the teaching of APA style with the course content.
- Regardless of how much responsibility you assume for teaching APA style, much of your time will be devoted to matters of style, time that could be spent on course content.
- Because there has been no systematic method for teaching APA style, instructors and students have had to reinvent the wheel, that is, develop their own means. There also has been no tool to enable mastery of APA style.

How *Mastering APA Style* Can Help You, the Instructor

Mastering APA Style offers a systematic way of teaching and learning APA style so that neither you nor your students are unduly burdened by the task. The process of mastering APA style is outlined in Table 1. *Mastering APA Style* is intended to minimize the amount of time spent by students who are learning and instructors who are teaching APA style. Broadly defined, the goals of the module are as follows:
- to serve the teaching needs of instructors in any field who give any of a variety of writing assignments to their students
- to serve the needs of instructors who have different amounts of time and skill available to devote to teaching the use of APA style
- to provide an organized, systematic, and effective way for students to learn and achieve mastery and instructors to teach.

Mastering APA Style is a training module that consists of two companion volumes: The *Instructor's Resource Guide* and the *Student's Workbook and Training Guide*. Although the fundamental goal of the module is identical for instructors and students—achieving mastery of APA style—the focus of the two volumes is different. Each volume was written specifically to address the needs of its audience.

The Student's Workbook and Training Guide

In the introduction to the *Student's Workbook and Training Guide* we explain what style is in general and what APA style is in particular. We thoroughly describe the rationale for using APA style, focusing on what is in it for the student. This material is essential reading: It provides the impetus for learning by showing students how APA style will benefit them personally. We then describe the teaching materials contained in the workbook and provide clear instructions for how to use the materials. If the workbook is effective and if students use it as they are instructed, the amount of time spent teaching APA style should be greatly reduced.

The contents of the *Student's Workbook and Training Guide* are almost entirely different from those of the *Instructor's Resource Guide*. For example, only the workbook contains the familiarization tests and the practice tests, the exercises, and detailed instructions for taking tests and completing exercises. Thus, you must read both books thoroughly.

The *Student's Workbook and Training Guide* is divided into two sections: the term paper unit and the research report unit. Students are instructed to always begin with the term paper unit, taking the familiarization test to assess their basic knowledge of APA style. On the basis of their scores, students can determine the areas (e.g., punctuation, grammar, numbers) in which they need the most practice. Students then move on to the learning exercises, which cover various style points. The right-hand page contains "draft" exercises that may or may not need correcting; the particular style point being targeted is shaded. The left-hand page shows the corrected version. Students can write answers directly

Table 1

The Process of Mastering APA Style

Step and learning activity	Function
Prewriting phase	
1. Familiarization tests	Assess baseline knowledge Define learning tasks
2. Learning exercises	Teach basic skills Reinforce application skills
3. Integrative exercises	Teach self-editor skills Reinforce basic skills
4. Practice tests	Diagnose learning weaknesses Forecast mastery test performance
5. Mastery tests	Assess knowledge and application skills Provide formative feedback for additional learning
6. Review exercises	Provide a remedial learning activity Rehearse integrative processes
Writing phase	
7. Structured paper writing	Instructor feedback assists further learning of style and technical composition
8. Free paper writing	Instructor feedback helps perfect logic and technical composition

in the workbook. At the end of each set of exercises on a specific topic, there are integrative exercises. These exercises, which consist of a paragraph or page of text that students are instructed to edit, incorporate the style points that students should have learned while doing the learning exercises.

After completing the integrative exercises, students take a practice test to determine whether they need more help learning style points or are ready to take a mastery test. If they require more help, students can do the review exercises. Students move on to the research report unit and complete it in the same manner they completed the term paper unit.

The Instructor's Resource Guide

In the Foreword of this manual, we explain how *Mastering APA Style* was developed. Chapter 2 offers advice and instructions for using the training module in your courses. How to integrate teaching APA style with course content, how to motivate students, and how to administer mastery tests and give feedback are described, and other resources and materials that you can use are suggested. The mastery tests, answer sheets/feedback reports, and answer keys are in chapter 3. The master test files (a complete list of all questions contained in all of the tests) can be found in chapter 4. At the end of the *Instructors' Resource Guide*, you will find a "Request for Comments." Your experiences as you use the module may show ways in which it can be improved. We value your comments and suggestions, both positive and negative, and will consider them for any future editions of *Mastering APA Style.*

What's new in APA Style?
Visit the APA *Publication Manual*
Web site:
www.apastyle.org

CHAPTER 2

How to Teach APA Style

2

Instructor's Preparation

Deciding How You Will Use the Training Module

The first decision that you must make is how actively you will teach APA style using this training module. To make this decision, you will need to assess the time and skill that you have available and also to consider the needs and skills that each new group of students brings to the learning task. The *Student's Workbook and Training Guide* is designed for self-instruction and contains an extensive description of each part of the package, except that it does not contain the mastery tests that are in the *Instructor's Resource Guide;* therefore, it is possible to assign *Mastering APA Style* as independent study. However, the more support you can offer to students and the more involved you become in this learning task, the more likely students are to be motivated to achieve the goals of the module. Their level of commitment to the task will mirror your own; therefore, whatever your level of involvement, it is important to convey to students your own belief that learning APA style is valuable.

Your involvement can take many different forms and occur on many different levels. The range of possibilities may be illustrated as follows:

- *Free independent study.* Assign the *Student's Workbook and Training Guide* as independent study. That is, have students take the familiarization tests, do exercises, and take the practice tests outside of class, at their own pace. You may spend a small amount of class time on strategic issues, such as giving an overview of the workbook; setting goals and standards; and, most important, administering mastery tests. We have found that free independent study works well with graduate students or advanced undergraduates.

- *Guided independent study.* Have students work independently, but assign deadlines for completing units. In this manner, you can help ensure that students will adequately prepare themselves before their writing assignments are due. You might schedule class times at regular intervals for discussing goals or particular style points, how to use the workbook, and so forth. You might think of other ways to support students without actually having to devote class time to it (e.g., have students pair up with a classmate whom they can meet with regularly for study sessions).

- *Fully integrated learning.* Integrate the training module into the course. For example, include goals, assignments, and test dates for learning APA style in the course syllabus alongside deadlines for course content. Designate class dates on which particular APA style issues will be discussed or on which only APA style will be discussed. Coordinate APA style assignments with other course assignments so that achievements complement each other. For example, set goals for completing the term paper unit before the first term paper is due. We have found this approach to work the best with the majority of students.

Even if you expect students to work independently, it will be useful for you to provide them with adequate background on both APA style and the module to enable them to use the workbook effectively. Probably the easiest way to accomplish this is to devote class time at the beginning of the course to presenting an overview or introduction. To prepare such an overview you will need to acquaint yourself and your students with the module.

To begin, you should read the table of contents for both volumes and have students read the table of contents for the workbook. The chapter titles and section headings describe clearly and succinctly what the volumes contain. It would also be useful for students to have read chapters 1 and 2 of the workbook and to have looked at the exercises and tests at least briefly before you give your overview.

The importance of this kind of preparation cannot be overemphasized. Your own familiarity with the materials will aid you in integrating APA style instruction into your courses. You will be better able to set goals and deadlines and anticipate potential problems, and you will save yourself a lot of time. Familiarizing students with the materials can be very reassuring for them. They can see even before they begin that the work is broken into manageable units; that feedback will be available to them immediately; that learning will take place preemptively (i.e., before papers are due); and that mastery can be achieved by the end of their course, if not sooner.

What to Tell Your Students During Orientation

The *Student's Workbook and Training Guide* contains a section outlining the benefits of APA style for students ("Why Should You Use APA Style?"). It is important for students to understand and internalize the reasons for learning APA style, beyond the fact that it is a requirement, because by doing so, they motivate themselves to learn. Self-motivation is a more powerful incentive than any you could provide. You can play an important role, however, in motivating students and in creating conditions for them to motivate themselves. An important way of motivating students at the outset is to give them an orientation to APA style and to *Mastering APA Style.* Chapters 1 and 2 of the *Instructor's Resource Guide* and the *Student's Workbook and Training Guide* contain a great deal of information that you can use. (Students may also be interested in knowing how the module was developed, which is explained in the Foreword to this volume.) The following checklist, which highlights some of the points made in these chapters, may assist you in developing your own presentation at the beginning of your course:

• Describe what the *Publication Manual* contains and how it is arranged. Clarify the distinction between a reference book and a how-to book, emphasizing that the *Publication Manual* is the former.

• Give a brief, realistic, and enthusiastic talk about the value of learning APA style, focusing on the benefits that students will derive. (Refer to the section "Why Should You Use APA Style?" in the *Student's Workbook and Training Guide.*)

• Explain how *Mastering APA Style* is designed to help students learn APA style. You might point out, for example, that it teaches by hands-on practice, provides feedback in the workbook, and allows students to pace themselves.

• Emphasize that good writers are usually good at editing their own work. One role of a critical reader or editor is to identify stylistic errors and suggest improvements in a manuscript. Students (and authors) rely on such readers or editors regardless of whether the editor is a course instructor, a mentor, a committee, or a journal editor. To become good writers, students must learn to anticipate the reactions of that editor to significantly reduce the need for the editor to comment on or demand changes in the presentation of the manuscript. Essentially, then, the goal is for students to become their own editors and to learn to think critically while writing.

• Make students aware that there are also other resources available to help them with writing, learning style, and using the workbook (e.g., sample manuscripts, other style guides, and their peers). (Direct them to chapter 9 of the *Publication Manual* for other published resources.)

• Specify your level of involvement in teaching APA style, and define deadlines and goals. Explain that, although the workbook is designed for self-study, it is important to pace the learning so that what is learned can be applied to writing assignments.

• Explain the kinds of feedback and reinforcement available to students, including the built-in feedback provided by test answer keys, APA codes indicating the applicable section of the *Publication*

Manual, and feedback versions of exercises and the kinds of feedback that you or other resources may provide.

- Make a distinction between fundamental style knowledge and secondary style knowledge. Examples of fundamental style rules, which students should be able to apply from memory, are those for punctuation, grammar, and so forth. Some style rules (secondary) are used infrequently and do not have to be memorized, but students are expected to know how to locate them when the need arises.

- Point out that the order in which the workbook materials are used will be different for each student, depending on his or her prior knowledge and skills and current needs.

- Describe how credit or grades are given, if any.

- Explain the concept of mastery and the criteria for demonstrating it.

- If you plan to use mastery tests, explain their use, how they will be graded, and so forth.

- Explain briefly how *Mastering APA Style* was developed (see the Foreword to the *Instructor's Resource Guide*), and invite students to share their experiences and to offer comments and suggestions as they use the workbook.

Setting Goals and Standards of Performance

Mastery as a Prerequisite

We urge you to administer the familiarization tests and the mastery tests yourself to let students know you are serious about the task. Require students to first master the unit on term papers, as reflected in their successful completion of the term paper mastery test, before they are allowed to submit their first written assignment. A similar requirement should be set for mastery of the unit on research reports before the students submit appropriate written assignments using those skills. In both cases, students should be required to demonstrate mastery at least 2 days prior to the due date of the assignment to underscore the expectation that students' mastery will be reflected in their work. To fit that timing, you may have to schedule administrations of the mastery test several times before that 2-day cutoff.

Some students (and instructors) may find this an intimidating requirement; however, we have found that this alternative works (students do meet the deadline!) and is more effective than allowing students to submit a written assignment and then subtracting points on the work for not achieving the mastery criterion. Subtracting points (versus requiring a prior qualifying score on a mastery test) encourages students to turn in work that is generally fraught with errors and that requires a great deal of work (for you as well as for the student) to correct. It is more effective to accept written assignments late, once mastery on the test has been achieved, and then to subtract points on the basis of the degree of lateness of submission. If you accept assignments late, you should set a cutoff date after which no points will be awarded for the assignment.

Standards of Performance

Set a rigorous standard (e.g., 80% on Term Paper Mastery Test 1) for acceptable mastery before the first written assignment can be submitted. To qualify for submitting the next written assignment, require students to achieve a higher level (e.g., 90%) of performance on another term paper mastery test (e.g., Term Paper Mastery Test 2).

Consistent with the focus on mastery, set no limit on how many times or how frequently a student may take the tests, subject to an announced schedule of when the tests may be taken. However, do not give a student the same mastery test repeatedly. These tests are designed to be given in the following order if a student does not achieve criterion: Mastery Test 1, Mastery Test 2, Mastery Test 3, Mastery Test 4, Mastery Test 1, and so on.

Follow the same procedure for research report mastery, setting the criterion initially at 80% and then at 90% for mastery tests before submission of subsequent written assignments using the same style components categorized as being for research reports.

Grades and Awarding Credit

Consistent with the mastery approach and with the view that the students are developing their skills as a means to achieve the goal of effective writing, students' grades in the course should not be based directly on test or exercise performance. Rather, the incentive for mastery of APA style should be that the students must demonstrate mastery to qualify for turning in a written assignment and that their grades on their written assignments will reflect the mastery they achieved.

Because we know that students will generally get the best results if they do the exercises, we have been tempted to provide incentive by having students turn in their exercises and then grading them. However, we have learned that such a practice is counterproductive. The students learn to read the items—at best—and simply copy the correct answers from the feedback to the exercise section of their workbook. One way of providing incentive for working through the exercises is to check that the students are using the workbook—even to award points for it—regardless of the accuracy of their performance.

Administering Tests

Familiarization Tests and Practice Tests

The *Student's Workbook and Training Guide* contains two types of tests (familiarization tests and practice tests) for each of the two units (term paper and research report). The familiarization tests help students to identify the areas of style that they are unfamiliar with and direct them to the sections of the *Publication Manual* that pertain to those style issues. The practice tests help students assess the level of mastery they have obtained after completing the exercises. The feedback that students garner by grading their own tests helps them to decide whether they need more work or are ready to take a mastery test. All of the material relating to these tests is contained only in the *Student's Workbook and Training Guide*.

Although these tests are designed so that students can administer them to themselves (or they can ask another classmate to give them), you may decide to administer these tests yourself or at least to provide class time for students to take the tests as a group. The value of administering these tests yourself is that you can gain a sense of where the class stands as a whole. Making the tests a group activity is also a supportive gesture.

Mastery Tests

The mastery tests are only in the *Instructor's Resource Guide*, and you or your assistants are the only ones who should administer them. The mastery tests have two functions: (a) to assess learning level and (b) to diagnose weaknesses and guide further learning. They are the primary means by which you can evaluate a student's readiness to prepare writing assignments and, in the case of the student who is not ready, they guide and support additional learning. Chapter 3 of this manual contains eight mastery tests: Term Paper Mastery Tests 1–4 and Research Report Mastery Tests 1–4. Although the topics covered overlap extensively and some items appear on more than one test, the individual test items are mostly dissimilar. Thus, memorization of the items on one test will not enable a student to answer the questions on another test. Furthermore, none of the tests cover all of the major style issues; each contains a representative sampling.

To retain the integrity of the mastery tests, you must administer these tests yourself and should never allow students to keep the test questions.

The procedure for administering mastery tests is as follows:

- Briefly describe the purpose of the test.
- Give each student a test and a blank answer sheet/feedback report.
- Inform students that, unlike the procedure for taking the familiarization tests and practice tests, they may not use the *Publication Manual* during the tests.
- Monitor students during the test.
- Collect all tests and answer sheets/feedback reports.

Answer Sheets/Feedback Reports and Answer Keys

Answer keys for the familiarization tests and practice tests are in the *Student's Workbook and Training Guide*; answer keys for the mastery tests are only in the *Instructor's Resource Guide*.

You must grade the mastery tests yourself to maintain the confidentiality of the answers. Feedback is given differently for mastery tests in that students are not told the correct answers. The procedure that you should use is as follows:

- Grade the mastery tests, and give feedback to students as soon as possible after the test.
- Compare the student's answer sheet/feedback report with the appropriate mastery test answer key, and circle the number of the questions that are incorrectly answered.
- Calculate a grade if grades are being assigned, and write it on the student's answer sheet/feedback report; record the grades on student and class record sheets.
- Give students a blank answer sheet/feedback report showing their score (or grade) and the items they answered incorrectly. (APA codes for each question are listed beside each answer blank so students can look up questions they missed.)

> Note: Do not allow students to keep the mastery test questions or their corrected answer sheets/feedback reports (give them feedback on blank ones); also, do not let students see the Instructor's Resource Guide because it contains the mastery tests and the answer keys to them.

Keeping Records and Providing Feedback

You may wish to create two types of record sheets: (a) a student record sheet and (b) a class record sheet. You can use the student record sheet to record each student's performance. It should provide spaces to record the date on which a student took a test, which test was taken, and the student's score. The scores may be recorded by you or by a student assistant, or by students themselves in the case of the familiarization tests and practice tests. On the class record sheet, you can record the date, which test was taken, and the score for each student in the class. Both record sheets are useful to you. The student record sheet will allow you to determine a baseline measure of each student's performance, whereas the class record sheet will reveal the standing of the class as a whole. Furthermore, by keeping a record of which form of a mastery test was taken, you can determine which test to administer next if a student needs to repeat the mastery test several times.

Feedback on performance is extremely useful to students, and the workbook has several forms of feedback built in:

- All of the exercises in the *Student's Workbook and Training Guide* in need of correction appear on right-hand pages; this is called the "draft version." (Note that not all exercises contain errors: Some are correct as is, and it is up to the student to determine that.) The style issue being targeted by a particular question is highlighted by a shaded box. The left-hand pages contain the feedback version of the same questions (i.e., the corrected style issue is shaded or the statement "correct as is" is at the bottom of the exercise).
- Answers to the familiarization tests and practice tests are provided, along with the APA codes that pertain to each question.

• APA codes are cited for each exercise so that students can consult the *Publication Manual* for review or further information.

The exercises also provide feedback and reinforcement that are less obvious. For example, each exercise not only targets a style issue that may need to be learned but also provides a model of how to use APA style correctly. Furthermore, although an exercise may target only one element of style, other points of style are taught incidentally. The exercises also contain much information about psychology; therefore, they may be interesting and informative aside from their purpose of teaching APA style. For example, some of the exercises describe particular research findings.

Once you have gotten students oriented and working through their workbooks, you may choose not to work directly or in class with students except for administering and scoring mastery tests, giving students feedback on the mastery tests, and keeping record sheets for each of them and for the class. However, once students begin to do some actual writing, giving feedback regularly and formally is valuable; by supplying feedback to students on their writing, you not only help them learn the material, you also provide them with a model: that of editor. Eventually students learn to edit their own work. Feedback that you give to the whole class is valuable as well. To be able to supply such feedback, you need to observe the students' progress in using the workbook and monitor performance on the practice tests and mastery tests. In this way you can pinpoint problems being experienced by both individuals and the class as a whole.

It may be appropriate to devote some class time to reviewing a particular style component that is presenting problems in the written papers of most students. As you review and evaluate writing assignments, be sensitive to patterns of incorrect usage and to whether students are trying to apply APA style mechanically, without thinking about the purpose of the style component. You can also encourage the exchange of feedback between students. Perhaps you can arrange to have more skilled writers work with students who are less skilled. The "master" writer can provide some of the critique you would provide and act as a tutor for the "apprentice" student. The experience is useful for the more skilled writer as well; he or she will have to think critically to give useful feedback to a fellow student and fulfill the role of editor.

Using the Master Test Files

All of the test items in the module are drawn from a pool of items. Chapter 4 of the *Instructor's Resource Guide* contains all of the items, divided into two categories—term paper and research report —and listed in the order of the sections of the *Publication Manual*. Each question appears with the section of the *Publication Manual* (APA code) addressed by the question, the number of the question in the group of questions provided for that section of the *Publication Manual*, its correct answer, the designated tests that contain the item, and some room for you to record information about the item's use. The files are provided for those of you who would like to construct additional forms of tests or tests with different mixes of items.

Using Other Resources

The Publication Manual of the American Psychological Association

It is essential that every student have a copy of the most recent edition (fifth edition) of the *Publication Manual*. The *Publication Manual* is the official repository of information about APA format and style, and it contains the standards for written materials in psychology as well as in many other fields. *Mastering APA Style* is designed to teach about using, not to supplant, the *Publication Manual*. The module does not cover all of the rules, standards, and guidelines that are contained in the *Publication Manual*. It focuses on key elements of style and on teaching, by application, how to use the *Publication Manual* as a resource.

Other Style and Writing Guides

The *Publication Manual* is not exhaustive in its coverage of style guidelines. Students need to be aware that there are other writing and style guides to consult on matters for which the *Publication Manual* does not provide guidance. Many institutions use the *Chicago Manual of Style* as their authority, as do the publishing departments of the American Psychological Association regarding matters outside the scope of the *Publication Manual*. Some style guides are written for specific disciplines, such as *A Uniform System of Citation* for the legal profession and *Mathematics Into Type* for people who need to format complicated mathematical text. These kinds of style guides may be consulted when a special need arises.

The *Publication Manual* does devote two chapters to writing style. Again, although the information in these chapters presents fundamentals of good writing that apply to any kind of writing, the information is not exhaustive and focuses only on the more pertinent issues faced by writers of research articles. Should students discover that they need more assistance in writing, it would be useful for them to know that there are many good books on the topic; some of these are listed in chapter 9 of the *Publication Manual*. Students can also consult their reference librarian.

Model Manuscripts and Articles

One of the most effective ways to learn is through observing models. You should assemble a set of examples of written work (published and unpublished), preferably ones that are relevant to the subject being taught, and distribute them to students. Bad examples can be as instructive as good ones, and some of each should be supplied (and clearly designated as a model to emulate or not emulate). There are several kinds of models that would be useful for teaching APA style:

- published articles or chapters
- earlier drafts of published articles or chapters, which students can compare with the final version
- manuscripts written by other students (so students can gain a sense of how they stand among their peers)
- written work that illustrates a successful way of handling a complicated or unusual style matter that APA style does not cover (e.g., atypical references, presentation of case studies).

Supplemental Exercises and Tests

Some of you may want to develop your own exercises to supplement those provided in the workbook. Your experiences with teaching APA style, with using this module, and with using model manuscripts will probably indicate topics or skills that are not adequately covered by the module, that your particular class or a particular student needs more assistance with, or that might be presented in a better way. Your suggestions and your students' suggestions for improving this training module are most welcome. Send them to us, and we will consider them for future revisions (see "Request for Comments" at the end of this manual).

Human Resources

As we have already mentioned, instructors and fellow students can be valuable resources. One of the most important skills a writer can have is that of being able to edit his or her own work. Rare is the person who produces a perfect first draft; the ability to revise and to correct errors comes with experience. Students often lack this experience, and it is often difficult for one to be objective about one's own work. *Mastering APA Style* is written in a way that fosters editorial skills. Students are directed to give themselves feedback, by referring to the feedback version of exercises and to relevant sections of the *Publication Manual*, and to apply that feedback to new situations.

Instructors and fellow students can provide more opportunities for giving, receiving, and applying feedback. The instructor's feedback is important because the student views it as having authority. However, an equally valuable experience is to encourage the exchange of feedback between students. By editing another student's paper, a student gains more experience being an editor, can be more objective about the flaws in a manuscript, and can practice giving constructive criticism, all skills that will be useful to the student when he or she is editing his or her own work.

CHAPTER 3

Testing Materials and Record Sheets

3

TERM PAPER MASTERY TEST 1

1. If a paper you have written is too long, shorten it by stating points clearly, confining discussion to the specific problem under investigation, writing in the active voice, and

    a. deleting or combining tables.
    b. using more figures.
    c. developing new theories.
    d. repeating the major points.
    e. Do none of the above.

2. In an introduction, controversial issues may be discussed when relevant; however, an author must

    a. present both sides of the issue.
    b. develop sound ad hominem arguments.
    c. cite authorities out of context.
    d. disguise his or her bias.
    e. do none of the above.

3. Report your conclusions in

    a. the past tense.
    b. the past perfect tense.
    c. the present tense.
    d. any of the above.

4. Which of the following phrases is an example of economical writing?

    a. absolutely essential
    b. four groups saw
    c. one and the same
    d. the reason is because

5. Identify problems with clarity in the following sentences:

    We read instructions to the students. This was done to reduce experimenter bias.

    a. Both sentences are expressed clearly.
    b. The first sentence is clear, but the second starts with *this*, a vague reference pronoun, and is in the passive voice.
    c. The first sentence uses a first-person pronoun.
    d. Instructions should be read to subjects, not students.
    e. Both sentences are unclear.

6. Edit the following for verb tense:

    After completing the preliminary battery of rating scales, each worker watched one of the six videotapes of a problem-solving session.

    a. leave as is

    b. After completing the preliminary battery of rating scales, each worker would watch one of the six videotapes of a problem-solving session.

    c. After completing the preliminary battery of rating scales, each worker had watched one of the six videotapes of a problem-solving session.

    d. After completing the preliminary battery of rating scales, each worker was watching one of the six videotapes of a problem-solving session.

7. Edit the following for the use of pronouns:

    The students that were assigned to the delay condition were asked to return at the same time in 3 days.

    a. leave as is

    b. The students who were assigned to the delay condition were asked to return at the same time in 3 days.

    c. The students whom were assigned to the delay condition were asked to return at the same time in 3 days.

    d. The students which were assigned to the delay condition were asked to return at the same time in 3 days.

8. Edit the following for the choice and placement of modifiers:

Hopefully, the different types of music will induce different levels of arousal in the listeners.

a. leave as is

b. The different types of music will, hopefully, induce different levels of arousal in the listeners.

c. Hopefully the different types of music will induce different levels of arousal in the listeners.

d. We hope that the different types of music will induce different levels of arousal in the listeners.

9. Edit the following for the use of relative pronouns:

The pictorial feedback, which was interpreted more rapidly than the verbal feedback, was remembered better.

a. leave as is

b. The pictorial feedback which was interpreted more rapidly than the verbal feedback was remembered better.

c. The pictorial feedback, which was interpreted more rapidly than the verbal feedback was remembered better.

d. The pictorial feedback that was interpreted more rapidly than the verbal feedback was remembered better.

10. Edit the following for the use of nonsexist language:

Accumulating evidence suggests that a supervisor will be more effective if he allows his workers to participate in decision making in a meaningful way.

a. leave as is

b. Accumulating evidence suggests that a supervisor will be more effective if he or she allows workers to participate in decision making in a meaningful way.

c. Accumulating evidence suggests that a supervisor who allows workers to participate in decision making in a meaningful way will be more effective.

d. Both b and c are correct.

11. Edit the following for language that shows consideration of the reader:

> The relative frequency of testing for AIDS was assessed in normal and homosexual populations.

    a. leave as is

    b. The relative frequency of testing for AIDS was assessed in sexually normal (heterosexual) and sexually abnormal (homosexual) populations.

    c. The relative frequency of testing for AIDS was assessed in heterosexual as well as in gay and lesbian populations.

    d. The relative frequency of testing for AIDS was assessed in straight and deviant populations.

12. End a complete declarative sentence with a

    a. prepositional clause followed by a question mark.
    b. semicolon.
    c. period.
    d. comma.

13. Edit the following for punctuation:

> The participants were introduced to each of the trainers, but they were not allowed to choose their own trainer.

    a. leave as is

    b. The participants were introduced to each of the trainers but they were not allowed to choose their own trainer.

    c. The participants were introduced to each of the trainers; but they were not allowed to choose their own trainer.

    d. The participants were introduced to each of the trainers. But they were not allowed to choose their own trainer.

14. What punctuation should follow *volunteers* in the example below?

> The participants in the first study were unpaid volunteers those in the second study were paid for their participation.

    a. comma
    b. colon
    c. dash
    d. semicolon

15. Edit the following for punctuation:

Human beings also undergo conditioning procedures that develop taste aversions ... bacteria in the food or an unrelated event such as chemotherapy may cause severe nausea following the ingestion of a novel, distinctively flavored food.

a. leave as is

b. Human beings also undergo conditioning procedures that develop taste aversions: Bacteria in the food or an unrelated event such as chemotherapy may cause severe nausea following the ingestion of a novel, distinctively flavored food.

c. Human beings also undergo conditioning procedures that develop taste aversions: bacteria in the food or an unrelated event such as chemotherapy may cause severe nausea following the ingestion of a novel, distinctively flavored food.

d. Human beings also undergo conditioning procedures that develop taste aversions--Bacteria in the food or an unrelated event such as chemotherapy may cause severe nausea following the ingestion of a novel, distinctively flavored food.

16. Edit the following for punctuation:

The book--that the client selected to read aloud--was given to the client as a reward for completing the task.

a. leave as is

b. The book that the client selected to read aloud was given to the client as a reward for completing the task.

c. The book, that the client selected to read aloud, was given to the client as a reward for completing the task.

d. The book (that the client selected to read aloud) was given to the client as a reward for completing the task.

17. Edit the following for highlighted key terms:

   According to Freud, the *latent dream* is censored by the defense mechanisms and replaced by a less threatening *manifest dream*.

   a. leave as is

   b. According to Freud, the "latent dream" is censored by the defense mechanisms and replaced by a less threatening "manifest dream."

   c. According to Freud, the 'latent dream' is censored by the defense mechanisms and replaced by a less threatening 'manifest dream.'

   d. According to Freud, the LATENT DREAM is censored by the defense mechanisms and replaced by a less threatening MANIFEST DREAM.

18. Edit the following for the punctuation of a reference citation in text:

   Masters and Johnson, 1966, found a similarity in the phases of the sexual response of men and women.

   a. leave as is

   b. Masters and Johnson, in 1966, found a similarity in the phases of the sexual response of men and women.

   c. Masters and Johnson, *1966*, found a similarity in the phases of the sexual response of men and women.

   d. Masters and Johnson (1966) found a similarity in the phases of the sexual response of men and women.

19. Edit the following for punctuation:

Clients on the waiting list who were assigned to the delayed-treatment condition (whose mean age and educational level (see Table 2) did not differ from those assigned to the immediate-treatment condition) were asked to return in 6 weeks.

a. leave as is

b. Clients on the waiting list who were assigned to the delayed-treatment condition [whose mean age and educational level (see Table 2) did not differ from those assigned to the immediate-treatment condition] were asked to return in 6 weeks.

c. Clients on the waiting list who were assigned to the delayed-treatment condition (whose mean age and educational level [see Table 2] did not differ from those assigned to the immediate-treatment condition) were asked to return in 6 weeks.

d. Clients on the waiting list who were assigned to the delayed-treatment condition (whose mean age and educational level, see Table 2, did not differ from those assigned to the immediate-treatment condition) were asked to return in 6 weeks.

20. Of the following examples, which represents correct hyphenation?
   a. randomly-assigned participants
   b. higher-scoring students
   c. self-report technique
   d. all of the above

21. Do not capitalize
   a. names of laws, theories, and hypotheses.
   b. trade and brand names.
   c. references to a specific department within a specific university.
   d. all of the above.
   e. b and c of the above.

22. Select the alternative that corrects the error of abbreviation in the following sentence. (Assume that the abbreviations are being used for the first time in text.)

The TAT was given to all LH women after they watched 30 hours of TV commercials.

a. The Thematic Apperception Test was given

b. to all left-handed women after

c. they watched 30 hr of

d. TV commercials

e. a, b, and c

23. Which Latin abbreviations are used correctly in the following example?

> Not all traditional sex role expectancies (e.g., women may cry, men should not cry) transfer into all organizational cultures, i.e., an organization's social environment. Some organizations punish traditional sex role behavior in women but not in men, for example, military organizations, heavy industries, etc.

   a. e.g.
   b. i.e.
   c. etc.
   d. all of the above
   e. none of the above

24. Edit the following by selecting the correct format:

> *Scenario and settings*. The same action scenario was described in the context of eight different settings, designed to represent the eight physical-social conditions of the experiment.

   a. leave as is

   b. *Scenario and settings*: The same action scenario was described in the context of eight different settings, designed to represent the eight physical-social conditions of the experiment.

   c.   *Scenario and settings*. The same action scenario was described in the context of eight different settings, designed to represent the eight physical-social conditions of the experiment.

   d.   *Scenario and Settings*. The same action scenario was described in the context of eight different settings, designed to represent the eight physical-social conditions of the experiment.

25. Within a paragraph or sentence, identify elements in a series by
   a. arabic numerals in parentheses.
   b. arabic numerals underlined.
   c. lowercase letters in parentheses.
   d. lowercase letters followed by a colon.

26. When citing the source of a direct quotation,
   a. it is not necessary to give source information in text as it will be given in the reference list.
   b. the citation may be enclosed in parentheses and is always placed immediately after the quotation mark.
   c. the citation is enclosed in parentheses after the final period of the quotation if the quoted passage is set off in a block and not put in quotation marks.
   d. b and c are correct.

27. Edit the following for the citation of a reference in text:

Milgram (1963) was interested in the degree to which people would obey an authority. A much higher percentage of the participants in Milgram's (1963) experiment obeyed the authority than was predicted by various groups of judges, including psychiatrists.

a. leave as is

b. Milgram (1963) was interested in the degree to which people would obey an authority. A much higher percentage of the participants in Milgram's experiment obeyed the authority than was predicted by various groups of judges, including psychiatrists.

c. Milgram (1963) was interested in the degree to which people would obey an authority. A much higher percentage of the participants in Milgram's (ibid.) experiment obeyed the authority than was predicted by various groups of judges, including psychiatrists.

d. Milgram (1963) was interested in the degree to which people would obey an authority. A much higher percentage of the participants in Milgram's (see Milgram, 1963) experiment obeyed the authority than was predicted by various groups of judges, including psychiatrists.

28. Edit the following for the citation of a reference in text:

Vroom & Yetton (1973) took a more practical approach to leadership and decision making.

a. leave as is

b. Vroom/Yetton (1973) took a more practical approach to leadership and decision making.

c. Vroom, and Yetton (1973) took a more practical approach to leadership and decision making.

d. Vroom and Yetton (1973) took a more practical approach to leadership and decision making.

29. Order the citations of two or more works within the same parentheses in order of their
    a. appearance in the reference list.
    b. importance.
    c. dates of publication.
    d. None of the above is correct.

30. Edit the following for the citation of a specific part of a source:

Rogers's theory developed out of his experiences as a psychotherapist. He was impressed by the extent to which his clients spoke in terms of the self (Rogers, 1959, pages 200-201).

a. leave as is

b. Rogers's theory developed out of his experiences as a psychotherapist. He was impressed by the extent to which his clients spoke in terms of the self (Rogers, 1959, p. 200-201).

c. Rogers's theory developed out of his experiences as a psychotherapist. He was impressed by the extent to which his clients spoke in terms of the self (Rogers, 1959, pp. 200-201).

d. Rogers's theory developed out of his experiences as a psychotherapist. He was impressed by the extent to which his clients spoke in terms of the self (Rogers, 1959, *200-201*).

31. Cite personal communications
   a. in the text.
   b. in the reference list.
   c. Do not cite personal communications.
   d. Do a and b.

32. Edit the following for ordering the references in a reference list. Choose the sequence of numbers that indicates the correct order of the four references. (*Note:* The numbers are not part of APA style but are used here for brevity.)

   1. Tulving, E., & Pearlstone, Z. (1966). Availability versus accessibility of information in memory for words. *Journal of Verbal Learning and Verbal Behavior, 5,* 381-391.

   2. Tulving, E., & Thomson, D. M. (1973). Encoding specificity and retrieval processes in episodic memory. *Psychological Review, 80,* 352-373.

   3. Craik, F. I. M., & Tulving, E. (1975). Depth of processing and the retention of words in episodic memory. *Journal of Experimental Psychology: General, 104,* 268-294.

   4. Tulving, E. (1983). *Elements of episodic memory.* New York: Oxford University Press.

   a. leave as is (i.e., 1, 2, 3, 4)
   b. 1, 3, 4, 2
   c. 3, 4, 1, 2
   d. 4, 3, 1, 2

33. The general rule to follow in alphabetizing surnames that contain articles and prepositions (e.g., DeVries, von Helmholtz) is to

   a. always treat the prefix as part of the surname.
   b. always treat the prefix as part of the middle name.
   c. treat the prefix as part of the surname if it is commonly used that way or as part of the middle name if it is not customarily used.
   d. None of the above is correct.

34. Edit the following for the application of APA reference style:

   Eagly, A. H., and Carli, L. L. *1981*. "Sex of researchers and sex-typed communications as determinants of sex differences in influenceability: A meta-analysis of social influences studies." *Psychological Bulletin, 90,* 1-20.

   a. leave as is

   b. Eagly, A. H., & Carli, L. L. (1981). Sex of researchers and sex-typed communications as determinants of sex differences in influenceability: A meta-analysis of social influence studies. *Psychological Bulletin, 90,* 1-20.

   c. Eagly, A. H., & Carli, L. L. *1981*. Sex of Researchers and Sex-Typed Communications as Determinants of Sex Differences in Influenceability: A Meta-Analysis of Social Influence Studies. *Psychological Bulletin, 90,* 1-20.

   d. Eagly, A. H., and Carli, L. L. (1981). *Sex of researchers and sex-typed communications as determinants of sex differences in influenceability: A meta-analysis of social influence studies.* Psychological Bulletin, *90,* 1-20.

35. In entries in the reference list

   a. periods are used to separate major elements (e.g., names of authors, dates, titles).
   b. a comma is used to separate the name of a periodical from volume and page number information.
   c. a colon is used in references for books, reports, proceedings, films, and audiotapes to separate the place of publication from the publisher's name.
   d. punctuation may vary in format according to the type of source.
   e. All of the above are correct.

36. Edit the following for line spacing:

Experiment 1

Method

 Participants. The participants were 44 sets of parents who were bringing their firstborn infant children to a well-baby clinic in a university hospital. The ages of the parents ranged from 19 to 38.

a. leave as is

b.
Experiment 1

Method

 Participants. The participants were 44 sets of parents who were bringing their firstborn infant children to a well-baby clinic in a university hospital. The ages of the parents ranged from 19 to 38.

c.
Experiment 1

Method

 Participants. The participants were 44 sets of parents who were bringing their firstborn infant children to a well-baby clinic in a university hospital. The ages of the parents ranged from 19 to 38.

d.
Experiment 1

Method
 Participants. The participants were 44 sets of parents who were bringing their firstborn infant children to a well-baby clinic in a university hospital. The ages of the parents ranged from 19 to 38.

37. Margin size

 a. depends on the style of the typeface.
 b. should always be 1 in. (2.54 cm) at the top, bottom, and sides of the paper.
 c. depends on what section of the paper is being typed.
 d. should be 2 in. (5.08 cm) at the top and bottom and 1/2 in. (1.27 cm) at the left and right sides.

38. Indentation at paragraphs

 a. is not necessary if there is triple-spaced typing between paragraphs.
 b. should be at least 10 spaces.
 c. is not necessary if block-style typing format is used for the entire page.
 d. is required in all but a few instances.

39. Put no space after

   a. the colon in ratios.
   b. periods in the initials of personal names.
   c. periods that separate parts of a reference.
   d. all of the above.
   e. none of the above.

40. Edit the following for typing a reference entry:

   Muñoz, R. F., Glish, M., Soo-Hoo, T., & Robertson, J. (1982). The San Francisco mood survey project: Preliminary work toward the prevention of depression. *American Journal of Community Psychology, 10,* 317-330.

   a. leave as is

   b. Muñoz, R. F., Glish, M., Soo-Hoo, T., & Robertson, J. (1982). The San Francisco mood survey project: Preliminary work toward the prevention of depression. *American Journal of Community Psychology, 10,* 317-330.

   c. Muñoz, R. F., Glish, M., Soo-Hoo, T., & Robertson, J. (1982). The San Francisco mood survey project: Preliminary work toward the prevention of depression. *American Journal of Community Psychology, 10,* 317-330.

   d. Muñoz, R. F., Glish, M., Soo-Hoo, T., & Robertson, J. (1982). The San Francisco mood survey project: Preliminary work toward the prevention of depression. *American Journal of Community Psychology, 10,* 317-330.

TERM PAPER MASTERY TEST 1
ANSWER SHEET AND FEEDBACK REPORT

Student Name _____   Date _____

Question Number	Answer	APA Codes	Question Number	Answer	APA Codes
1	_____	1.03–1.05	21	_____	3.12–3.18
2	_____	1.06–1.08	22	_____	3.20–3.29
3	_____	2.01–2.02	23	_____	3.20–3.29
4	_____	2.03–2.05	24	_____	3.30–3.33
5	_____	2.03–2.05	25	_____	3.30–3.33
6	_____	2.06–2.07	26	_____	3.34–3.41
7	_____	2.08–2.12	27	_____	3.94–3.103
8	_____	2.08–2.12	28	_____	3.94–3.103
9	_____	2.08–2.12	29	_____	3.94–3.103
10	_____	2.13–2.17	30	_____	3.94–3.103
11	_____	2.13–2.17	31	_____	3.94–3.103
12	_____	3.01–3.09	32	_____	4.01–4.04
13	_____	3.01–3.09	33	_____	4.01–4.04
14	_____	3.01–3.09	34	_____	4.01–4.04
15	_____	3.01–3.09	35	_____	4.01–4.04
16	_____	3.01–3.09	36	_____	5.01–5.08
17	_____	3.01–3.09, 3.19	37	_____	5.01–5.08
18	_____	3.01–3.09, 3.95	38	_____	5.01–5.08
19	_____	3.01–3.09	39	_____	5.09–5.13
20	_____	3.10–3.11	40	_____	5.17–5.18

NUMBER CORRECT _____

TERM PAPER MASTERY TEST 1
ANSWER KEY

Question Number	Answer	APA Codes	Question Number	Answer	APA Codes
1	a	1.03–1.05	21	a	3.12–3.18
2	a	1.06–1.08	22	e	3.20–3.29
3	c	2.01–2.02	23	a	3.20–3.29
4	b	2.03–2.05	24	c	3.30–3.33
5	b	2.03–2.05	25	c	3.30–3.33
6	a	2.06–2.07	26	c	3.34–3.41
7	b	2.08–2.12	27	b	3.94–3.103
8	d	2.08–2.12	28	d	3.94–3.103
9	a	2.08–2.12	29	a	3.94–3.103
10	d	2.13–2.17	30	c	3.94–3.103
11	c	2.13–2.17	31	a	3.94–3.103
12	c	3.01–3.09	32	c	4.01–4.04
13	a	3.01–3.09	33	c	4.01–4.04
14	d	3.01–3.09	34	b	4.01–4.04
15	b	3.01–3.09	35	e	4.01–4.04
16	b	3.01–3.09	36	c	5.01–5.08
17	a	3.01–3.09, 3.19	37	b	5.01–5.08
18	d	3.01–3.09, 3.95	38	d	5.01–5.08
19	c	3.01–3.09	39	a	5.09–5.13
20	c	3.10–3.11	40	a	5.17–5.18

TERM PAPER MASTERY TEST 2

1. It is important that headings convey to the reader

    a. a sense of style.
    b. the relative importance of the parts of the paper.
    c. the author's biases.
    d. all of the above.

2. A finished report should possess

    a. no recognizable theme or logical structure.
    b. disconnected but logical subsections.
    c. an orderly presentation of ideas.
    d. inferential statistical tests of the data.

3. You can check your writing for smoothness of expression by

    a. looking for sudden shifts in topic, tense, or person.
    b. having a colleague search the paper for abrupt transitions.
    c. reading the paper aloud.
    d. doing all of the above.
    e. doing a and b.

4. Redundancy, wordiness, jargon, evasiveness, and circumlocution contribute to

    a. poor economy of expression.
    b. clear scientific writing.
    c. smoothness of expression.
    d. erudite precision.
    e. a more readable, less pompous style of writing.

5. The best person to select to critique your manuscript is

    a. your spouse or another person whom you know very well.
    b. a colleague who is very familiar with your work.
    c. a colleague who does not follow your work closely.
    d. a stranger off the street.

6. Edit the following for verb tense:

If the theory of learned helplessness was not considered relevant to human behavior, clinically depressed clients would be treated differently by many therapists.

a. leave as is

b. If the theory of learned helplessness was not considered relevant to human behavior, clinically depressed clients would have been treated differently by many therapists.

c. If the theory of learned helplessness was not considered relevant to human behavior, clinically depressed clients would be being treated differently by many therapists.

d. If the theory of learned helplessness were not considered relevant to human behavior, clinically depressed clients would be treated differently by many therapists.

7. Edit the following for the use of pronouns:

The volunteer whom the confederate selected had to use nonverbal gestures to convey the emotion to the other volunteers.

a. leave as is

b. The volunteer that the confederate selected had to use nonverbal gestures to convey the emotion to the other volunteers.

c. The volunteer who the confederate selected had to use nonverbal gestures to convey the emotion to the other volunteers.

d. The volunteer which the confederate selected had to use nonverbal gestures to convey the emotion to the other volunteers.

8. Misplaced modifiers can be avoided by

a. placing adjectives and adverbs at the end of sentences wherever possible.
b. placing adjectives and adverbs as close as possible to the words that they modify.
c. using the word *only* for clarification.
d. writing in the passive voice.

9. Edit the following for sentence structure:

The results of experiments with animals and humans indicated that continuous reinforcement resulted in faster acquisition but partial reinforcement was more resistant to extinction.

   a. leave as is

   b. The results of experiments with animals and humans indicated that continuous reinforcement resulted in faster acquisition, but partial reinforcement was more resistant to extinction.

   c. The results of experiments with animals and humans indicated that continuous reinforcement resulted in faster acquisition and partial reinforcement was more resistant to extinction.

   d. The results of experiments with animals and humans indicated that continuous reinforcement resulted in faster acquisition but that partial reinforcement was more resistant to extinction.

10. Edit the following for the use of nonsexist language:

A telephone operator must decode numerous messages daily from voices she has never previously heard.

   a. leave as is

   b. A telephone operator must decode numerous messages daily from male or female voices she has never previously heard.

   c. A telephone operator must decode numerous messages daily from voices he has never previously heard.

   d. A telephone operator must decode numerous messages daily from voices the operator has never previously heard.

11. Edit the following for avoiding ethnic bias:

Black and White participants were asked to rate the attractiveness of Black and White models pictured in black-and-white photographs.

   a. leave as is

   b. Black (Negro) and White participants were asked to rate the attractiveness of Black (Negro) and White models pictured in black-and-white photographs.

   c. Negro and Caucasian participants were asked to rate the attractiveness of Negro and Caucasian models pictured in black-and-white photographs.

   d. Black and Caucasian participants were asked to rate the attractiveness of Black and Caucasian models pictured in black-and-white photographs.

12. Edit the following for punctuation:

Blind sleepers also show a cyclical pattern of sleep stages, they do not, however, display eye movements (Schwartz et al., 1978).

   a. leave as is

   b. Blind sleepers also show a cyclical pattern of sleep stages: They do not, however, display eye movements (Schwartz et al., 1978).

   c. Blind sleepers also show a cyclical pattern of sleep stages. They do not, however, display eye movements (Schwartz et al., 1978).

   d. Blind sleepers also show a cyclical pattern of sleep stages--They do not, however, display eye movements (Schwartz et al., 1978).

13. Edit the following for punctuation:

Damage to the left temporal cortex may impair language comprehension; whereas damage to the left frontal cortex may impair language production.

   a. leave as is

   b. Damage to the left temporal cortex may impair language comprehension. Whereas damage to the left frontal cortex may impair language production.

   c. Damage to the left temporal cortex may impair language comprehension, whereas damage to the left frontal cortex may impair language production.

   d. Damage to the left temporal cortex may impair language comprehension-- whereas damage to the left frontal cortex may impair language production.

14. Edit the following for punctuation:

Decay theory attributes forgetting to the passage of time, interference theory attributes it to other activities.

   a. leave as is

   b. Decay theory attributes forgetting to the passage of time: Interference theory attributes it to other activities.

   c. Decay theory attributes forgetting to the passage of time; interference theory attributes it to other activities.

   d. Decay theory attributes forgetting to the passage of time; and interference theory attributes it to other activities.

15. Which of the following examples is correctly punctuated?

   a. They have agreed on the outcome, informed participants perform better than uninformed participants.

   b. They have agreed on the outcome; Informed participants perform better than uninformed participants.

   c. They have agreed on the outcome: Informed participants perform better than uninformed participants.

   d. None of the above is correct.

16. Edit the following for punctuation:

   The stimuli were six songs--matched for length, complexity of melody, and familiarity of lyrics.

   a. leave as is

   b. The stimuli were six songs: matched for length, complexity of melody, and familiarity of lyrics.

   c. The stimuli were six songs ... matched for length, complexity of melody, and familiarity of lyrics.

   d. The stimuli were six songs matched for length, complexity of melody, and familiarity of lyrics.

17. Edit the following for the correct way to identify an ironic, coined, or invented expression:

   In Selfridge's (1959) pandemonium model of pattern recognition, feature detectors are represented by demons in the sensory system who shout to the next level of analysis when their feature is present in the stimulus.

   a. leave as is

   b. In Selfridge's (1959) pandemonium model of pattern recognition, feature detectors are represented by DEMONS in the sensory system who SHOUT to the next level of analysis when their feature is present in the stimulus.

   c. In Selfridge's (1950) pandemonium model of pattern recognition, feature detectors are represented by *demons* in the sensory system who *shout* to the next level of analysis when their feature is present in the stimulus.

   d. In Selfridge's (1959) pandemonium model of pattern recognition, feature detectors are represented by "demons" in the sensory system who "shout" to the next level of analysis when their feature is present in the stimulus.

18. Edit the following for punctuation:

   Scores were higher when participants were tested in the same environment as the one in which they learned (the effect of environmental similarity is reflected in the interaction between study environment and test environment).

   a. leave as is

   b. Scores were higher when participants were tested in the same environment as the one in which they learned. (The effect of environmental similarity is reflected in the interaction between study environment and test environment.)

   c. Scores were higher when participants were tested in the same environment as the one in which they learned. (The effect of environmental similarity is reflected in the interaction between study environment and test environment).

   d. Scores were higher when participants were tested in the same environment as the one in which they learned (The effect of environmental similarity is reflected in the interaction between study environment and test environment.).

19. Edit the following for punctuation:

   One possibility (as Winer, 1971, suggested) is to pool the error terms.

   a. leave as is

   b. One possibility (as Winer (1971) suggested) is to pool the error terms.

   c. One possibility (as Winer [1971] suggested) is to pool the error terms.

   d. One possibility [as Winer (1971) suggested] is to pool the error terms.

   e. One possibility (as Winer [1971], suggested) is to pool the error terms.

20. Which of the following words with a prefix require a hyphen?
   a. compounds in which the base word is an abbreviation (e.g., pre-UCS)
   b. *self* compounds (e.g., self-esteem)
   c. words that could be misunderstood or misread (e.g., un-ionized)
   d. all of the above
   e. none of the above

21. Which of the following examples shows the wrong way to capitalize proper nouns?

   a. All psychology departments are reviewing their instructional effectiveness.

   b. Lennox (1988) also has a theory of self-monitoring.

   c. Dolphins are pro-Skinnerian.

   d. The eustachian tube was inserted.

   e. None of the above is incorrect.

22. Edit the following for the use of abbreviations to describe a procedural sequence:

All the men read about (R), danced with (D), or smelled (S) potential romantic partners. The bachelor group received one of four romantic interest arousal sequences: RDS, SDR, RSD, or SRD.

a. leave as is

b. read about, danced with, smelled; smelled, danced with, read about; read about, smelled, danced with; or smelled, read about, danced with.

c. read, danced, smelled; smelled, danced, read; read, smelled, danced; or smelled, read, danced.

d. read about then danced with then smelled; smelled then danced with then read about; read about then smelled then danced with; or smelled then read about then danced with.

23. Is the Latin abbreviation *i.e.* used incorrectly in the following example?

Some lonely individuals appear to be shy but are in fact isolated because of social rejection (i.e., are actively avoided and excluded by others).

a. The parentheses should be removed.
b. The Latin abbreviation *i.e.* should be *viz*.
c. The abbreviation *i.e.* should be spelled out as *that is*.
d. In the above example, *i.e.* is used correctly.

24. Articles in APA journals use

a. centered uppercase headings only.
b. centered, underlined, uppercase headings only.
c. flush left lowercase headings only.
d. a and c.
e. as many as five levels of headings.

25. When quoting,

a. provide the author's name in the text.
b. provide the year and page citation in the text.
c. include a complete reference in the reference list.
d. do only a and c.
e. do a, b, and c.

26. At the end of a block quote,

a. cite the quoted source in parentheses after the final punctuation mark.
b. cite the quoted source in parentheses before the final punctuation mark.
c. use a footnote with a superscript number and cite the quoted source in the footnote.
d. None of the above is correct.

27. From the examples below, identify the correct forms of citation:
    a. According to Wagner (1988), depressed people reveal inappropriately.
    b. Individual differences in memory have been found (Gelfand, 1987).
    c. In 1988, Scarano and Walker found that androgynous women respond to self-worth dilemmas differently than do stereotypic women.
    d. Lavin (1986) observed that TV serves as a surrogate parent for some young adults. Lavin found that "soap addicts" spend more time watching TV than being with their parents.
    e. All of the above are correct.

28. Edit the following for the citation of a reference in text:
    Briddell, Rimm, Caddy, Krawitz, Scholis, and Wunderlin (1978) showed that some of the inhibition-releasing effects of alcohol are due to expectations aroused by drinking rather than to the chemical effects on bodily functions.

    a. leave as is
    b. Briddell & Rimm & Caddy & Krawitz & Scholis, & Wunderlin (1978) showed that some of the inhibition-releasing effects of alcohol are due to expectations aroused by drinking rather than to the chemical effects on bodily functions.
    c. Briddell et al. (1978) showed that some of the inhibition-releasing effects of alcohol are due to expectations aroused by drinking rather than to the chemical effects on bodily functions.
    d. Briddell, et al. (1978) showed that some of the inhibition-releasing effects of alcohol are due to expectations aroused by drinking rather than to the chemical effects on bodily functions.

29. Edit the following for the citation of references in text:

   A nativist (e.g., J. J. Gibson, 1950; J. J. Gibson, 1966; S. G. Gibson, 1979) would try to identify the invariants in the stimulus situation that accounted for a particular perceptual experience.

   a. leave as is

   b. A nativist (e.g., J. J. Gibson, 1950, J. J. Gibson, 1966; S. G., Gibson, 1979) would try to identify the invariants in the stimulus situation that accounted for a particular perceptual experience.

   c. A nativist (e.g., J. J. Gibson, 1950; 1966; S. G. Gibson, 1979) would try to identify the invariants in the stimulus situation that accounted for a particular perceptual experience.

   d. A nativist (e.g., J. J. Gibson, 1950, 1966; S. G. Gibson, 1979) would try to identify the invariants in the stimulus situation that accounted for a particular perceptual experience.

30. Edit the following for the citation of a quotation in text:

   Although literary style certainly affects readers, "the elegance of presentation is of no importance as a measure of whether the theory will prove an empirically useful tool" (Hall & Linzey, 1957).

   a. leave as is

   b. Although literary style certainly affects readers, "the elegance of presentation is of no importance as a measure of whether the theory will prove an empirically useful tool" (Hall & Linzey, 1957, p. 551).

   c. Although literary style certainly affects readers, "the elegance of presentation is of no importance as a measure of whether the theory will prove an empirically useful tool" (Hall & Linzey, 1957, chap. 14).

   d. Although literary style certainly affects readers, "the elegance of presentation is of no importance as a measure of whether the theory will prove an empirically useful tool" (Hall & Linzey, 1957, pp. 551).

31. A reference list
   a. cites all works supportive of or contradictory to the text.
   b. is a synonym for bibliography.
   c. should include only the references cited anywhere in the article.
   d. should never be used in short articles.

32. Edit the following for ordering the references in a reference list. Choose the sequence of numbers that indicates the correct order of the four references. (*Note:* The numbers are not part of APA style but are used here for brevity.)

  1. Bandura, A. (1973). *Aggression: A social learning analysis.* Englewood Cliffs, NJ: Prentice Hall.

  2. Bandura, A., & Menlove, F. L. (1968). Factors determining vicarious extinction and avoidance behavior through symbolic modeling. *Journal of Personality and Social Psychology, 8,* 99-108.

  3. Bandura, A. (1965). Influence of models' reinforcement contingencies on the acquisition of imitative responses. *Journal of Personality and Social Psychology, 1,* 589-595.

  4. Bandura, A., & Walters, R. H. (1963). *Social learning and personality development.* New York: Holt, Rinehart & Winston.

  a. leave as is (i.e., 1, 2, 3, 4)
  b. 1, 3, 2, 4
  c. 3, 1, 2, 4
  d. 4, 3, 2, 1

33. A reference list entry should have

  a. the author's surname and initials in inverted order (e.g., McMahon, P. M.).
  b. the title of the article, page number, ISBN code, and book title.
  c. the author's surname only.
  d. only b and c.

34. Edit the following for the application of APA reference style:

  Feldman-Summers, S., Gordon, P. E., & Meagher, J. R. (1979). The impact of rape on sexual satisfaction. *Journal of Abnormal Psychology, 88,* 101-105.

  a. leave as is

  b. Feldman-Summers, S., Gordon, P. E., & Meagher, J. R. (1979). "The Impact of Rape on Sexual Satisfaction." *JOURNAL OF ABNORMAL PSYCHOLOGY,* 88, 101-105.

  c. Feldman-Summers, S., Gordon, P. E., & Meagher, J. R. (1979, *88,* 101-105). The impact of rape on sexual satisfaction. *Journal of Abnormal Psychology.*

  d. Feldman-Summers, S., Gordon, P. E., & Meagher, J. R. (1979). "The impact of rape on sexual satisfaction." *Journal of Abnormal Psychology, 88,* 101-105.

35. The paper on which your article is printed should be

    a. onionskin, to save filing space.
    b. erasable bond for ease of correcting.
    c. heavy, nonerasable, white bond for durability.
    d. legal-size paper.

36. Edit the following by selecting the correct spacing arrangement:

    Effects of Academic Stress on Interpersonal Relationships
    of Male and Female Students

    Whatever the academic standards of a college or university, there always seem to be students who do not meet the standards.

    a. leave as is

    b.
    Effects of Academic Stress on Interpersonal Relationships
    of Male and Female Students

    Whatever the academic standards of a college or university, there always seem to be students who do not meet the standards.

    c.
    Effects of Academic Stress on Interpersonal Relationships
    of Male and Female Students

    Whatever the academic standards of a college or university, there always seem to be students who do not meet the standards.

    d.
    Effects of Academic Stress on Interpersonal Relationships
    of Male and Female Students

    Whatever the academic standards of a college or university, there always seem to be students who do not meet the standards.

37. Identify the numbering error in the following example of the first page of text of a manuscript that has a title page and an abstract page:

    Slug Love

    3

    a. The numbering is correct.
    b. The first text page is numbered with a 1.
    c. A number is not put on the first page.
    d. Page numbers are typed flush with the left margin.

38. The typing instruction "type in capital and lowercase letters" means
    a. capitalize only the first letters of important words.
    b. type it twice, once in capitals and once in lowercase letters.
    c. type all of the letters of important words in capital letters.
    d. type the heading in all capital letters and the body of the text in lowercase letters.

39. Edit the following for the spacing of punctuation:

    Some therapists select the method of treatment on a case--by--case basis.

    a. leave as is

    b. Some therapists select the method of treatment on a case by case basis.

    c. Some therapists select the method of treatment on a case-by-case basis.

    d. Some therapists select the method of treatment on a case - by - case basis.

40. Edit the following for the typing of a reference list:

    1. Garcia, J. (1981). The logic and limits of mental aptitude testing. *American Psychologist, 36,* 1172-1180.

    2. Kamin, L. (1974). *The science and politics of I.Q.* Hillsdale, NJ: Erlbaum.

    a. leave as is

    b. Garcia, J. (1981). The logic and limits of mental aptitude testing. *American Psychologist, 36,* 1172-1180.

    Kamin, L. (1974). *The science and politics of I.Q.* Hillsdale, NJ: Erlbaum.

    c. Garcia, J. (1981). The logic and limits of mental aptitude testing. *American Psychologist, 36,* 1172-1180.

    Kamin, L. (1974). *The science and politics of I.Q.* Hillsdale, NJ: Erlbaum.

    d. Garcia, J. (1981). The logic and limits of mental aptitude testing. *American Psychologist, 36,* 1172-1180.

    Kamin, L. (1974). *The science and politics of I.Q.* Hillsdale, NJ: Erlbaum.

TERM PAPER MASTERY TEST 2
ANSWER SHEET AND FEEDBACK REPORT

Student Name _____ Date _____

Question Number	Answer	APA Codes	Question Number	Answer	APA Codes
1	_____	1.03–1.05	21	_____	3.12–3.18
2	_____	2.01–2.02	22	_____	3.20–3.29
3	_____	2.01–2.02	23	_____	3.20–3.29
4	_____	2.03–2.05	24	_____	3.30–3.33
5	_____	2.03–2.05	25	_____	3.34–3.41
6	_____	2.06–2.07	26	_____	3.34–3.41
7	_____	2.08–2.12	27	_____	3.94–3.103
8	_____	2.08–2.12	28	_____	3.94–3.103
9	_____	2.08–2.12	29	_____	3.94–3.103
10	_____	2.13–2.17	30	_____	3.94–3.103
11	_____	2.13–2.17	31	_____	4.01–4.04
12	_____	3.01–3.09	32	_____	4.01–4.04
13	_____	3.01–3.09	33	_____	4.01–4.04
14	_____	3.01–3.09	34	_____	4.01–4.04
15	_____	3.01–3.09	35	_____	5.01–5.08
16	_____	3.01–3.09	36	_____	5.01–5.08
17	_____	3.01–3.09	37	_____	5.01–5.08
18	_____	3.01–3.09	38	_____	5.09–5.13
19	_____	3.01–3.09	39	_____	5.09–5.13
20	_____	3.10–3.11	40	_____	5.18

NUMBER CORRECT _____

TERM PAPER MASTERY TEST 2
ANSWER KEY

Question Number	Answer	APA Codes	Question Number	Answer	APA Codes
1	b	1.03–1.05	21	e	3.12–3.18
2	c	2.01–2.02	22	a	3.20–3.29
3	d	2.01–2.02	23	d	3.20–3.29
4	a	2.03–2.05	24	e	3.30–3.33
5	c	2.03–2.05	25	e	3.34–3.41
6	d	2.06–2.07	26	a	3.34–3.41
7	a	2.08–2.12	27	e	3.94–3.103
8	b	2.08–2.12	28	c	3.94–3.103
9	d	2.08–2.12	29	d	3.94–3.103
10	d	2.13–2.17	30	b	3.94–3.103
11	a	2.13–2.17	31	c	4.01–4.04
12	c	3.01–3.09	32	c	4.01–4.04
13	c	3.01–3.09	33	a	4.01–4.04
14	c	3.01–3.09	34	a	4.01–4.04
15	c	3.01–3.09	35	c	5.01–5.08
16	d	3.01–3.09	36	a	5.01–5.08
17	d	3.01–3.09	37	a	5.01–5.08
18	b	3.01–3.09	38	a	5.09–5.13
19	a	3.01–3.09	39	c	5.09–5.13
20	d	3.10–3.11	40	c	5.18

TERM PAPER MASTERY TEST 3

1. Before you begin to write, you should plan the sequence and levels of importance of

    a. voicing.
    b. statistical analyses.
    c. headings.
    d. the hypotheses.
    e. all of the above.

2. In scientific writing, continuity

    a. is achieved partly by proper use of punctuation marks and transitional words.
    b. requires abandoning familiar syntax.
    c. is enhanced by using many commas.
    d. is not really necessary.

3. Verb tense should

    a. be varied to keep the reader's interest.
    b. never change.
    c. always be the past or past perfect.
    d. be consistent within paragraphs.

4. A writer must be careful when using the pronouns *this*, *that*, *these*, and *those*. The writer can eliminate or reduce the vagueness of these pronouns by

    a. referring the reader to a specific previous sentence.
    b. using them to modify a noun (e.g., this frenulum, that hypothalamus, these electrodes, those mice).
    c. using them frequently.
    d. clarifying what is being referred to for the reader.
    e. All of the above except c may be done.

5. Which of the following is a good strategy for improving writing style?

    a. Revise the first draft after a delay.
    b. Use an outline.
    c. Ask a colleague for criticism.
    d. Do all of the above.

6. Edit the following for grammar:

    The six stimulus were presented to each participant simultaneously.

    a. leave as is

    b. The six stimuli were presented to each participant simultaneously.

    c. The six stimuli was presented to each participant simultaneously.

    d. The six stimuluses were presented to each participant simultaneously.

7. Edit the following for the use of pronouns:

   The team achieved a 38% improvement in their scores after undergoing imagery training.

   a. leave as is

   b. The team achieved a 38% improvement in its scores after undergoing imagery training.

   c. The team achieved a 38% improvement in each of their scores after undergoing imagery training.

   d. The team achieved a 38% improvement in scores after undergoing imagery training.

8. Which of the following sentences illustrates the correct use of the word *while* in scientific writing?

   a. Bragg (1965) found that participants performed well, while Bohr (1969) found that participants did poorly.

   b. While these findings are unusual, they are not unique.

   c. Bragg found that participants performed well while listening to music.

   d. All of the above are correct.

9. Edit the following for sentence structure:

   Successful problem solvers were both more adept at representing the problem and using heuristics.

   a. leave as is

   b. Successful problem solvers were both more adept at representing the problem as well as using heuristics.

   c. Successful problem solvers were more adept both at representing the problem and at using heuristics.

   d. Successful problem solvers were more adept at both representing the problem and at using heuristics.

10. Edit the following for the use of nonsexist language:

Before an experienced computer programmer attempts a particular solution, he tries to relate the problem structure to other problems he has solved successfully.

a. leave as is

b. Before an experienced computer programmer attempts a particular solution, he/she tries to relate the problem structure to other problems he/she has solved successfully.

c. Before experienced computer programmers attempt a particular solution, they try to relate the problem structure to other problems they have solved successfully.

d. Before an experienced computer programmer attempts a particular solution, the programmer (he or she) tries to relate the problem structure to other problems he (or she if she really is experienced) has solved successfully.

11. Edit the following for avoiding ethnic bias:

In each age group, the American citizens who were foreigners performed better on the American history test than did the Americans.

a. leave as is

b. In each age group, the American citizens who were foreigners performed better on the American history test than did the American citizens who were native-born.

c. In each age group, the naturalized American citizens performed better on the American history test than did the native-born American citizens.

d. In each age group, the foreigners who became American citizens performed better on the American history test than did the Americans.

12. Edit the following for punctuation:

Optimal-level theories of motivation follow a homeostatic model. Opponent-process theories were advanced to account for addiction and other phenomena.

a. leave as is

b. Optimal-level theories of motivation follow a homeostatic model, opponent-process theories were advanced to account for addiction and other phenomena.

c. Optimal-level theories of motivation follow a homeostatic model--Opponent-process theories were advanced to account for addiction and other phenomena.

d. Optimal-level theories of motivation follow a homeostatic model; Opponent-process theories were advanced to account for addiction and other phenomena.

13. Edit the following for correct punctuation:

   The floor was covered with cedar shavings and paper was available for shredding and nest building.

   a. The sentence is correct as it stands.
   b. Put a semicolon after *shavings*.
   c. Put a comma after *shavings*.
   d. Put a comma after *floor*.

14. Edit the following for punctuation:

   Thus, the light status for the three trials in the four conditions was on, off, on: off, on, off: on, on, on: or off, off, off.

   a. leave as is

   b. Thus, the light status for the three trials in the four conditions was on, off, on, off, on, off, on, on, on, or off, off, off.

   c. Thus, the light status for the three trials in the four conditions was on, off, and on, or off, on, and off, or on, on, and on, or off, off, and off.

   d. Thus, the light status for the three trials in the four conditions was on, off, on; off, on, off; on, on, on; or off, off, off.

15. Which sentence is correct?
   a. The digits were shown in the following order: 3, 2, 4, 1.
   b. The digits were shown in the following order, 3, 2, 4, 1.
   c. The digits were shown in the following order; 3, 2, 4, 1.
   d. The digits were shown in the following order--3, 2, 4, 1.

16. Edit the following for punctuation:

   The 4 participants--2 in the vicarious condition, 1 in the direct condition, and 1 in the control condition--who recognized the confederate as a fellow student were excused from the second part of the experiment.

   a. leave as is

   b. The 4 participants, 2 in the vicarious condition, 1 in the direct condition, and 1 in the control condition, who recognized the confederate as a fellow student were excused from the second part of the experiment.

   c. The 4 participants: 2 in the vicarious condition, 1 in the direct condition, and 1 in the control condition: who recognized the confederate as a fellow student were excused from the second part of the experiment.

   d. The 4 participants ... 2 in the vicarious condition, 1 in the direct condition, and 1 in the control condition ... who recognized the confederate as a fellow student were excused from the second part of the experiment.

17. When using slang or a coined phrase, set the expression off with

    a. double quotation marks the first time the expression is used.
    b. double quotation marks every time it is used.
    c. dashes every time it is used.
    d. single quotation marks the first time it is used.

18. Edit the following for punctuation:

    The length of utterances increases dramatically between the ages of 18 and 60 months. See Figure 1.

    a. leave as is

    b. The length of utterances increases dramatically between the ages of 18 and 60 months (see Figure 1).

    c. The length of utterances increases dramatically between the ages of 18 and 60 months (see Figure 1.).

    d. The length of utterances increases dramatically between the ages of 18 and 60 months, see Figure 1.

19. The standard spelling reference for APA journals is

    a. the most recent edition of *Merriam-Webster's Collegiate Dictionary*.
    b. the *British-American Speller*.
    c. the *Random House Dictionary*.
    d. any of the above.

20. Identify the example with incorrect use of capitalization:

    a. The conclusion is obvious: forgiveness is not granted to the stronger partner in an inequitable relationship.

    b. Familiar tasks appear to accelerate the acquaintanceship process in groups of strangers.

    c. Schizophrenia is sometimes associated with visual creativity.

    d. The brain stem is the "on switch" of consciousness.

21. Which noun is incorrectly capitalized in the following example?

    Bem's Theory of Self-Perception suggests that a woman will like a stranger more after she dances with him.

    a. Theory
    b. Self
    c. Peception
    d. Bem's
    e. All of the above are incorrect except d.

22. Edit the following for correct use of abbreviations:

> Three kinds of scene identification tasks were given to the police officers: a murder scene, a robbery scene, and an assault scene. The identification tasks were given in either an MS-RS-AS or AS-RS-MS sequence.

    a. Define the abbreviations earlier by putting them within parentheses following the terms they abbreviated.
    b. Use no abbreviations because they are not known by most readers.
    c. Make no change because the connection between terms and abbreviations is obvious.
    d. Make no change because the writer used standard abbreviations.

23. Which abbreviations are used only in parentheses?

    a. vs., kg, i.e.
    b. i.e., cf., viz.
    c. e.g., etc., p.
    d. none of the above.
    e. all of the above.

24. Level 5 (centered uppercase) headings are used

    a. only when the article requires five levels of headings.
    b. in short articles where one level of heading is sufficient.
    c. after any other type of heading in single-experiment papers.
    d. only in multiexperiment papers.

25. Identify the error in the following quotation:

> Zwycewicz (1976) concluded the following:
>
> > "Children appear to employ the same schemata as adults. Like adults, they are predisposed to structure intragroup relations with an ordering schema more readily than with a grouping schema. Thus, their readiness to arrange inanimate stimuli along a vertical dimension as opposed to a horizontal dimension is seen as well with social stimuli." (p. 61)

    a. There are no errors.
    b. The quote should not be in block form.
    c. The quote does not need quotation marks.
    d. There is no need to cite the page number.

26. Any direct, short quotation (less than 500 words) of text from an APA journal must

    a. be accompanied by a reference citation.
    b. include a page number.
    c. be used only with the permission of the copyright owner.
    d. be footnoted if copyrighted.
    e. Answers a and b are correct.

27. When a work has more than two authors and fewer than six authors, cite

    a. all of the authors every time the reference occurs in text.
    b. all of the authors the first time the reference occurs in text; use the surname of the first author followed by *et al.* in subsequent citations.
    c. the surname of the first author followed by *et al.* every time the reference occurs in text.
    d. none of the above.

28. When a reference source is cited in the text,

    a. each author's surname must be cited every time a reference occurs in the text when there are two authors of a single work.
    b. every author's surname is used only the first time a reference is made when a work has more than two and less than six authors.
    c. only the first author's surname is used followed by *et al.* every time the reference is made when a work has six or more authors.
    d. All of the above are correct.
    e. Only b and c are correct.

29. Edit the following for the citation of references in text:

    Others (e.g., Hoffman, 1975, 1975, 1976) have taken a developmental approach to the study of altruism.

    a. leave as is

    b. Others (e.g., Hoffman, 1975a, b, 1976) have taken a developmental approach to the study of altruism.

    c. Others (e.g., Hoffman, 1975a, 1975b, 1976) have taken a developmental approach to the study of altruism.

    d. Others (e.g., Hoffman, 1975a/b, 1976) have taken a developmental approach to the study of altruism.

30. Edit the following for the citation of a specific part of a reference in text:

    Cook and Campbell (1979, 2) considered two other criteria, statistical conclusion validity and constant validity.

    a. leave as is

    b. Cook and Campbell (1979, Ch. 2) considered two other criteria, statistical conclusion validity and construct validity.

    c. Cook and Campbell (1979, Ch. #2) considered two other criteria, statistical conclusion validity and construct validity.

    d. Cook and Campbell (1979, chap. 2) considered two other criteria, statistical conclusion validity and construct validity.

31. Each entry in the reference list must be

    a. relevant to other entries.
    b. cited in text also.
    c. published in a credible journal.
    d. all of the above.

32. Edit the following for ordering the references in a reference list. Choose the sequence of numbers that indicates the correct order of the four references. (*Note:* The numbers are not part of APA style but are used here for brevity.)

    1. Miller, G. A. (1956b). The magical number seven plus or minus two: Some limits on our capacity for processing information. *Psychological Review, 63,* 81-97.

    2. Miller, G. A. (1956a). Human memory and the storage of information. *IRE Transactions on Information Theory, IT-2,* 129-137.

    3. Miller, G. A., Galanter, E., & Pribram, K. H. (1960). *Plans and the structure of behavior.* New York: Holt, Rinehart & Winston.

    4. Miller, G. A., & Selfridge, J. (1950). Verbal context and the recall of meaningful material. *American Journal of Psychology, 63,* 176-185.

    a. leave as is (i.e., 1, 2, 3, 4)
    b. 4, 1, 2, 3
    c. 2, 3, 1, 4
    d. 2, 1, 3, 4

33. Edit the following for the application of APA reference style:

    Brickman, P., Coates, D., & Janoff-Bulman, R. (1978). Lottery Winners and Accident Victims: Is Happiness Relative? *Journal of Personality and Social Psychology, 36,* 917-927.

    a. leave as is

    b. Brickman, P., Coates, D., & Janoff-Bulman, R. (1978). *Lottery Winners and Accident Victims: Is Happiness Relative? Journal of Personality and Social Psychology, 36,* 917-927.

    c. Brickman, P., Coates, D., & Janoff-Bulman, R. (1978). Lottery winners and accident victims: Is happiness relative? *Journal of Personality and Social Psychology, 36,* 917-927.

    d. Brickman, P., Coates, D., & Janoff-Bulman, R. (1978). "Lottery Winners and Accident Victims: Is Happiness Relative?" *Journal of Personality and Social Psychology, 36,* 917-927.

34. Edit the following for the application of APA reference style:

> Bronfenbrenner, U. (1970). *Two worlds of childhood: U.S. and U.S.S.R.* New York: Russell Sage Foundation.

   a. leave as is

   b. Bronfenbrenner, U. *Two worlds of childhood: U.S. and U.S.S.R.* New York: Russell Sage Foundation. (1970).

   c. Bronfenbrenner, U. (1970). "Two words of childhood: U.S. and U.S.S.R." New York: Russell Sage Foundation.

   d. Bronfenbrenner, U. (1970). *Two Worlds of Childhood: U.S. and U.S.S.R.* Russell Sage Foundation: New York.

35. A manuscript should be printed on
   a. erasable white bond paper.
   b. heavy, white nonerasable bond paper.
   c. white onionskin paper.
   d. any professional-looking paper.

36. Edit the following by selecting the correct spacing arrangement:

Naturalistic Observation of the Duration and Distribution
of Sleep Across the Life Span

Although individual differences within each age group are certainly recognized, our society has general notions about the sleep patterns--duration and distribution--of people at different ages.

a. leave as is

b.

Naturalistic Observation of the Duration and Distribution

of Sleep Across the Life Span

Although individual differences within each age group are certainly

recognized, our society has general notions about the sleep patterns--duration

and distribution--of people at different ages.

c.

Naturalistic Observation of the Duration and Distribution
of Sleep Across the Life Span

Although individual differences within each age group are certainly

recognized, our society has general notions about the sleep patterns--duration

and distribution--of people at different ages.

d.

Naturalistic Observation of the Duration and Distribution

of Sleep Across the Life Span

Although individual differences within each age group are certainly

recognized, our society has general notions about the sleep patterns--duration

and distribution--of people at different ages.

37. Edit the following for numbering of an abstract page:

Firefly Helplessness

1

a. leave as is
b. Change the page number 1 to the number 2.
c. The page number is correct, but it should not be typed flush with the right margin.
d. The page number is correct, but the short title should not appear on the abstract page.

38. A heading that is flush left

a. should be typed in uppercase and lowercase letters.
b. need not be underlined.
c. may be typed in all uppercase letters or all lowercase letters depending on the heading's level.
d. must end with a period.

39. Edit the following for spacing and punctuation:

Physical and psychological measures of the members of the medical emergency staff--nurses and doctors--were taken immediately and 48 hr after the crisis.

a. leave as is

b. Physical and psychological measures of the members of the medical emergency staff - nurses and doctors - were taken immediately and 48 hr after the crisis.

c. Physical and psychological measures of the members of the medical emergency staff-nurses and doctors-were taken immediately and 48 hr after the crisis.

d. Physical and psychological measures of the members of the medical emergency staff -- nurses and doctors -- were taken immediately and 48 hr after the crisis.

40. Edit the following for the typing of a reference list:

REFERENCES

Baron, J. B., & Sternberg, R. J. (1987). *Teaching thinking skills: Theory and practice*. San Francisco: Freeman.

Nickerson, R. S., Perkins, D. N., & Smith, E. E. (1985). *The teaching of thinking*. Hillsdale, NJ: Erlbaum.

a. leave as is

b.
                                        References

Baron, J. B., & Sternberg, R. J. (1987). *Teaching thinking skills: Theory and practice*. San Francisco: Freeman.

Nickerson, R. S., Perkins, D. N., & Smith, E. E. (1985). *The teaching of thinking*. Hillsdale, NJ: Erlbaum.

c.
                                        References

Baron, J. B., & Sternberg, R. J. (1987). *Teaching thinking skills: Theory and practice*. San Francisco: Freeman.

Nickerson, R. S., Perkins, D. N., & Smith, E. E. (1985). *The teaching of thinking*. Hillsdale, NJ: Erlbaum.

d.
                                        References

Baron, J. B., & Sternberg, R. J. (1987). *Teaching thinking skills: Theory and practice*. San Francisco: Freeman.

Nickerson, R. S., Perkins, D. N., & Smith, E. E. (1985). *The teaching of thinking*. Hillsdale, NJ: Erlbaum.

TERM PAPER MASTERY TEST 3
ANSWER SHEET AND FEEDBACK REPORT

Student Name _____ Date _____

Question Number	Answer	APA Codes	Question Number	Answer	APA Codes
1	_____	1.03–1.05	21	_____	3.12–3.18
2	_____	2.01–2.02	22	_____	3.20–3.29
3	_____	2.01–2.02	23	_____	3.20–3.29
4	_____	2.03–2.05	24	_____	3.30–3.33
5	_____	2.03–2.05	25	_____	3.34–3.41
6	_____	2.06–2.07	26	_____	3.34–3.41
7	_____	2.08–2.12	27	_____	3.94–3.103
8	_____	2.08–2.12	28	_____	3.94–3.103
9	_____	2.08–2.12	29	_____	3.94–3.103
10	_____	2.13–2.17	30	_____	3.94–3.103
11	_____	2.13–2.17	31	_____	4.01–4.04
12	_____	3.01–3.09	32	_____	4.01–4.04
13	_____	3.01–3.09	33	_____	4.01–4.04
14	_____	3.01–3.09	34	_____	4.01–4.04
15	_____	3.01–3.09	35	_____	5.01–5.08
16	_____	3.01–3.09	36	_____	5.01–5.08
17	_____	3.01–3.09	37	_____	5.01–5.08
18	_____	3.01–3.09	38	_____	5.09–5.13
19	_____	3.10–3.11	39	_____	5.09–5.13
20	_____	3.12–3.18	40	_____	5.18

NUMBER CORRECT _____

TERM PAPER MASTERY TEST 3
ANSWER KEY

Question Number	Answer	APA Codes	Question Number	Answer	APA Codes
1	c	1.03–1.05	21	e	3.12–3.18
2	a	2.01–2.02	22	a	3.20–3.29
3	d	2.01–2.02	23	b	3.20–3.29
4	e	2.03–2.05	24	a	3.30–3.33
5	d	2.03–2.05	25	c	3.34–3.41
6	b	2.06–2.07	26	e	3.34–3.41
7	b	2.08–2.12	27	b	3.94–3.103
8	c	2.08–2.12	28	d	3.94–3.103
9	c	2.08–2.12	29	c	3.94–3.103
10	c	2.13–2.17	30	d	3.94–3.103
11	c	2.13–2.17	31	b	4.01–4.04
12	a	3.01–3.09	32	d	4.01–4.04
13	c	3.01–3.09	33	c	4.01–4.04
14	d	3.01–3.09	34	a	4.01–4.04
15	a	3.01–3.09	35	b	5.01–5.08
16	a	3.01–3.09	36	d	5.01–5.08
17	a	3.01–3.09	37	b	5.01–5.08
18	b	3.01–3.09	38	a	5.09–5.13
19	a	3.10–3.11	39	a	5.09–5.13
20	a	3.12–3.18	40	c	5.18

TERM PAPER MASTERY TEST 4

1. Headings are important in a report because they

    a. satisfy the requirements of APA style.
    b. communicate the logical structure of the paper.
    c. fulfill a tradition in scientific writing.
    d. are used in place of paragraph indentation.
    e. All of the above are correct.

2. Ideas appear more orderly when

    a. punctuation supports meaning.
    b. transition words of time (*then* or *next*) or causation (*therefore* or *consequently*) are used.
    c. contrast links (*however* or *whereas*) are used.
    d. all of the above are present.
    e. only a and b are present.

3. Synonyms should be used

    a. with care because they may suggest subtle differences.
    b. as much as possible to make the manuscript interesting.
    c. whenever the same word is mentioned three or more times in one paragraph.
    d. only in the conclusion.

4. Colloquial expressions such as *the wind in his sails died* or approximations of quantity such as *the lion's share of*

    a. reduce word precision and clarity.
    b. add warmth to dull scientific prose.
    c. have a place even in serious scientific writing.
    d. can be used to enhance communication.
    e. are more acceptable in written than in oral communication.

5. Choose the best strategy for improving your writing style:

    a. Write from an outline.
    b. Put aside the first draft, then reread it after a delay.
    c. Ask a colleague to critique the first draft for you.
    d. Begin writing close to a deadline to enhance your motivation.
    e. Any of the above except d can be used, but the strategy must match your personality and work habits.

6. Which of the following sentences is an example of correct agreement between subject and verb?

    a. The percentage of correct responses increase with practice.

    b. The data indicate that Brenda was correct.

    c. The phenomena occurs every 100 years.

    d. Neither the participants nor the confederate were in the perfumery.

7. Edit the following for the placement of modifiers:

    The victims reported to trained volunteers still experiencing anxiety.

    a. leave as is

    b. The victims reported to trained volunteers, still experiencing anxiety.

    c. The victims, still experiencing anxiety, reported to trained volunteers.

    d. The victims, reported to trained volunteers, still experiencing anxiety.

8. Which of the following sentences is incorrect according to the preferred style stated in the APA *Publication Manual*?

    a. While these findings are unusual, they are not unique.

    b. Although these findings are unusual, they are not unique.

    c. These findings are unusual, but they are not unique.

    d. All of the above are incorrect.

9. Edit the following for sentence structure:

    Interviewees are often instructed to dress conservatively, to pay attention to their nonverbal communications, and that they should ask a few job-related questions of the interviewer.

    a. leave as is

    b. Interviewees are often instructed to dress conservatively, to pay attention to their nonverbal communications, and to ask a few job-related questions of the interviewer.

    c. Interviewees are often instructed to dress conservatively, pay attention to their nonverbal communications, and that they should be prepared to ask a few job-related questions of the interviewer.

    d. Interviewees are often instructed to dress conservatively and pay attention to their nonverbal communications, and that they should ask a few job-related questions of the interviewer.

10. Edit the following for the use of nonsexist language:

> They predicted that men would be selected more frequently as partners for the cognitive tasks and that females would be chosen more frequently for the interpersonal tasks.

a. leave as is

b. They predicted that males would be selected more frequently as partners for the cognitive tasks and that nonmales would be chosen more frequently for the interpersonal tasks.

c. They predicted that men would be selected more frequently as partners for the cognitive tasks and that women would be chosen more frequently for the interpersonal tasks.

d. They predicted that guys would be selected more frequently as partners for the cognitive tasks and that girls would be chosen more frequently for the interpersonal tasks.

11. Edit the following for avoiding ethnic bias:

> Participation in ethnic celebrations was compared for oriental immigrants and their first-, second-, and third-generation counterparts of the same cohort.

a. leave as is

b. Participation in ethnic celebrations was compared for immigrants from oriental countries and their first-, second-, and third-generation counterparts of the same cohort.

c. Participation in ethnic celebrations was compared for oriental immigrants and first-, second-, and third-generation orientals of the same cohort.

d. Participation in ethnic celebrations was compared for Asian immigrants and for first-, second-, and third-generation Asian Americans of the same cohort.

12. Edit the following for punctuation:

   According to Piaget, the four stages of intellectual development are the sensorimotor stage, the preoperational stage, the concrete-operational stage, and the formal-operational stage.

   a. leave as is

   b. According to Piaget, the four stages of intellectual development are the sensorimotor stage, the preoperational stage, the concrete-operational stage and the formal-operational stage.

   c. According to Piaget, the four stages of intellectual development are the sensorimotor stage; the preoperational stage; the concrete-operational stage; and the formal-operational stage.

   d. According to Piaget, the four stages of intellectual development are the sensorimotor stage--the preoperational stage--the concrete-operational stage--and the formal-operational stage.

13. Use a comma
   a. before *and* and *or* in a series of three or more items.
   b. between the two parts of a compound predicate.
   c. to separate two independent clauses joined by a conjunction.
   d. in all of the above instances.
   e. in instances a and c above.

14. Edit the following for punctuation:

   From shortest to longest wavelength, the colors of the visible spectrum appear in the following order: blue-purple, blue, blue-green, green, yellow-green, yellow, orange, and red.

   a. leave as is

   b. From shortest to longest wavelength, the colors of the visible spectrum appear in the following order--blue-purple, blue, blue-green, green, yellow-green, yellow, orange, and red.

   c. From shortest to longest wavelength, the colors of the visible spectrum appear in the following order: Blue-purple, blue, blue-green, green, yellow-green, yellow, orange, and red.

   d. From shortest to longest wavelength, the colors of the visible spectrum appear in the following order ... blue-purple, blue, blue-green, green, yellow-green, yellow, orange, and red.

15. The dash is used

   a. to indicate a sudden interruption in the continuity of a sentence.
   b. in APA articles only with permission of the technical editor.
   c. frequently in APA articles in the statistical section.
   d. by Type A psychologists.

16. Edit the following for punctuation:

   Harlow's (1959) article, *Love in Infant Monkeys*, made the case for the role of contact comfort in infant development.

   a. leave as is

   b. Harlow's (1959) article, titled Love in Infant Monkeys, made the case for the role of contact comfort in infant development.

   c. Harlow's (1959) article, 'Love in Infant Monkeys,' made the case for the role of contact comfort in infant development.

   d. Harlow's (1959) article, "Love in Infant Monkeys," made the case for the role of contact comfort in infant development.

17. Use double quotation marks

   a. every time an invented expression is used.
   b. only the first time an invented expression is introduced.
   c. to introduce a technical or key term.
   d. Answers b and c are correct.

18. Edit the following for punctuation:

   Individuals with Type A personalities are more likely to develop coronary heart disease, CHD, than are those with Type B personalities.

   a. leave as is

   b. Individuals with Type A personalities are more likely to develop coronary heart disease, "CHD," than are those with Type B personalities.

   c. Individuals with Type A personalities are more likely to develop coronary heart disease--CHD--than are those with Type B personalities.

   d. Individuals with Type A personalities are more likely to develop coronary heart disease (CHD) than are those with Type B personalities.

19. Regarding spelling,

   a. the standard spelling reference is the most recent edition of *Merriam-Webster's Collegiate Dictionary*.
   b. APA accepts all the spelling choices listed in popular English dictionaries.
   c. APA has no standard and leaves the matter up to the individual journal editors.
   d. British spelling is preferred.

20. Which of the following words with a prefix require a hyphen?

    a. compounds in which the base word is an abbreviation (e.g., pre-UCS)
    b. *self* compounds (e.g., self-esteem)
    c. words that could be misunderstood or misread (e.g., un-ionized)
    d. all of the above
    e. none of the above

21. From the alternatives below, select the one that correctly uses capitalization:

    a. few significant differences were found.

    b. However, one important observation was made: Participatory followers do not like to be led by authoritarian leaders.

    c. Authoritarian followers behaved in a curious way: they acted in a participatory manner with participatory leaders.

    d. these results were reported by Black and Walker (1986).

22. In the following example, which abbreviation should be spelled out when it is first introduced?

    After the depressed clients received ECT treatments, changes in central nervous system activity were assessed with an EEG and effects on sleep were measured by observing REM periods.

    a. EEG
    b. ECT
    c. REM
    d. all of the above
    e. any that do not appear in the latest edition of *Merriam-Webster's Collegiate Dictionary*

23. Latin abbreviations, except *et al.*, should

    a. be spelled out each time they are used.
    b. not be used.
    c. be used only in parenthetical material.
    d. be spelled out the first time they are used.

24. In articles in which one level of heading is sufficient, use

    a. a centered upper case heading (level 5).
    b. a centered uppercase and lowercase heading (level 1).
    c. any type (level) of heading.
    d. none of the above.

25. Edit the following for a quotation of a source:

    Zwycewicz (1976) concluded that "children appear to employ the same schemata as adults. Like adults, they are predisposed to structure intragroup relations with an ordering schema more readily than with a grouping schema."

    a. leave as is
    b. The quote should be in block form.
    c. A page number should be cited.
    d. Quotation marks are not necessary.

26. From the examples below, identify the correct form of citation:

    a. According to McMahon (1988), math ability is acquired.

    b. Individual differences in memory have been found (Gelfand, 1987).

    c. In 1988, Scarano found that androgynous women respond to self-worth dilemmas differently than do stereotypic women.

    d. Lavin (1986) observed that TV serves as a surrogate parent for some young adults. Lavin found that "soap addicts" have limited parental contact.

    e. All of the above are correct.

27. Edit the following for the citation of a reference in text:

    Some researchers have recognized that people may not follow mathematical rules in judging the probability of events (Tversky & Kahneman, 1973). Tversky et al. reported evidence that people rely on an availability heuristic in making probability judgments.

    a. leave as is

    b. Some researchers have recognized that people may not follow mathematical rules in judging the probability of events (Tversky & Kahneman, 1973). Tversky & Kahneman reported evidence that people rely on an availability heuristic in making probability judgments.

    c. Some researchers have recognized that people may not follow mathematical rules in judging the probability of events (Tversky & Kahneman, 1973). Tversky and Kahneman reported evidence that people rely on an availability heuristic in making probability judgments.

    d. Some researchers have recognized that people may not follow mathematical rules in judging the probability of events (Tversky & Kahneman, 1973). Tversky/ Kahneman reported evidence that people rely on an availability heuristic in making probability judgments.

28. When a work has two authors, cite

    a. only one name every time the reference occurs in text.
    b. both names the first time the reference occurs in text and only one thereafter.
    c. both names every time the reference occurs in text.
    d. None of the above is correct.

29. Edit the following for the citation of references in text:

Many phobias have been treated successfully with systematic desensitization (Hekmat, Lubitz, & Deal, 1984; Land & Lazovik, 1963; Paul, 1966; Wolpe, 1958).

a. leave as is

b. Many phobias have been treated successfully with systematic desensitization (Hekmat, Lubitz, & Deal, 1984; Paul, 1966; Land & Lazovik, 1963; Wolpe, 1958).

c. Many phobias have been treated successfully with systematic desensitization (Wolpe, 1958; Land & Lazovik, 1963; Paul, 1966; Hekmat, Lubitz, & Deal, 1984).

d. Many phobias have been treated successfully with systematic desensitization (Paul, 1966; Wolpe, 1958; Land & Lazovik, 1963; Hekmat, Lubitz, & Deal, 1984).

30. Edit the following for the citation of a specific part of a reference in text:

Ecphory "is the process by which retrieval information is brought into interaction with stored information" (Tulving, 1983) [p. 178].

a. leave as is

b. Ecphory "is the process by which retrieval information is brought into interaction with stored information (p. 178)" (Tulving, 1983).

c. Ecphory "is the process by which retrieval information is brought into interaction with stored information" (Tulving, 1983, p. 178).

d. Ecphory "is the process by which retrieval information is brought into interaction with stored information" (Tulving, 1983).

31. Reference entries
a. may consist of the author's name only, if the bibliography is totally complete.
b. may contain only the author's name and title of publication, if the bibliography is totally complete.
c. should be complete and correct.
d. a or b

32. Edit the following for ordering the references in a reference list. Choose the sequence of numbers that indicates the correct order of the four references. (*Note:* The numbers are not part of APA style but are used here for brevity.)

    1. McKenzie, B., & Over, R. (1983). Young infants fail to imitate facial and manual gestures. *Infant Behavior and Development, 6*, 85-96.

    2. Martin, G. B., & Clark, R. D. (1982). Distress crying in neonates: Species and peer specificity. *Developmental Psychology, 18*, 3-9.

    3. Maurer, D., & Salapatek, P. (1976). Developmental changes in the scanning of faces by young infants. *Child Development, 47*, 523-527.

    4. Meltzoff, A. N., & Moore, M. K. (1977). Imitation of facial and manual gestures by human neonates. *Science, 198*, 75-78.

a. leave as is (i.e., 1, 2, 3, 4)
b. 3, 4, 2, 1
c. 3, 2, 4, 1
d. 2, 3, 1, 4

33. Edit the following for the application of APA reference style:

Bower, G. H. (1970). Analysis of a mnemonic device. *American Scientist, 58*, 496-510.

a. leave as is

b. Bower, G. H. (1970). Analysis of a mnemonic device. *AMERICAN SCIENTIST, 58*, 496-510.

c. Bower, G. H. (1970). Analysis of a mnemonic device. AMERICAN SCIENTIST, *58*, 496-510.

d. Bower, G. H. (1970). Analysis of a mnemonic device. "*American Scientist,*" *58*, 496-510.

34. Edit the following for the application of APA reference style:

Deaux, Kay. (1976). *The behavior of women and men.* Brooks/Cole: Monterey, CA.

a. leave as is

b. Deaux, Kay. (1976). *The Behavior of Women and Men.* Monterey, CA: Brooks/Cole.

c. Deaux, K. "The Behavior of Women and Men." Monterey, CA: Brooks/Cole, 1976.

d. Deaux, K. (1976). *The behavior of women and men.* Monterey, CA: Brooks/Cole.

35. Use a typeface that is
   a. dark.
   b. clear.
   c. readable.
   d. all of the above.

36. Edit the following by selecting the correct spacing arrangement:

Survey Methods

Telephone Survey

In urban environments, many respondents screen their calls or record them on answering machines. Simple random sampling is not easily done because direct contact with the respondent is difficult to achieve.

   a. leave as is

   b.
Survey Methods

Telephone Survey

In urban environments, many respondents screen their calls or record them on answering machines. Simple random sampling is not easily done because direct contact with the respondent is difficult to achieve.

   c.
Survey Methods

Telephone Survey

In urban environments, many respondents screen their calls or record them on answering machines. Simple random sampling is not easily done because direct contact with the respondent is difficult to achieve.

   d.
Survey Methods

Telephone Survey

In urban environments, many respondents screen their calls or record them on answering machines. Simple random sampling is not easily done because direct contact with the respondent is difficult to achieve.

37. Concerning page numbers,
   a. number your pages consecutively starting with the title page.
   b. place the numbers in the center of each page at the top margin.
   c. if a page is inserted after numbering is complete, number the inserted page with an *a* (e.g., 6a).
   d. pages used for figures are not numbered.
   e. a and d are correct.

38. One space should follow
    a. colons used in the text.
    b. all punctuation marks at the end of sentences.
    c. periods that separate parts of a reference.
    d. all of the above.
    e. none of the above.

39. Edit the following for spacing and punctuation:

    When the applicant's ethnic origin was stated explicitly, ethnic origin did affect selection (see Table 1,) but when ethnic origin was not stated explicitly, it did not affect selection (see Table 2) (The interviewers represented a variety of ethnic origins).

    a. leave as is

    b. When the applicant's ethnic origin was stated explicitly, ethnic origin did affect selection, (see Table 1), but when ethnic origin was not stated explicitly, it did not affect selection, (see Table 2). (The interviewers represented a variety of ethnic origins.).

    c. When the applicant's ethnic origin was stated explicitly, ethnic origin did affect selection (see Table 1), but when ethnic origin was not stated explicitly, it did not affect selection (see Table 2). (The interviewers represented a variety of ethnic origins.)

    d. When the applicant's ethnic origin was stated explicitly, ethnic origin did affect selection, (see Table 1), but when ethnic origin was not stated explicitly, it did not affect selection, (see Table 2). (The interviewers represented a variety of ethnic origins).

40. When typing a reference list,
    a. begin it after the last word of the Discussion section on the same page.
    b. type each reference with the first line indented and all of the remaining lines flush left.
    c. head the section with the word *References* even if you cite only one source.
    d. indent all lines of each reference except the first line at least five spaces.

41. Edit the following for the application of APA electronic reference style:

VandenBos, G., Knapp, S., & Doe, J. (2001). Role of reference elements in the selection of resources by psychology undergraduates. *Journal of Bibliographic Research, 5,* 117-123 (electronic version).

a. VandenBos, G., Knapp, S., & Doe, J. (2001). Role of reference elements in the selection of resources by psychology undergraduates [Electronic version]. *Journal of Bibliographic Research, 5,* 117-123.

b. VandenBos, G., Knapp, S., & Doe, J. (2001). Role of reference elements in the selection of resources by psychology undergraduates (electronic version). *Journal of Bibliographic Research, 5,* 117-123.

c. VandenBos, G., Knapp, S., & Doe, J. (2001). Role of reference elements in the selection of resources by psychology undergraduates [electronic version]. *Journal of Bibliographic Research, 5,* 117-123.

d. VandenBos, G., Knapp, S., & Doe, J. (2001). Role of reference elements in the selection of resources by psychology undergraduates. *Journal of Bibliographic Research, 5,* 117-123 [Electronic version].

42. Edit the following for the application of APA electronic reference style:

VandenBos, G., Knapp, S., & Doe, J. (2001, October 13). Role of reference elements in the selection of resources by psychology undergraduates. *Journal of Bibliographic Research, 5,* 117-123. Retrieved online from http://jbr.org/articles.html

a. leave as is

b. VandenBos, G., Knapp, S., & Doe, J. (2001). Role of reference elements in the selection of resources by psychology undergraduates. *Journal of Bibliographic Research, 5,* 117-123. Retrieved October 13, 2001, from http://jbr.org/articles.html

c. VandenBos, G., Knapp, S., & Doe, J. (2001, October 13). Role of reference elements in the selection of resources by psychology undergraduates. [Retrieved from http://jbr.org/articles.html]. *Journal of Bibliographic Research, 5,* 117-123.

d. VandenBos, G., Knapp, S., & Doe, J. (2001). Role of reference elements in the selection of resources by psychology undergraduates. *Journal of Bibliographic Research, 5,* 117-123 [retrieved October 13, 2001, from http://jbr.org/articles.html]

TERM PAPER MASTERY TEST 4
ANSWER SHEET AND FEEDBACK REPORT

Student Name _____ **Date** _____

Question Number	Answer	APA Codes	Question Number	Answer	APA Codes
1	_____	1.03–1.05	22	_____	3.20–3.29
2	_____	2.01–2.02	23	_____	3.20–3.29
3	_____	2.01–2.02	24	_____	3.30–3.33
4	_____	2.03–2.05	25	_____	3.34–3.41
5	_____	2.03–2.05	26	_____	3.94–3.103
6	_____	2.06–2.07	27	_____	3.94–3.103
7	_____	2.08–2.12	28	_____	3.94–3.103
8	_____	2.08–2.12	29	_____	3.94–3.103
9	_____	2.08–2.12	30	_____	3.94–3.103
10	_____	2.13–2.17	31	_____	4.01–4.04
11	_____	2.13–2.17	32	_____	4.01–4.04
12	_____	3.01–3.09	33	_____	4.01–4.04
13	_____	3.01–3.09	34	_____	4.01–4.04
14	_____	3.01–3.09	35	_____	5.01–5.08
15	_____	3.01–3.09	36	_____	5.01–5.08
16	_____	3.01–3.09	37	_____	5.01–5.08
17	_____	3.01–3.09	38	_____	5.09–5.13
18	_____	3.01–3.09	39	_____	5.09–5.13
19	_____	3.10–3.11	40	_____	5.18
20	_____	3.10–3.11	41	_____	4.16
21	_____	3.12–3.18	42	_____	4.16

NUMBER CORRECT _____

TERM PAPER MASTERY TEST 4
ANSWER KEY

Question Number	Answer	APA Codes	Question Number	Answer	APA Codes
1	b	1.03–1.05	22	e	3.20–3.29
2	d	2.01–2.02	23	c	3.20–3.29
3	a	2.01–2.02	24	b	3.30–3.33
4	a	2.03–2.05	25	c	3.34–3.41
5	e	2.03–2.05	26	e	3.94–3.103
6	b	2.06–2.07	27	c	3.94–3.103
7	c	2.08–2.12	28	c	3.94–3.103
8	a	2.08–2.12	29	a	3.94–3.103
9	b	2.08–2.12	30	c	3.94–3.103
10	c	2.13–2.17	31	c	4.01–4.04
11	d	2.13–2.17	32	d	4.01–4.04
12	a	3.01–3.09	33	a	4.01–4.04
13	e	3.01–3.09	34	d	4.01–4.04
14	a	3.01–3.09	35	d	5.01–5.08
15	a	3.01–3.09	36	c	5.01–5.08
16	d	3.01–3.09	37	e	5.01–5.08
17	b	3.01–3.09	38	d	5.09–5.13
18	d	3.01–3.09	39	c	5.09–5.13
19	a	3.10–3.11	40	d	5.18
20	d	3.10–3.11	41	a	4.16
21	b	3.12–3.18	42	b	4.16

RESEARCH REPORT MASTERY TEST 1

1. A report of an empirical study usually includes an introduction and sections called Method, _____ , and Discussion.

   a. Results
   b. Bibliography
   c. Statement of the Problem
   d. Conclusion

2. The abstract of an article should be

   a. a specific and concise summary of the entire report.
   b. about 25 to 50 words.
   c. an evaluation of the research report.
   d. all of the above.

3. The introduction section of a research report should

   a. include a thorough historical review of the literature.
   b. define all of the terms that would be unintelligible to a reader with no previous exposure to the field.
   c. present the specific problem to be explored and describe the research strategy.
   d. be clearly labeled.

4. When animals are the subjects in a study, it is not usually necessary to report

   a. the name of the supplier.
   b. details of their treatment and handling.
   c. their age, sex, and weight.
   d. the cost of maintaining them.

5. Results are sometimes difficult to read and understand; therefore, it is useful to

   a. start a Results section by stating your main findings and then reporting each data analysis in detail.
   b. introduce the reader to statistical theory before you report the results of even basic statistical analyses.
   c. let the statistics drive the logic of your Results section, not the logic you developed in your introduction (i.e., your hypotheses).
   d. report raw data, descriptive statistics, and the results of inferential analyses.

6. Speculation is permitted in the Discussion section if it is

   a. faithful to the intuition of the authors.
   b. related closely and logically to empirical data or theory.
   c. expressed verbosely and eloquently.
   d. none of the above.

7. In a paper that integrates several experiments, you should

   a. not try to relate the experiments to each other.
   b. have only one Results section for all of the experiments.
   c. make it at least twice as long as a one-experiment study.
   d. include a comprehensive general discussion of all of the work.

8. Past tense is usually appropriate for describing

    a. previous experiments.
    b. an experimental design.
    c. a procedure.
    d. all of the above.

9. Which of the following examples represents correct hyphenation?

    a. *t*-test results
    b. results from *t* tests
    c. 2-, 3-, and 10-min trials
    d. All of the above are correct.

10. Edit the following for capitalization:

    On the third day of Experiment 2 the children read Chapter 6 of their sex

    education text.

    a. leave as is
    b. *Experiment* and *Chapter* do not need to be capitalized.
    c. *Chapter* does not require capitalization.
    d. The terms *sex* and *education* should be capitalized.

11. Capitalize

    a. the word *factor* when it is followed by a number (e.g., Factor 6).
    b. effects or variables that do not appear with multiplication signs.
    c. names of conditions or groups in an experiment.
    d. all of the above.
    e. none of the above.

12. In general, use abbreviations

    a. if the reader is more familiar with the abbreviation than with the complete word or words being used.
    b. for long technical terms.
    c. if considerable space can be saved and repetition avoided.
    d. Answers a and c of the above are correct.
    e. All of the above are correct.

13. Choose the correct format for the use of three levels of headings:

a.

Experiment 2

Method

Participants

b.

METHOD

Procedure

   Pretraining period.

c. *Method*

   Procedure.

Participants

d.

Method

Procedure

   Pretraining period.

14. Edit the following for the expression of numbers:

Of the companies that participated, twenty-four were service companies, eleven were high-technology companies, and eight were heavy-industry companies.

a. leave as is

b. Of the companies that participated, 24 were service companies, eleven were high-technology companies, and eight were heavy-industry companies.

c. Of the companies that participated, 24 were service companies, 11 were high-technology companies, and eight were heavy-industry companies.

d. Of the companies that participated, 24 were service companies, 11 were high-technology companies, and 8 were heavy-industry companies.

15. Edit the following for the expression of numbers:

Procedural errors occurred while testing 2 rats in the drug condition and 3 rats in the placebo condition.

a. leave as is

b. Procedural errors occurred while testing 2.0 rats in the drug condition and 3.0 rats in the placebo condition.

c. Procedural errors occurred while testing two rats in the drug condition and three rats in the placebo condition.

d. Procedural errors occurred while testing two (2) rats in the drug condition and three (3) rats in the placebo condition.

16. Edit the following for the expression of numbers:

    The 3-dimensional conceptualization allows for 8 possible dyadic relationships.

    a. leave as is

    b. The 3-dimensional conceptualization allows for eight possible dyadic relationships.

    c. The three-dimensional conceptualization allows for eight possible dyadic relationships.

    d. The three-dimensional conceptualization allows for 8 possible dyadic relationships.

17. Edit the following for the expression of numbers:

    There were twenty 6-year-olds, eighteen 10-year-olds, and twenty-four 14-year-olds.

    a. leave as is

    b. There were 20 6-year-olds, 18 10-year-olds, and 24 14-year-olds.

    c. There were 20 six-year-olds, 18 ten-year-olds, and 24 fourteen-year-olds.

    d. There were twenty six-year-olds, eighteen 10-year-olds, and twenty-four 14-year-olds.

18. Edit the following for the expression of ordinal numbers:

    The 6th and 12th graders in each of the treatment conditions returned for a 5th session in which the performance measures were taken.

    a. leave as is

    b. The sixth and 12th graders in each of the treatment conditions returned for a fifth session in which the performance measures were taken.

    c. The sixth and twelfth graders in each of the treatment conditions returned for a fifth session in which the performance measures were taken.

    d. The 6th and 12th graders in each of the treatment conditions returned for a fifth session in which the performance measures were taken.

19. When using decimal numbers,

    a. a zero is used before the decimal point (0.05) only when the number cannot be greater than one (e.g., correlations, proportions, and levels of statistical significance; $r = -0.96$, $p < 0.05$).

    b. a zero is never used before the decimal point (.05).

    c. the author should check with the editor of each specific APA journal.

    d. a zero is always used before the decimal point (0.05) when numbers can take on values greater than one.

20. Edit the following for the presentation of numbers:

The interaction of class year and type of organization was not significant, $F(3, 1,590) = 1.85$, $p > .10$.

a. leave as is

b. The interaction of class year and type of organization was not significant, $F(3, 1590) = 1.85$, $p > .10$.

c. The interaction of class year and type of organization was not significant, $F(3, 1.590K) = 1.85$, $p > .10$.

21. Physical measurements should be reported in

a. metric units.
b. traditional nonmetric units.
c. units of the original measurement.
d. physical units.

22. Which of the following is correctly expressed?

a. 13 cms
b. 313 cm.
c. 31 cm
d. 313 cms.

23. Edit the following for the citation of a statistic in text:

A t test for related means was used to compare the number of targets found by birds in the experimental group with the number found by their yoked partners.

a. leave as is

b. A t test for related means (Hays, 1963) was used to compare the number of targets found by birds in the experimental group with the number found by their yoked partners.

c. A t test for related means (see any standard statistics reference work) was used to compare the number of targets found by birds in the experimental group with the number found by their yoked partners.

24. Edit the following for the presentation of a formula:

The frequencies of heterosexual intercourse per month by heterosexual and bisexual men were compared using a t test.

a. leave as is

b. The frequencies of heterosexual intercourse per month by heterosexual and bisexual men were compared using a t test (t = difference between means/ standard error of difference between means).

c. The frequencies of heterosexual intercourse per month by heterosexual and bisexual men were compared using a t test [$t = (M_H - M_B)$/standard error of difference between means].

d. The frequencies of heterosexual intercourse per month by heterosexual and bisexual men were compared using a t test [$(M_H - M_B)/(s_{H-B})$].

25. When presenting an inferential statistic in text, give
    a. the statistical symbol.
    b. degrees of freedom.
    c. the probability level.
    d. all of the above.
    e. none of the above.

26. Edit the following for the use of statistical symbols:

We first conducted a pilot study to determine the % of participants who could complete the task with different time limits.

a. leave as is

b. We first conducted a pilot study to determine the percentage of participants who could complete the task with different time limits.

c. We first conducted a pilot study to determine the % age of participants who could complete the task with different time limits.

d. We first conducted a pilot study to determine the percentage (%) of participants who could complete the task with different time limits.

27. Which of the following should be used to designate the number of members in a part of a total sample?
    a. N
    b. n
    c. n
    d. N

28. Edit the table below for tabular presentation:

Table 6

Mean Imaginal Scores of Students Reporting an Out-of-Body Experience

Condition	Imaginal scores
Visual	7.1
Auditory	4.0

 a. Means should be carried out to two decimal places.
 b. No standard deviations are given.
 c. Results consisting of only two means should be presented in the text, not in a table.
 d. b and c

29. Tables should be

 a. intelligible without reference to the text.
 b. referred to but not duplicated in the text.
 c. referred to in text by their numbers.
 d. all of the above.

30. Every table should have a title that is

 a. brief.
 b. clear.
 c. explanatory.
 d. all of the above.

31. Which of the following abbreviations need not be explained in table headings?

 a. abbreviations of technical terms
 b. standard abbreviations for nontechnical terms
 c. group names
 d. none of the above

32. A specific note to a table

 a. refers to a particular column or individual entry.
 b. is indicated by a superscript uppercase letter.
 c. is placed within the body of the table.
 d. does none of the above.

33. When inspecting a newly constructed table, what question should you *not* ask yourself?

 a. Should this table be vertically displayed?
 b. Is the table necessary?
 c. Does every column have a heading?
 d. Is it double-spaced?
 e. all of the above

34. What factors weigh against using a figure?

    a. It duplicates the text.
    b. It complements text and reduces lengthy discussions.
    c. It will be expensive to make.
    d. Answers a and c are correct.
    e. Answers a and b are correct.

35. What kind of figure is easy and inexpensive to prepare and reproduce?

    a. photograph
    b. line art
    c. halftone
    d. color
    e. laser

36. Select the figure caption that does not explain its figure effectively:

    a. *Figure 1.* Videocamera effects.

    b. *Figure 4.* Varimax rotation of factors.

    c. *Figure 2.* Outpatient and inpatient contrasts.

    d. All of the above captions are too brief and not sufficiently explanatory.

37. Which part of a research report should not always begin on a new page?

    a. abstract
    b. References
    c. Method
    d. author identification notes
    e. a and b

38. Edit the following for the typing of statistical copy:

    The problem-solving scores (see Table 3) yielded no significant effect due to the sex of the participant, F (1,152)=1.49, $p >$ .20.

    a. leave as is

    b. The problem-solving scores (see Table 3) yielded no significant effect due to the sex of the participant, $F(1,152) = 1.49$, $p>.20$.

    c. The problem-solving scores (see Table 3) yielded no significant effect due to the sex of the participant, $F(1,152)=1.49$, $p>.20$.

    d. The problem-solving scores (see Table 3) yielded no significant effect due to the sex of the participant, $F(1, 152) = 1.49$, $p > .20$.

39. The title page includes the title,

    a. author, and abstract.
    b. author and institutional affiliation, short title, and the page number 1.
    c. author and institutional affiliation, running head, short title, and the page number 1.
    d. author and institutional affiliation, and abstract.

40. Choose the correct statement about the placing of a table in a manuscript:

    a. Type the table in full exactly in the place in the text where it should be printed.
    b. Type the table on the back of the page that first refers to it.
    c. Try to type all of the tables on the same page.
    d. Type each table on a separate page.

RESEARCH REPORT MASTERY TEST 1
ANSWER SHEET AND FEEDBACK REPORT

Student Name _____ Date _____

Question Number	Answer	APA Codes	Question Number	Answer	APA Codes
1	_____	1.01–1.04	21	_____	3.50–3.52
2	_____	1.06–1.07	22	_____	3.50–3.52
3	_____	1.08–1.09	23	_____	3.53–3.59
4	_____	1.08–1.09	24	_____	3.53–3.59
5	_____	1.10–1.13	25	_____	3.53–3.59
6	_____	1.10–1.13	26	_____	3.53–3.59
7	_____	1.10–1.13	27	_____	3.53–3.59
8	_____	2.01–2.02	28	_____	3.62–3.72
9	_____	3.10–3.11	29	_____	3.62–3.72
10	_____	3.12–3.18	30	_____	3.62–3.72
11	_____	3.12–3.18	31	_____	3.62–3.72
12	_____	3.20–3.29	32	_____	3.62–3.72
13	_____	3.30–3.33	33	_____	3.74
14	_____	3.42–3.49	34	_____	3.75–3.81
15	_____	3.42–3.49	35	_____	3.75–3.81
16	_____	3.42–3.49	36	_____	3.83–3.84
17	_____	3.42–3.49	37	_____	5.01–5.08
18	_____	3.42–3.49	38	_____	5.09–5.14
19	_____	3.42–3.49	39	_____	5.15–5.25
20	_____	3.42–3.49	40	_____	5.15–5.25

NUMBER CORRECT _____

RESEARCH REPORT MASTERY TEST 1
ANSWER KEY

Question Number	Answer	APA Codes	Question Number	Answer	APA Codes
1	a	1.01–1.04	21	a	3.50–3.52
2	a	1.06–1.07	22	c	3.50–3.52
3	c	1.08–1.09	23	a	3.53–3.59
4	d	1.08–1.09	24	a	3.53–3.59
5	a	1.10–1.13	25	d	3.53–3.59
6	b	1.10–1.13	26	b	3.53–3.59
7	d	1.10–1.13	27	b	3.53–3.59
8	d	2.01–2.02	28	d	3.62–3.72
9	d	3.10–3.11	29	d	3.62–3.72
10	c	3.12–3.18	30	d	3.62–3.72
11	a	3.12–3.18	31	b	3.62–3.72
12	d	3.20–3.29	32	a	3.62–3.72
13	d	3.30–3.33	33	a	3.74
14	d	3.42–3.49	34	d	3.75–3.81
15	a	3.42–3.49	35	b	3.75–3.81
16	c	3.42–3.49	36	d	3.83–3.84
17	a	3.42–3.49	37	c	5.01–5.08
18	d	3.42–3.49	38	d	5.09–5.14
19	d	3.42–3.49	39	c	5.15–5.25
20	b	3.42–3.49	40	d	5.15–5.25

RESEARCH REPORT MASTERY TEST 2

1. When writing a report of original research, the sections should be arranged by

   a. order of importance.
   b. relation to each other.
   c. chronology in the experiment.
   d. none of the above.

2. The abstract of an article should contain

   a. statements of the problem, method, results, and conclusions.
   b. raw data statements with conclusions.
   c. conclusions not found in the text of the report.
   d. F values, degrees of freedom, and probability levels.

3. When closing the introduction section, questions to bear in mind include the following:

   a. What variables did I plan to manipulate?
   b. What was the rationale for each of my hypotheses?
   c. What statistical tests were used?
   d. all of the above.
   e. a and b.

4. When describing participants in your research, you should

   a. give major demographic characteristics.
   b. state how they were selected.
   c. report if they were provided incentives to participate.
   d. do all of the above.

5. When reporting statistics, include

   a. information about the magnitude or value of the test (e.g., t tests or F tests).
   b. information about degrees of freedom.
   c. descriptive statistics.
   d. all of the above.

6. The Discussion section is a part of the report in which you are

   a. free to discuss theory independent of your results.
   b. free to interpret your results and to discuss their implications.
   c. permitted to develop literature support for your hypotheses.
   d. encouraged to emphasize the flaws of your study.

7. In a paper that integrates several experiments, you should

   a. not try to relate the experiments to each other.
   b. have only one Results section for all of the experiments.
   c. include a comprehensive general discussion of all the work.
   d. make it at least twice as long as a one-experiment study.

8. Consistency of verb tense helps to smooth expression. Select the preferred match of paper section with verb tense from the choices below:

    a. conclusion: present tense
    b. literature review: present tense
    c. Results: past tense
    d. Method: past tense
    e. all of the above except b

9. Which of the following examples represents correct hyphenation?

    a. *t*-test results
    b. results from *t* tests
    c. 2-, 3-, and 10-min trials
    d. All of the above are correct.

10. Which of the following examples demonstrates correct use of capitalization?

    a. Trial 3 and Item 4
    b. trial *n* and item *x*
    c. chapter 4
    d. Table 2 and Figure 3
    e. All of the above are correct.

11. Edit the following for capitalization of names of variables, factors, or effects:

    All of the manipulated variables were counterbalanced. Fats, carbohydrates, and fiber were introduced into the clients' diets in different orders.

    a. leave as is
    b. Names of variables such as *fats*, *carbohydrates*, and *fiber* should be capitalized.
    c. The word *variables* should be capitalized.
    d. The names of variables or effects should be capitalized unless followed by a multiplication sign.

12. Abbreviations appearing in several figures or tables

    a. must be explained in the figure caption or table note for every figure or table in which they are used.
    b. must be explained in the figure caption or table note of only the first figure or table in which they are used.
    c. should only be explained in the text.
    d. need not be explained.

13. Edit the following by selecting the correct arrangement of headings:

Method

Subjects

Procedure

Results

Discussion

a. leave as is

b.
Method

Subjects.

Procedure.

Results

Discussion

c.
Method

Subjects

Procedure

Results

Discussion

d.
METHOD

Subjects

Procedure

RESULTS

DISCUSSION

14. **Edit the following for the expression of numbers:**

The maze consisted of a series of 18 choice points.

a. leave as is

b. The maze consisted of a series of eighteen choice points.

c. 18 choice points composed the maze.

15. **Edit the following for the expression of numbers:**

The survey had a sampling error of four %.

a. leave as is

b. The survey had a sampling error of four percent.

c. The survey had a sampling error of 4%.

d. The survey had a sampling error of 4 percent.

16. Edit the following for the expression of numbers:

> To test the program, schools were sought in which at least one fourth of the students did not finish the year above grade level on the criterion measure.

   a. leave as is

   b. To test the program, schools were sought in which at least 1/4 of the students did not finish the year above grade on the criterion measure.

   c. To test the program, schools were sought in which at least 1/4th of the students did not finish the year above grade level on the criterion measure.

   d. To test the program, schools were sought in which at least one/fourth of the students did not finish the year above grade level on the criterion measure.

17. Edit the following for the expression of numbers:

> Each client was asked to describe his or her actual and ideal selves on 16 5-point rating scales.

   a. leave as is

   b. Each client was asked to describe his or her actual and ideal selves on 16, 5-point rating scales.

   c. Each client was asked to describe his or her actual and ideal selves on sixteen 5-point rating scales.

   d. Each client was asked to describe his or her actual and ideal selves on 16 five-point rating scales.

18. Edit the following for the expression of decimal fractions:

> The dots appeared simultaneously on the screen, .5 cm apart.

   a. leave as is

   b. The dots appeared simultaneously on the screen, 0.5 cm apart.

   c. The dots appeared simultaneously on the screen, .50 cm apart.

19. According to the *Publication Manual of the American Psychological Association*,
   a. roman and arabic numbers can be used in equal frequency.
   b. arabic numerals should be used wherever possible except when roman numerals are part of an established terminology.
   c. roman numerals should never be used.
   d. roman numerals should be used wherever possible.

20. Edit the following for the punctuation of numbers:

   A content analysis was performed on 1,480 episodes of soap operas that had been televised in the preceding 5 years.

   a. leave as is

   b. A content analysis was performed on 1480 episodes of soap operas that had been televised in the preceding 5 years.

21. Experimenters who use instruments that record measurements in nonmetric units
   a. should report the measurement as recorded.
   b. may report the nonmetric units but must also report the SI (metric) equivalents.
   c. can report either the nonmetric units or the SI (metric) equivalents.
   d. None of the above is correct.

22. Spell out the metric unit
   a. when the unit does not appear with a numeric value.
   b. when the unit appears with a numeric value.
   c. in table headings.
   d. None of the above is correct.

23. Edit the following for citing the source of a statistic in text:

   A one-way analysis of variance (see any standard statistics text) was used to assess the effect of drug dosage.

   a. leave as is

   b. A one-way analysis of variance was used to assess the effect of drug dosage.

   c. A one-way analysis of variance (Winer, 1971) was used to assess the effect of drug dosage.

24. Include formulas for
   a. new or rare statistics or mathematical expressions.
   b. a statistical or mathematical expression essential to a paper.
   c. all statistics and mathematical expressions.
   d. a and b.
   e. none of the above.

25. Edit the following for the presentation of statistics:

The interaction between depression status of the participant and content of the message had a significant effect on mood judgments (see Table 2), $F(1, 92) = 4.26$, $p < .05$.

a. leave as is

b. The interaction between depression status of the participant and content of the message had a significant effect on mood judgments (see Table 2), $p < .05$.

c. The interaction between depression status of the participant and content of the message had a significant effect on mood judgments (see Table 2), $F = 4.26$, $p < .05$.

d. The interaction between depression status of the participant and content of the message had a significant effect on mood judgments (see Table 2), $F(1/92)$, $p < .05$.

26. Edit the following for the presentation of statistics:

The volunteers who appeared for the orientation session (sample size = 120) were then randomly assigned to one of the three conditions.

a. leave as is

b. The volunteers who appeared for the orientation session (N = 120) were then randomly assigned to one of the three conditions.

c. The volunteers who appeared for the orientation session (N = 120) were then randomly assigned to one of the three conditions.

d. The volunteers who appeared for the orientation session (n = 120) were then randomly assigned to one of the three conditions.

27. A table should be used

a. whenever numbers are involved.
b. when an article is more than five pages.
c. when it compresses data and allows relationships to be seen that are not readily seen in text.
d. for all of the above.

28. Edit the following table for tabular presentation:

Table 4

Mean Imaginal Scores of Students Reporting an Out-of-Body Experience

Condition	Imaginal scores
Visual	7.1
Auditory	4.0

    a. Table 4 should be Table IV.
    b. Results consisting of only two means should be presented in the text, not in a table.
    c. No standard deviations are given.
    d. b and c

29. For all tables within one paper, use

    a. the same terminology.
    b. similar formats.
    c. the same title.
    d. a and b.

30. A table title should be

    a. brief (i.e., no more than four to six words).
    b. clear about what data are in the table, yet concise.
    c. detailed about all independent and dependent variables.
    d. a and b are correct.

31. The left-hand column of a table (the *stub*) has a heading (the *stubhead*) that usually describes the

    a. elements in that column.
    b. dependent variables.
    c. independent variables.
    d. data.
    e. a and c.

32. In the word-processed manuscript, all rules used in a table should be

    a. drawn with the underline key.
    b. drawn with the table border function.
    c. used only to clarify divisions.
    d. all of the above.

33. The word *figure* refers to

    a. halftones.
    b. graphs and charts.
    c. illustrations.
    d. all of the above.

34. A figure is not necessary if it

   a. augments text.
   b. duplicates text.
   c. eliminates lengthy discussion from the text.
   d. does none of the above.

35. A figure legend should be positioned

   a. within the figure.
   b. to the left of the figure.
   c. below the figure.
   d. above the figure.

36. Figure captions

   a. serve as the explanation and as the title of the figure.
   b. should describe the contents of the figure in a brief sentence or phrase.
   c. should be typed on a separate sheet for submission to a journal.
   d. all of the above.

37. Which of the following is the correct ordering of manuscript sections in a research report?

   a. title page, abstract, introduction
   b. Method, Results, Discussion
   c. References, tables, footnotes
   d. a and b

38. Edit the following for typing statistical and mathematical copy:

   A 2 x 2 x 3 (Sex of Participant x Sex of Target x Activity Profile) analysis of variance was performed on the attractiveness scores.

   a. leave as is

   b. A 2x2x3 (Sex of Participant x Sex of Target x Activity Profile) analysis of variance was performed on the attractiveness scores.

   c. A 2X2X3 (Sex of Participant X Sex of Target X Activity Profile) analysis of variance was performed on the attractiveness scores.

   d. A 2 X 2 X 3 (Sex of Participant X Sex of Target X Activity Profile) analysis of variance was performed on the attractiveness scores.

39. A running head to be used in a research report should be

   a. centered at the bottom of the title page in all uppercase letters.
   b. flush left at the top of the title page.
   c. centered at the bottom of the title page in uppercase and lowercase letters.
   d. flush right at the bottom of the title page.

40. Table numbers and titles should be

    a. centered in uppercase and lowercase letters.
    b. single-spaced at the top of the table.
    c. flush with the left margin in uppercase and lowercase letters.
    d. according to a and b.

RESEARCH REPORT MASTERY TEST 2
ANSWER SHEET AND FEEDBACK REPORT

Student Name _____ **Date** _____

Question Number	Answer	APA Codes	Question Number	Answer	APA Codes
1	_____	1.01–1.04	21	_____	3.50–3.52
2	_____	1.06–1.07	22	_____	3.50–3.52
3	_____	1.08–1.09	23	_____	3.53–3.59
4	_____	1.08–1.09	24	_____	3.53–3.59
5	_____	1.10–1.13	25	_____	3.53–3.59
6	_____	1.10–1.13	26	_____	3.53–3.59
7	_____	1.10–1.13	27	_____	3.62–3.72
8	_____	2.01–2.02	28	_____	3.62–3.72
9	_____	3.10–3.11	29	_____	3.62–3.72
10	_____	3.12–3.18	30	_____	3.62–3.72
11	_____	3.12–3.18	31	_____	3.62–3.72
12	_____	3.20–3.29	32	_____	3.62–3.72
13	_____	3.30–3.33	33	_____	3.75–3.81
14	_____	3.42–3.49	34	_____	3.75–3.81
15	_____	3.42–3.49	35	_____	3.75–3.81
16	_____	3.42–3.49	36	_____	3.83–3.84
17	_____	3.42–3.49	37	_____	5.01–5.08
18	_____	3.42–3.49	38	_____	5.09–5.14
19	_____	3.42–3.49	39	_____	5.15–5.25
20	_____	3.42–3.49	40	_____	5.15–5.25

NUMBER CORRECT _____

RESEARCH REPORT MASTERY TEST 2
ANSWER KEY

Question Number	Answer	APA Codes	Question Number	Answer	APA Codes
1	c	1.01–1.04	21	b	3.50–3.52
2	a	1.06–1.07	22	a	3.50–3.52
3	e	1.08–1.09	23	b	3.53–3.59
4	d	1.08–1.09	24	d	3.53–3.59
5	d	1.10–1.13	25	a	3.53–3.59
6	b	1.10–1.13	26	c	3.53–3.59
7	c	1.10–1.13	27	c	3.62–3.72
8	e	2.01–2.02	28	d	3.62–3.72
9	d	3.10–3.11	29	d	3.62–3.72
10	e	3.12–3.18	30	b	3.62–3.72
11	a	3.12–3.18	31	e	3.62–3.72
12	a	3.20–3.29	32	d	3.62–3.72
13	c	3.30–3.33	33	d	3.75–3.81
14	a	3.42–3.49	34	b	3.75–3.81
15	c	3.42–3.49	35	a	3.75–3.81
16	a	3.42–3.49	36	d	3.83–3.84
17	c	3.42–3.49	37	d	5.01–5.08
18	b	3.42–3.49	38	a	5.09–5.14
19	b	3.42–3.49	39	a	5.15–5.25
20	a	3.42–3.49	40	c	5.15–5.25

RESEARCH REPORT MASTERY TEST 3

1. A research report usually includes an introduction and sections called _____ , Results, and Discussion.

    a. Method
    b. Bibliography
    c. Statement of the Problem
    d. Hypotheses

2. A poorly written abstract is not self-contained. Which of the sentences below violates the criterion of being self-contained?

    a. The DSM treatment group was superior to the control group.

    b. Salt-sensitive clients are more reactive than are non-salt-sensitive clients.

    c. According to Smith (1990), "male-dominant sexual activity is seen in cultures where rape receives little or no punishment" (p. 221).

    d. all of the above
    e. a and c of the above

3. When citing references in the introduction,

    a. avoid exhaustive historical reviews.
    b. cite select studies pertinent to the problem issue.
    c. refer the reader to reviews if they are available.
    d. do all of the above.
    e. do only a and b.

4. The Method section should be described in enough detail to

    a. permit a reader to evaluate the reality of your hypotheses.
    b. permit an experienced investigator to replicate your study.
    c. allow a perfect duplication of your investigation.
    d. allow an editor to judge the external validity of your study.

5. In the Results section, you should

    a. summarize data collected.
    b. discuss the statistical treatment of data.
    c. discuss the implications of the findings.
    d. do all of the above.
    e. do a and b of the above.

6. Speculation can be used in the Discussion section when it

    a. bravely goes beyond empirical data and the theory being tested.
    b. is expressed concisely.
    c. is identified as speculation.
    d. does all of the above.
    e. does b and c of the above.

7. Consistency of verb tense helps to smooth expression. Select the preferred match of paper section with verb tense from the choices below:

   a. conclusion: present tense
   b. literature review: present tense
   c. Results: past tense
   d. Method: past tense
   e. all of the above except b

8. The present tense is usually appropriate when you are

   a. presenting past research.
   b. describing the demographic details of the subjects.
   c. discussing results and presenting conclusions.
   d. describing the results.
   e. The present tense is never used.

9. Identify the example with incorrect use of capitalization:

   a. The conclusion is obvious: forgiveness is not granted to the stronger partner in an inequitable relationship.

   b. Familiar tasks appear to accelerate the acquaintanceship process in groups of strangers.

   c. Schizophrenia is sometimes associated with visual creativity.

   d. The brain stem is the "on switch" of consciousness.

10. Edit the following for capitalization of experimental conditions:

    The Sex-education and No-sex-education groups were then asked to view a film on the ethics of physical intimacy.

    a. leave as is
    b. The names of experimental conditions or groups should not be capitalized.
    c. All nouns following hyphens should be capitalized.
    d. The word *groups* also should be capitalized.

11. Capitalize

    a. the word *factor* when it is followed by a number (e.g., Factor 6).
    b. effects or variables that do not appear with multiplication signs.
    c. sources of effect variance, but not sources of error variance.
    d. all of the above.
    e. none of the above.

12. The abbreviations S, E, and O (for subject, experimenter, and observer, respectively)

    a. are treated the same as other abbreviations in the text.
    b. are not used in APA articles.
    c. should only be used in table notes and figure captions.
    d. None of the above is correct.

13. Edit the following by selecting the correct arrangement of headings:

Results

Pretraining Phase

Accuracy.

   a. leave as is

   b.

RESULTS

Pretraining Phase

Accuracy.

   c.

RESULTS

Pretraining Phase

Accuracy.

   d.

Results

Pretraining Phase

Accuracy.

14. Edit the following for the expression of numbers:

The stimulus presentations were separated by a masking field that lasted for 2 ms.

   a. leave as is

   b. The stimulus presentations were separated by a masking field that lasted for two ms.

15. Edit the following for the expression of numbers:

Each critical word was preceded by zero, one, two, or three priming words in the list.

   a. leave as is

   b. Each critical word was preceded by zero, 1, 2, or 3 priming words in the list.

   c. Each critical word was preceded by 0, 1, 2, or 3 priming words in the list.

   d. Each critical word was preceded by zero (0), one (1), two (2), or three (3) priming words in the list.

16. Edit the following for the expression of numbers:

Each participant evaluated each of the 12 social portraits on each of 6 dimensions.

a. leave as is

b. Each participant evaluated each of the twelve social portraits on each of six dimensions.

c. Each participant evaluated each of the 12 social portraits on each of six dimensions.

d. Each participant evaluated each of the twelve social portraits on each of 6 dimensions.

17. Edit the following for the expression of numbers:

There were 20 4-person teams in each leadership-style condition.

a. leave as is

b. There were twenty four-person teams in each leadership-style condition.

c. There were 20 four-person teams in each leadership-style condition.

d. There were twenty 4-person teams in each leadership-style condition.

18. Edit the following for the expression of decimal fractions:

The correlation between scores on the two measures of job satisfaction was .84.

a. leave as is

b. The correlation between scores on the two measures of job satisfaction was 0.84.

c. The correlation between scores on the two measures of job satisfaction was 84×10^{-2}.

d. The correlation between scores on the two measures of job satisfaction was .8400.

19. Edit the following for the expression of numbers:

Experiment I was a normative study to determine the reactions of hospital staff members to different diseases and illnesses.

a. leave as is

b. Experiment One was a normative study to determine the reactions of hospital staff members to different diseases and illnesses.

c. Experiment 1 was a normative study to determine the reactions of hospital staff members to different diseases and illnesses.

d. Experiment one was a normative study to determine the reactions of hospital staff members to different diseases and illnesses.

20. Edit the following for the expression of numbers:

The tones were presented at 6,000 Hz for varying durations.

a. leave as is

b. The tones were presented at 6000 Hz for varying durations.

c. The tones were presented at 6×10^3 Hz for varying durations.

21. The APA policy on the use of metric units in writing states that

a. due to the complex nature of the metric system it should only be used for publication in international journals.
b. the metric system is used in journals if possible; when not possible, nonmetric units must also be accompanied by their equivalents (in parentheses) in the International System of Units.
c. either system, metric or nonmetric, is acceptable.
d. the use of nonmetric units is completely unacceptable.

22. When you include statistics from another source in a research report, cite the reference

a. for less common statistics.
b. for statistics used in a controversial way.
c. when the statistic itself is the focus of an article.
d. all of the above.

23. Edit the following for citing the source of a statistic in text:

A chi-square test (Ferguson, 1981) was used to compare the preference distributions for girls and boys.

a. leave as is

b. A chi-square test (see any standard statistics text) was used to compare the preference distributions for girls and boys.

c. A chi-square test was used to compare the preference distributions for girls and boys.

24. Edit the following for the presentation of statistics:

Suggested starting salary was significantly lower when the applicant was described as a woman (M = \$19,600) than when the applicant was described as a man (M = \$22,080), $t(df = 62)$ = 2.58, $p < .01$.

a. leave as is

b. Suggested starting salary was significantly lower when the applicant was described as a woman (M = \$19,600) than when the applicant was described as a man (M = \$22,080), t_{62} = 2.58, $p < .01$.

c. Suggested starting salary was significantly lower when the applicant was described as a woman (M = \$19,600) than when the applicant was described as a man (M = \$22,080), $t(62)$ = 2.58, $p < .01$.

d. Suggested starting salary was significantly lower when the applicant was described as a woman (M = \$19,600) than when the applicant was described as a man (M = \$22,080), t = 2.58, $p < .01$.

25. Edit the following for the presentation of statistics:

The grade distributions of instructors who conducted extra help sessions were significantly different from those of instructors who did not, $\chi_4^2(1,208)$ = 10.25, $p < .05$.

a. leave as is

b. The grade distributions of instructors who conducted extra help sessions were significantly different from those of instructors who did not, $\chi_{1,208}^2(df = 4)$ = 10.25, $p < .05$.

c. The grade distributions of instructors who conducted extra help sessions were significantly different from those of instructors who did not, $\chi^2(4, N = 1,208)$ = 10.25, $p < .05$.

d. The grade distributions of instructors who conducted extra help sessions were significantly different from those of instructors who did not, χ^2 = 10.25 ($df = 4$, N = 1,208), $p < .05$.

26. Edit the following for the presentation of statistics:

   The applicants in the support condition (n = 18) were given a training course in résumé writing and interview techniques.

   a. leave as is

   b. The applicants in the support condition (n = 18) were given a training course in résumé writing and interview techniques.

   c. The applicants in the support condition (N = 18) were given a training course in résumé writing and interview techniques.

   d. The applicants in the support condition (sample size = 18) were given a training course in résumé writing and interview techniques.

27. Tables should be used for

   a. any data relevant to the article.
   b. important data directly related to the content of the article.
   c. any data presented in the text.
   d. all of the above.

28. Tables should be an integral part of the text, yet be readable alone. To accomplish this end,

   a. use extensive footnotes (one third of a page).
   b. explain all but the most common statistical abbreviations.
   c. cite the table in the text by saying "in the above table."
   d. put tables in an appendix.
   e. do all of the above.

29. For all tables within one paper, use

   a. the same terminology.
   b. similar formats.
   c. the same title.
   d. a and b.

30. The left-hand column of a table (the *stub*) usually lists

   a. mean values.
   b. the major independent variables.
   c. decked heads.
   d. none of the above.

31. The body of a table

   a. always contains data that are rounded off to the nearest tenth.
   b. contains columns of data even if those data can be easily calculated from other columns.
   c. contains words or numerical data.
   d. does all of the above.

32. When ruling tables,

    a. almost never use vertical rules.
    b. use both horizontal and vertical rules.
    c. you may substitute appropriately positioned white spaces for rules.
    d. do a and c.
    e. do all of the above.

33. The word *figure* is used to refer to

    a. tables of data.
    b. graphs and charts.
    c. statistical symbols.
    d. all of the above.

34. What type of graph is useful to represent the intersection of two variables?

    a. bar
    b. scatter
    c. line
    d. circle

35. What kind of lettering should not be used when lettering a figure?

    a. careful freehand
    b. professional
    c. typewritten
    d. dry-transfer or stencil
    e. a and c

36. A good figure caption

    a. describes the figure in detail no matter how lengthy it becomes.
    b. should refer the reader to a place in the text for explanation of the figure.
    c. is concise but explanatory.
    d. does none of the above.

37. Which of the following is the correct ordering of manuscript sections in a research report?

    a. Method, Results, tables, Discussion
    b. References, tables, figure captions, figures
    c. author notes, figures, figure captions, tables
    d. none of the above

38. Edit the following for typing statistical and mathematical copy:

    The students' use of the computer for word processing was independent of their knowledge of computer programming, Chi^2(1, $N = 86$) = 1.23, $p > .25$.

    a. leave as is
    b. The students' use of the computer for word processing was independent of their knowledge of computer programming, χ^2(1, $N = 86$) = 1.23, $p > .25$.
    c. The students' use of the computer for word processing was independent of their knowledge of computer programming, χ^2(1, $N=86$) = 1.23, $p > .25$.
    d. The students' use of the computer for word processing was independent of their knowledge of computer programming, X^2(1, $N = 86$)=1.23, $p>.25$.

39. The title page of a manuscript includes the

   a. author's name
   b. author's institutional affiliation.
   c. running head.
   d. short title.
   e. All of the above are included.

40. Edit the following for placement of a table in text:

   Insert Table 99 about here

   ---

   a. leave as is
   b. A table insert should not be centered.
   c. The lines above and below the insert should be dotted.
   d. "Insert" instructions should be more precise. The word *about* should be deleted.
   e. It is not necessary to indicate table placement other than by citing it in text.

RESEARCH REPORT MASTERY TEST 3
ANSWER SHEET AND FEEDBACK REPORT

Student Name _____ Date _____

Question Number	Answer	APA Codes	Question Number	Answer	APA Codes
1	_____	1.01–1.04	21	_____	3.50–3.52
2	_____	1.06–1.07	22	_____	3.53–3.59
3	_____	1.08–1.09	23	_____	3.53–3.59
4	_____	1.08–1.09	24	_____	3.53–3.59
5	_____	1.10–1.13	25	_____	3.53–3.59
6	_____	1.10–1.13	26	_____	3.53–3.59
7	_____	2.01–2.02	27	_____	3.62–3.72
8	_____	2.01–2.02	28	_____	3.62–3.72
9	_____	3.12–3.18	29	_____	3.62–3.72
10	_____	3.12–3.18	30	_____	3.62–3.72
11	_____	3.12–3.18	31	_____	3.62–3.72
12	_____	3.20–3.29	32	_____	3.62–3.72
13	_____	3.30–3.33	33	_____	3.75–3.81
14	_____	3.42–3.49	34	_____	3.75–3.81
15	_____	3.42–3.49	35	_____	3.75–3.81
16	_____	3.42–3.49	36	_____	3.83–3.84
17	_____	3.42–3.49	37	_____	5.01–5.08
18	_____	3.42–3.49	38	_____	5.09–5.14
19	_____	3.42–3.49	39	_____	5.15–5.25
20	_____	3.42–3.49	40	_____	5.15–5.25

NUMBER CORRECT _____

RESEARCH REPORT MASTERY TEST 3
ANSWER KEY

Question Number	Answer	APA Codes	Question Number	Answer	APA Codes
1	a	1.01–1.04	21	b	3.50–3.52
2	e	1.06–1.07	22	d	3.53–3.59
3	d	1.08–1.09	23	c	3.53–3.59
4	b	1.08–1.09	24	c	3.53–3.59
5	e	1.10–1.13	25	c	3.53–3.59
6	e	1.10–1.13	26	a	3.53–3.59
7	e	2.01–2.02	27	b	3.62–3.72
8	c	2.01–2.02	28	b	3.62–3.72
9	a	3.12–3.18	29	d	3.62–3.72
10	b	3.12–3.18	30	b	3.62–3.72
11	a	3.12–3.18	31	c	3.62–3.72
12	b	3.20–3.29	32	d	3.62–3.72
13	d	3.30–3.33	33	b	3.75–3.81
14	a	3.42–3.49	34	b	3.75–3.81
15	c	3.42–3.49	35	e	3.75–3.81
16	c	3.42–3.49	36	c	3.83–3.84
17	d	3.42–3.49	37	b	5.01–5.08
18	a	3.42–3.49	38	b	5.09–5.14
19	c	3.42–3.49	39	e	5.15–5.25
20	b	3.42–3.49	40	e	5.15–5.25

RESEARCH REPORT MASTERY TEST 4

1. Which of the following must identify the specific variables investigated and the relation between them?

   a. the first sentence of the introduction section
   b. the conclusion of the Discussion section
   c. the title of the report
   d. the first table that is cited

2. Abstracts of empirical studies are between 100 and 120 words and contain

   a. a one-sentence statement of the problem.
   b. pertinent details from the Method section.
   c. all statistical findings, degrees of freedom, F or t values, and significance levels.
   d. all of the above.
   e. a and b of the above.

3. Before writing the introduction, questions to bear in mind include the following:

   a. What is the point of the study?
   b. How does the study relate to past research?
   c. What are the theoretical implications of the study?
   d. How will the study's hypotheses be derived from the literature?
   e. all of the above.

4. The usual subsections of the Method section include

   a. introduction, procedures, and design.
   b. procedures, procedure tests, and participants.
   c. participants, apparatus, and procedure.
   d. none of the above.

5. An analysis of variance on your 2 × 2 design has revealed two main effects without an interaction effect (fewer errors were made with easy tasks, and 6-month-olds did better than 1-month-olds in all tasks). In planning your Results section, the best alternative from among the possibilities is to include

   a. no figure.
   b. one figure to show the main effect of age.
   c. a simple table showing the main effect means.
   d. both a table and a figure.

6. The Discussion section should begin with

   a. a statement regarding implications for future research.
   b. a statement of the support or nonsupport of your original hypothesis.
   c. a reformulation of the important points of the paper.
   d. an analysis of the flaws in your study.

7. On the basis of verb tense, in which part of a report is the following text segment likely to appear?

> College students judged time differently than did college faculty. Faculty were more accurate in judging the amount of time required to do academic tasks.

   a. Method
   b. hypotheses
   c. Discussion
   d. conclusion

8. Informal verb use such as *the participant felt that*, colloquial expressions such as *lab report*, or approximations of quantity such as *in large measure*

   a. have a place in serious scientific writing.
   b. add warmth to dull scientific prose.
   c. reduce word precision and clarity.
   d. can be used to enhance communication.
   e. are more acceptable in written than in oral communication.

9. In table headings and figure captions,

   a. capitalize only the first word and proper nouns.
   b. capitalize all major words.
   c. do not capitalize any words.
   d. capitalization will depend on the message you wish to convey.

10. Edit the following for the capitalization of names of experimental conditions:

> Participants in the tobacco-chewing therapy condition and in the no-therapy control condition then each received two wads of chewing tobacco.

   a. leave as is
   b. The names of experimental conditions should always be capitalized.
   c. The names of treatments such as *two wads* should be capitalized.
   d. Because *chewing tobacco* is a commercial term, it should be capitalized.

11. Which of the following should not be italicized?

   a. *a priori*

   b. 1973, *26*, 46-77

   c. $F(1, 53) = 10.03$

   d. *Journal of Experimental Psychology*

12. The abbreviations S, E, and O (for subject, experimenter, and observer, respectively)

   a. should always be used in articles.
   b. should only be used in journals that deal with physiological aspects of psychology.
   c. should be used only in the Method section.
   d. are not used in APA articles.

13. The general rule on expressing numbers is
    a. use words to express all numbers.
    b. use figures to express all numbers.
    c. use words to express numbers below 10 and figures to express numbers 10 and above.
    d. use figures to express numbers in tables and graphs and words to express numbers in the text.

14. Edit the following for the expression of numbers:

    The number of times the client used *I* in each therapy sessions is shown in Figure Two.

    a. leave as is

    b. The number of times the client used *I* in each therapy session is shown in Figure II.

    c. The number of times the client used *I* in each therapy session is shown in Figure 2.

    d. The number of times the client used *I* in each therapy session is shown in Figure two.

15. Edit the following for the expression of numbers:

    The investigation compared the effectiveness of 3 methods for disseminating health information in the local community.

    a. leave as is

    b. The investigation compared the effectiveness of three methods for disseminating health information in the local community.

    c. Both a and b are correct.

16. Edit the following for the expression of numbers:

    Sixty percent of the victims' closest relatives, but only twenty-eight percent of the victims themselves, showed signs of anxiety and stress on the delayed tests.

    a. leave as is

    b. Sixty percent of the victims' closest relatives, but only 28% of the victims themselves, showed signs of anxiety and stress on the delayed tests.

    c. 60% of the victims' closest relatives, but only 28% of the victims themselves, showed signs of anxiety and stress on the delayed tests.

    d. Sixty percent (60%) of the victims' closest relatives, but only 28% of the victims themselves, showed signs of anxiety and stress on the delayed tests.

17. Edit the following for the expression of ordinal numbers:

The sequence of events changed on the fourth trial.

a. leave as is

b. The sequence of events changed on the 4th trial.

c. The sequence of events changed on the IVth trial.

18. Edit the following for the expression of decimal fractions:

The main effect of training condition was significant, $F(3, 150) = 5.28$, $p < 0.01$.

a. leave as is

b. The main effect of training condition was significant, $F(3, 150) = 5.28$, $p < .01$.

c. The main effect of training condition was significant, $F(3, 150) = 5.28$, $p < .010$.

19. Edit the following for the expression of numbers:

The differential treatments were implemented on Trial 2.

a. leave as is

b. The differential treatments were implemented on Trial II.

c. The differential treatments were implemented on Trial Two.

d. The differential treatments were implemented on trial two.

20. Edit the following for the punctuation of numbers:

We counted the number of times that incumbent and nonincumbent candidates referred to themselves and their opposition in a total of 1663 speeches during the 1984 and the 1988 political campaigns.

a. leave as is

b. We counted the number of times that incumbent and nonincumbent candidates referred to themselves and their opposition in a total of 1,663 speeches during the 1,984 and the 1,988 political campaigns.

c. We counted the number of times that incumbent and nonincumbent candidates referred to themselves and their opposition in a total of 1,663 speeches during the 1984 and the 1988 political campaigns.

21. The APA policy on the use of metric units in writing states that
    a. due to the complex nature of the metric system it should only be used for publication in international journals.
    b. the metric system is used in journals if possible; when not possible, nonmetric units must also be accompanied by their equivalents (in parentheses) in the International System of Units.
    c. either system, metric or nonmetric, is acceptable.
    d. the use of nonmetric units is completely unacceptable.

22. Formulas for statistics should be given
    a. at all times.
    b. for common statistics and for a statistic that is used only once in the article.
    c. for a statistic not yet widely known or for one that is the focus of the article.
    d. None of the above is correct.

23. Edit the following for the presentation of formulas:

    The participants were divided into high and low self-monitors by a median split (*Mdn* = 50th percentile).

    a. leave as is

    b. The participants were divided into high and low self-monitors by a median split (*Mdn* = 50th %ile).

    c. The participants were divided into high and low self-monitors by a median split [*Mdn* = (*n* + 1)/2].

    d. The participants were divided into high and low self-monitors by a median split.

24. Which of the following is the correct way to present a statistic in text?
    a. $t = 2.62(22)$, p< .01
    b. $t = 2.62(22)$, *p* <. 01
    c. t(22) = 2.62, *p*<. 01
    d. any of the above
    e. none of the above

25. Edit the following for the presentation of statistics:

    The means for the no-treatment, placebo, and drug conditions were 8.8, 7.2, and 4.6, respectively.

    a. leave as is

    b. The means for the three conditions were 8.8, 7.2, and 4.6.

    c. The means for the three conditions were 8.8, 7.2, and 4.6, respectively.

26. Edit the following for the expression of statistical terms:

    The *M*s for the alcohol and no-alcohol conditions were 18.4 and 13.6, respectively.

    a. leave as is

    b. The means for the alcohol and no-alcohol conditions were 18.4 and 13.6, respectively.

    c. The MEANS for the alcohol and no-alcohol conditions were 18.4 and 13.6, respectively.

    d. The $\overline{X}$s for the alcohol and no-alcohol conditions were 18.4 and 13.6, respectively.

27. A table should be used

    a. whenever data analyses are involved.
    b. when an article is more than 1,200 words.
    c. when it compresses data and allows relationships to be seen that are not readily seen in text.
    d. for all of the above.

28. Tables should be an integral part of the text, yet be readable alone. To accomplish this end,

    a. use extensive footnotes (one third of a page).
    b. explain all but the most common statistical abbreviations.
    c. cite the table in the text by saying "in the above table."
    d. put tables in an appendix.
    e. do all of the above.

29. Tables should be numbered in the order

    a. in which they are first mentioned in the text.
    b. that seems most logical to the author.
    c. that seems most logical to an editor.
    d. of any of the above.

30. The column spanner of a table

    a. is a thick line used to mark the top of the table.
    b. is exclusively used to list the dependent variables.
    c. labels the column head variables.
    d. should be no more than 20 characters wide.

31. The body of a table

    a. always contains data rounded off to the nearest tenth.
    b. contains columns of data even if those data can be easily calculated from other columns.
    c. contains words or numerical data.
    d. does all of the above.

32. When ruling tables, use

    a. horizontal rules only.
    b. vertical rules only.
    c. both horizontal and vertical rules.
    d. well-positioned white space rather than horizontal rules.
    e. b and d.

33. A good figure

    a. conveys only essential facts.
    b. is easy to understand.
    c. is prepared in the same style as similar figures in the same article.
    d. does all of the above.

34. If a graph could be misinterpreted because the origin of the coordinates is not zero,

    a. do not include the graph in the research report.
    b. break the axes with a double slash.
    c. specify the origin in the notes to the table.
    d. separate the axes by at least 1 cm.

35. From the following examples, select the correct way to refer to a figure in text:

    a. see the figure above

    b. see the figure on page 14

    c. see Figure 2

    d. see Figure 2 above on page 14

36. Table notes

    a. are placed below the bottom rule of a table.
    b. explain table data or provide additional information.
    c. acknowledge the source of a reprinted table.
    d. do all of the above.
    e. do none of the above.

37. Which of the following should be placed on a separate page of a manuscript?

    a. the abstract
    b. appendixes
    c. figure captions
    d. all of the above
    e. none of the above

38. Edit the following for typing statistical and mathematical copy:

    The students' use of the computer for word processing was independent of their knowledge of computer programming, $\text{Chi}^2(1, N = 86) = 1.23, p > .25$.

    a. leave as is

    b. The students' use of the computer for word processing was independent of their knowledge of computer programming, $\chi^2(1, N = 86) = 1.23, p > .25$.

    c. The students' use of the computer for word processing was independent of their knowledge of computer programming, $\chi^2(1, N=86) = 1.23, p > .25$.

    d. The students' use of the computer for word processing was independent of their knowledge of computer programming, $X^2(1, N = 86)=1.23, p>.25$.

39. The abstract should be typed as

    a. a single paragraph in block format.
    b. one or more paragraphs with the first line indented.
    c. a single paragraph with the first line indented.
    d. more than one paragraph with space between paragraphs.

40. Table numbers and titles should be typed

    a. centered in uppercase and lowercase letters.
    b. single-spaced at the top of the table.
    c. flush with the left margin in uppercase and lowercase letters.
    d. according to a and b.

RESEARCH REPORT MASTERY TEST 4
ANSWER SHEET AND FEEDBACK REPORT

Student Name _____ Date _____

Question Number	Answer	APA Codes	Question Number	Answer	APA Codes
1	_____	1.06–1.07	21	_____	3.50–3.52
2	_____	1.06–1.07	22	_____	3.53–3.59
3	_____	1.08–1.09	23	_____	3.53–3.59
4	_____	1.08–1.09	24	_____	3.53–3.59
5	_____	1.10–1.13	25	_____	3.53–3.59
6	_____	1.10–1.13	26	_____	3.53–3.59
7	_____	2.01–2.02	27	_____	3.62–3.72
8	_____	2.03–2.05	28	_____	3.62–3.72
9	_____	3.12–3.18	29	_____	3.62–3.72
10	_____	3.12–3.18	30	_____	3.62–3.72
11	_____	3.19	31	_____	3.62–3.72
12	_____	3.20–3.29	32	_____	3.62–3.72
13	_____	3.42–3.49	33	_____	3.75–3.81
14	_____	3.42–3.49	34	_____	3.75–3.81
15	_____	3.42–3.49	35	_____	3.83–3.84
16	_____	3.42–3.49	36	_____	3.87–3.89
17	_____	3.42–3.49	37	_____	5.01–5.08
18	_____	3.42–3.49	38	_____	5.09–5.14
19	_____	3.42–3.49	39	_____	5.15–5.25
20	_____	3.42–3.49	40	_____	5.15–5.25

NUMBER CORRECT _____

RESEARCH REPORT MASTERY TEST 4
ANSWER KEY

Question Number	Answer	APA Codes	Question Number	Answer	APA Codes
1	c	1.06–1.07	21	b	3.50–3.52
2	e	1.06–1.07	22	c	3.53–3.59
3	e	1.08–1.09	23	d	3.53–3.59
4	c	1.08–1.09	24	e	3.53–3.59
5	a	1.10–1.13	25	a	3.53–3.59
6	b	1.10–1.13	26	b	3.53–3.59
7	c	2.01–2.02	27	c	3.62–3.72
8	c	2.03–2.05	28	b	3.62–3.72
9	a	3.12–3.18	29	a	3.62–3.72
10	a	3.12–3.18	30	c	3.62–3.72
11	a	3.19	31	c	3.62–3.72
12	d	3.20–3.29	32	a	3.62–3.72
13	c	3.42–3.49	33	d	3.75–3.81
14	c	3.42–3.49	34	b	3.75–3.81
15	b	3.42–3.49	35	c	3.83–3.84
16	b	3.42–3.49	36	d	3.87–3.89
17	a	3.42–3.49	37	d	5.01–5.08
18	b	3.42–3.49	38	b	5.09–5.14
19	a	3.42–3.49	39	a	5.15–5.25
20	c	3.42–3.49	40	c	5.15–5.25

CHAPTER 4

The Master Test Files

TERM PAPER MASTER TEST FILE

In contrast to empirical or theoretical articles, review articles
   a.   define and clarify a problem.
   b.   summarize previous investigations.
   c.   identify relations, contradictions, or inconsistencies in the literature.
   d.   suggest steps for future research.
   e.   do all of the above.

APA CODE: 1.04
INDEX NUMBER: 01
answer: e
TP-FAMILIARIZATION

Which characteristic of a manuscript helps readers grasp the paper's outline and the relative importance of its parts?
   a.   voice
   b.   verb tense
   c.   hypotheses
   d.   headings
   e.   all of the above

APA CODE: 1.05
INDEX NUMBER: 01
answer: d
TP-PRACTICE

If a paper you have written is too long, shorten it by stating points clearly, confining discussion to the specific problem under investigation, writing in the active voice, and
   a.   deleting or combining tables.
   b.   using more figures.
   c.   developing new theories.
   d.   repeating the major points.
   e.   Do none of the above.

APA CODE: 1.05
INDEX NUMBER: 02
answer: a
TP-MASTERY 1

It is important that headings convey to the reader
   a.   a sense of style.
   b.   the relative importance of the parts of the paper.
   c.   the author's biases.
   d.   all of the above.

APA CODE: 1.05
INDEX NUMBER: 03
answer: b
TP-MASTERY 2

Before you begin to write, you should plan the sequence and levels of importance of
   a.   voicing.
   b.   statistical analyses.
   c.   headings.
   d.   the hypotheses.
   e.   all of the above.

APA CODE: 1.05
INDEX NUMBER: 04
answer: c
TP-MASTERY 3

Headings are important in a report because they
   a.   satisfy the requirements of APA style.
   b.   communicate the logical structure of the paper.
   c.   fulfill a tradition in scientific writing.
   d.   are used in place of paragraph indentation.
   e.   All of the above are correct.

APA CODE: 1.05
INDEX NUMBER: 05
answer: b
TP-MASTERY 4

When listing an author of a paper, it is incorrect to

    a.   give titles (PhD or OFM).
    b.   spell out the middle name.
    c.   use informal names (Ronnie Reagan).
    d.   do all of the above.

APA CODE: 1.06
INDEX NUMBER: 01
answer: d
TP-FAMILIARIZATION

A manuscript title should

    a.   use abbreviations wherever possible.
    b.   contain at least 30 words.
    c.   be fully explanatory when standing alone.
    d.   begin with the words *A Study of*.

APA CODE: 1.06
INDEX NUMBER: 02
answer: c
TP-PRACTICE

In an introduction, controversial issues may be discussed when relevant; however, an author must

    a.   present both sides of the issue.
    b.   develop sound ad hominem arguments.
    c.   cite authorities out of context.
    d.   disguise his or her bias.
    e.   do none of the above.

APA CODE: 1.08
INDEX NUMBER: 01
answer: a
TP-MASTERY 1

A finished report should possess

    a.   no recognizable theme or logical structure.
    b.   disconnected but logical subsections.
    c.   an orderly presentation of ideas.
    d.   inferential statistical tests of the data.

APA CODE: 2.01
INDEX NUMBER: 01
answer: c
TP-MASTERY 2

In scientific writing, continuity

    a.   is achieved partly by proper use of punctuation marks and transitional words.
    b.   requires abandoning familiar syntax.
    c.   is enhanced by using many commas.
    d.   is not really necessary.

APA CODE: 2.01
INDEX NUMBER: 02
answer: a
TP-MASTERY 3

Ideas appear more orderly when

    a.   punctuation supports meaning.
    b.   transition words of time (*then* or *next*) or causation (*therefore* or *consequently*) are used.
    c.   contrast links (*however* or *whereas*) are used.
    d.   all of the above are present.
    e.   only a and b are present.

APA CODE: 2.01
INDEX NUMBER: 03
answer: d
TP-MASTERY 4

In casual conversation the word *since* is synonymous with _____ , but in scientific writing it should be used only in its temporal meaning.

    a.   *however*
    b.   *because*
    c.   *after*
    d.   all of the above

APA CODE: 2.01
INDEX NUMBER: 04
answer: b
TP-FAMILIARIZATION

The orderly presentation of ideas will become disorderly if the writer

    a.   cues the reader to the subordination of ideas with punctuation.
    b.   misplaces words.
    c.   abandons familiar syntax.
    d.   does all of the above.
    e.   does b and c.

APA CODE: 2.01
INDEX NUMBER: 05
answer: e
TP-PRACTICE

Report your conclusions in

    a.   the past tense.
    b.   the past perfect tense.
    c.   the present tense.
    d.   any of the above.

APA CODE: 2.02
INDEX NUMBER: 01
answer: c
TP-MASTERY 1

You can check your writing for smoothness of expression by

    a.   looking for sudden shifts in topic, tense, or person.
    b.   having a colleague search the paper for abrupt transitions.
    c.   reading the paper aloud.
    d.   doing all of the above.
    e.   doing a and b.

APA CODE: 2.02
INDEX NUMBER: 02
answer: d
TP-MASTERY 2

Verb tense should

    a.   be varied to keep the reader's interest.
    b.   never change.
    c.   always be the past or past perfect.
    d.   be consistent within paragraphs.

APA CODE: 2.02
INDEX NUMBER: 03
answer: d
TP-MASTERY 3

Synonyms should be used

    a.   with care because they may suggest subtle differences.
    b.   as much as possible to make the manuscript interesting.
    c.   whenever the same word is mentioned three or more times in one paragraph.
    d.   only in the conclusion.

APA CODE: 2.02
INDEX NUMBER: 04
answer: a
TP-MASTERY 4

Good economy of expression may be achieved through using

    a.   short words.
    b.   short sentences.
    c.   simple declarative sentences.
    d.   short paragraphs.
    e.   all of the above.

APA CODE: 2.03
INDEX NUMBER: 01
answer: e
TP-FAMILIARIZATION

Which of the following phrases is redundant?

    a.   a total of 68 respondents
    b.   has been previously found
    c.   in close proximity
    d.   all of the above
    e.   none of the above

APA CODE: 2.03
INDEX NUMBER: 02
answer: d
TP-PRACTICE

Which of the following phrases is an example of economical writing?

    a.   absolutely essential
    b.   four groups saw
    c.   one and the same
    d.   the reason is because

APA CODE: 2.03
INDEX NUMBER: 03
answer: b
TP-MASTERY 1

Redundancy, wordiness, jargon, evasiveness, and circumlocution contribute to

    a.   poor economy of expression.
    b.   clear scientific writing.
    c.   smoothness of expression.
    d.   erudite precision.
    e.   a more readable, less pompous style of writing.

APA CODE: 2.03
INDEX NUMBER: 04
answer: a
TP-MASTERY 2

A writer must be careful when using the pronouns *this*, *that*, *these*, and *those*. The writer can eliminate or reduce the vagueness of these pronouns by

    a.   referring the reader to a specific previous sentence.
    b.   using them to modify a noun (e.g., this frenulum, that hypothalamus, these electrodes, those mice).
    c.   using them frequently.
    d.   clarifying what is being referred to for the reader.
    e.   All of the above except c may be done.

APA CODE: 2.04
INDEX NUMBER: 01
answer: e
TP-MASTERY 3

Colloquial expressions such as *the wind in his sails died* or approximations of quantity such as *the lion's share of*

    a.   reduce word precision and clarity.
    b.   add warmth to dull scientific prose.
    c.   have a place even in serious scientific writing.
    d.   can be used to enhance communication.
    e.   are more acceptable in written than in oral communication.

APA CODE: 2.04
INDEX NUMBER: 02
answer: a
TP-MASTERY 4

The phrase "the experiment demonstrated" is an example of which of the following writing errors?

    a.   ambiguity
    b.   redundancy
    c.   attributing a human characteristic to a nonhuman source
    d.   none of the above

APA CODE: 2.04
INDEX NUMBER: 03
answer: c
TP-FAMILIARIZATION

Colloquial expressions such as *write-up*, approximations of quantity such as *quite a large part*, and informal or imprecise use of verbs such as *the client felt that*

    a.   reduce word precision and clarity.
    b.   add warmth to dull scientific prose.
    c.   have a place even in serious scientific writing.
    d.   can be used to enhance communication.
    e.   are more acceptable in written as compared with oral communication.

APA CODE: 2.04
INDEX NUMBER: 04
answer: a
TP-PRACTICE

Identify problems with clarity in the following sentences:

    We read instructions to the students. This was done to reduce experimenter bias.

    a.   Both sentences are expressed clearly.
    b.   The first sentence is clear, but the second starts with *this*, a vague reference pronoun, and is in the passive voice.
    c.   The first sentence uses a first-person pronoun.
    d.   Instructions should be read to subjects, not students.
    e.   Both sentences are unclear.

APA CODE: 2.04
INDEX NUMBER: 05
answer: b
TP-MASTERY 1

The best person to select to critique your manuscript is

    a.   your spouse or another person whom you know very well.
    b.   a colleague who is very familiar with your work.
    c.   a colleague who does not follow your work closely.
    d.   a stranger off the street.

APA CODE: 2.05
INDEX NUMBER: 01
answer: c
TP-MASTERY 2

Which of the following is a good strategy for improving writing style?

    a.   Revise the first draft after a delay.
    b.   Use an outline.
    c.   Ask a colleague for criticism.
    d.   Do all of the above.

APA CODE: 2.05
INDEX NUMBER: 02
answer: d
TP-MASTERY 3

Choose the best strategy for improving your writing style:

    a.   Write from an outline.
    b.   Put aside the first draft, then reread it after a delay.
    c.   Ask a colleague to critique the first draft for you.
    d.   Begin writing close to a deadline to enhance your motivation.
    e.   Any of the above except d can be used, but the strategy must match your personality and work habits.

APA CODE: 2.05
INDEX NUMBER: 03
answer: e
TP-MASTERY 4

Which of the following sentences contains the preferable use of verb tense and voice?

    a.   The same results have been shown by Ramirez (1980).

    b.   Ramirez (1980) shows the same results.

    c.   Ramirez (1980) showed the same results.

    d.   Ramirez (1980) had shown the same results.

APA CODE: 2.06
INDEX NUMBER: 01
answer: c
TP-FAMILIARIZATION

Edit the following for verb tense:

Wrightsman and Deaux (1981) would demonstrate the same effect.

a. leave as is

b. Wrightsman and Deaux (1981) demonstrated the same effect.

c. Wrightsman and Deaux (1981) demonstrate the same effect.

d. The same effect was demonstrated by Wrightsman and Deaux (1981).

APA CODE: 2.06
INDEX NUMBER: 02
answer: b
TP-PRACTICE

Edit the following for verb tense:

After completing the preliminary battery of rating scales, each worker watched one of the six videotapes of a problem-solving session.

a. leave as is

b. After completing the preliminary battery of rating scales, each worker would watch one of the six videotapes of a problem-solving session.

c. After completing the preliminary battery of rating scales, each worker had watched one of the six videotapes of a problem-solving session.

d. After completing the preliminary battery of rating scales, each worker was watching one of the six videotapes of a problem-solving session.

APA CODE: 2.06
INDEX NUMBER: 03
answer: a
TP-MASTERY 1

Edit the following for verb tense:

If the theory of learned helplessness was not considered relevant to human behavior, clinically depressed clients would be treated differently by many therapists.

a. leave as is

b. If the theory of learned helplessness was not considered relevant to human behavior, clinically depressed clients would be being treated differently by many therapists.

c. If the theory of learned helplessness were not considered relevant to human behavior, clinically depressed clients were being treated differently by many therapists.

d. If the theory of learned helplessness were not considered relevant to human behavior, clinically depressed clients would be treated differently by many therapists.

APA CODE: 2.06
INDEX NUMBER: 04
answer: d
TP-MASTERY 2

Edit the following for grammar:

The six stimulus were presented to each participant simultaneously.

a.   leave as is

b.   The six stimuli were presented to each participant simultaneously.

c.   The six stimuli was presented to each participant simultaneously.

d.   The six stimuluses were presented to each participant simultaneously.

APA CODE: 2.07
INDEX NUMBER: 01
answer: b
TP-MASTERY 3

Which of the following sentences is an example of correct agreement between subject and verb?

a.   The percentage of correct responses increase with practice.

b.   The data indicate that Brenda was correct.

c.   The phenomena occurs every 100 years.

d.   Neither the participants nor the confederate were in the perfumery.

APA CODE: 2.07
INDEX NUMBER: 02
answer: b
TP-MASTERY 4

Which of the following sentences is an example of correct agreement between the pronoun and its antecedent?

a.   The rats that completed the task successfully were rewarded.

b.   Neither the highest scorer nor the lowest scorer had any doubt about their competence.

c.   The group improved their scores 30%.

d.   All of the above are correct.
e.   None of the above is correct.

APA CODE: 2.08
INDEX NUMBER: 01
answer: a
TP-FAMILIARIZATION

Which of the following sentences is grammatically correct?

a.   Name the participant whom you found scored above the median.

b.   The rats that completed the test successfully were rewarded.

c.   We had nothing to do with them being the winners.

d.   None of the above is correct.

APA CODE: 2.08
INDEX NUMBER: 02
answer: b
TP-PRACTICE

Edit the following for the use of pronouns:

The students that were assigned to the delay condition were asked to return at the same time in 3 days.

a.   leave as is

b.   The students who were assigned to the delay condition were asked to return at the same time in 3 days.

c.   The students whom were assigned to the delay condition were asked to return at the same time in 3 days.

d.   The students which were assigned to the delay condition were asked to return at the same time in 3 days.

APA CODE: 2.08
INDEX NUMBER: 03
answer: b
TP-MASTERY 1

Edit the following for the use of pronouns:

The volunteer whom the confederate selected had to use nonverbal gestures to convey the emotion to the other volunteers.

a. leave as is

b. The volunteer that the confederate selected had to use nonverbal gestures to convey the emotion to the other volunteers.

c. The volunteer who the confederate selected had to use nonverbal gestures to convey the emotion to the other volunteers.

d. The volunteer which the confederate selected had to use nonverbal gestures to convey the emotion to the other volunteers.

APA CODE: 2.08
INDEX NUMBER: 04
answer: a
TP-MASTERY 2

Edit the following for the use of pronouns:

The team achieved a 38% improvement in their scores after undergoing imagery training.

a. leave as is

b. The team achieved a 38% improvement in its scores after undergoing imagery training.

c. The team achieved a 38% improvement in each of their scores after undergoing imagery training.

d. The team achieved a 38% improvement in scores after undergoing imagery training.

APA CODE: 2.08
INDEX NUMBER: 05
answer: b
TP-MASTERY 3

Edit the following for the placement of modifiers:

The victims reported to trained volunteers still experiencing anxiety.

a. leave as is

b. The victims reported to trained volunteers, still experiencing anxiety.

c. The victims, still experiencing anxiety, reported to trained volunteers.

d. The victims, reported to trained volunteers, still experiencing anxiety.

APA CODE: 2.09
INDEX NUMBER: 01
answer: c
TP-MASTERY 4

Edit the following for the placement of the modifier *only*:

> Although the authors reported the data for the mild and extreme patients in the placebo condition, they only reported the data for the extreme patients in the treatment condition.

a. leave as is

b. Although the authors reported the data for the mild and extreme patients in the placebo condition, they reported only the data for the extreme patients in the treatment condition.

c. Although the authors reported the data for the mild and extreme patients in the placebo condition, they reported the data for only the extreme patients in the treatment condition.

d. Although the authors reported the data for the mild and extreme patients in the placebo condition, they reported the data for the extreme patients only in the treatment condition.

APA CODE: 2.09
INDEX NUMBER: 02
answer: c
TP-FAMILIARIZATION

Edit the following for the placement of modifiers:

> To manipulate ego-involvement, the respondents were given different average scores for their norm group.

a. leave as is

b. To manipulate ego-involvement, we gave the respondents different average scores for their norm group.

c. Manipulating ego-involvement, the respondents were given different average scores for their norm group.

d. The respondents were given different average scores for their norm group to manipulate ego-involvement.

APA CODE: 2.09
INDEX NUMBER: 03
answer: b
TP-PRACTICE

Edit the following for the choice and placement of modifiers:

> Hopefully, the different types of music will induce different levels of arousal in the listeners.

a. leave as is

b. The different types of music will, hopefully, induce different levels of arousal in the listeners.

c. Hopefully the different types of music will induce different levels of arousal in the listeners.

d. We hope that the different types of music will induce different levels of arousal in the listeners.

APA CODE: 2.09
INDEX NUMBER: 04
answer: d
TP-MASTERY 1

Misplaced modifiers can be avoided by
    a.   placing adjectives and adverbs at the end of sentences wherever possible.
    b.   placing adjectives and adverbs as close as possible to the words that they modify.
    c.   using the word *only* for clarification.
    d.   writing in the passive voice.

APA CODE: 2.09
INDEX NUMBER: 05
answer: b
TP-MASTERY 2

Which of the following sentences illustrates the correct use of the word *while* in scientific writing?

    a.   Bragg (1965) found that participants performed well, while Bohr (1969) found that participants did poorly.

    b.   While these findings are unusual, they are not unique.

    c.   Bragg found that participants performed well while listening to music.

    d.   All of the above are correct.

APA CODE: 2.10
INDEX NUMBER: 01
answer: c
TP-MASTERY 3

Which of the following sentences is incorrect according to the preferred style stated in the APA *Publication Manual*?

    a.   While these findings are unusual, they are not unique.

    b.   Although these findings are unusual, they are not unique.

    c.   These findings are unusual, but they are not unique.

    d.   All of the above are incorrect.

APA CODE: 2.10
INDEX NUMBER: 02
answer: a
TP-MASTERY 4

Edit the following for the use of subordinate conjunctions:

    Since left-handers constitute a minority of the population, there are less likely to be appropriate models for them to watch.

    a.   leave as is

    b.   Because left-handers constitute a minority of the population, there are less likely to be appropriate models for them to watch.

    c.   Although left-handers constitute a minority of the population, there are less likely to be appropriate models for them to watch.

    d.   While left-handers constitute a minority of the population, there are less likely to be appropriate models for them to watch.

APA CODE: 2.10
INDEX NUMBER: 03
answer: b
TP-FAMILIARIZATION

Edit the following for the use of subordinate conjunctions:

    The more skilled athletes chose individual sports, while the less skilled athletes chose team sports.

    a.   leave as is

    b.   The more skilled athletes chose individual sports, and, at the same time, the less skilled athletes chose team sports.

    c.   The more skilled athletes chose individual sports, whereas the less skilled athletes chose team sports.

    d.   Both a and b are correct.

APA CODE: 2.10
INDEX NUMBER: 04
answer: c
TP-PRACTICE

Edit the following for the use of relative pronouns:

> The pictorial feedback, which was interpreted more rapidly than the verbal feedback, was remembered better.

a. leave as is

b. The pictorial feedback which was interpreted more rapidly than the verbal feedback was remembered better.

c. The pictorial feedback, which was interpreted more rapidly than the verbal feedback was remembered better.

d. The pictorial feedback that was interpreted more rapidly than the verbal feedback was remembered better.

APA CODE: 2.10
INDEX NUMBER: 05
answer: a
TP-MASTERY 1

Edit the following for sentence structure:

> The results of experiments with animals and humans indicated that continuous reinforcement resulted in faster acquisition but partial reinforcement was more resistant to extinction.

a. leave as is

b. The results of experiments with animals and humans indicated that continuous reinforcement resulted in faster acquisition, but partial reinforcement was more resistant to extinction.

c. The results of experiments with animals and humans indicated that continuous reinforcement resulted in faster acquisition and partial reinforcement was more resistant to extinction.

d. The results of experiments with animals and humans indicated that continuous reinforcement resulted in faster acquisition but that partial reinforcement was more resistant to extinction.

APA CODE: 2.11
INDEX NUMBER: 01
answer: d
TP-MASTERY 2

Edit the following for sentence structure:

> Successful problem solvers were both more adept at representing the problem and using heuristics.

a. leave as is

b. Successful problem solvers were both more adept at representing the problem as well as using heuristics.

c. Successful problem solvers were more adept both at representing the problem and at using heuristics.

d. Successful problem solvers were more adept at both representing the problem and at using heuristics.

APA CODE: 2.11
INDEX NUMBER: 02
answer: c
TP-MASTERY 3

Edit the following for sentence structure:

> Interviewees are often instructed to dress conservatively, to pay attention to their nonverbal communications, and that they should ask a few job-related questions of the interviewer.

a. leave as is

b. Interviewees are often instructed to dress conservatively, to pay attention to their nonverbal communications, and to ask a few job-related questions of the interviewer.

c. Interviewees are often instructed to dress conservatively, pay attention to their nonverbal communications, and that they should be prepared to ask a few job-related questions of the interviewer.

d. Interviewees are often instructed to dress conservatively and pay attention to their nonverbal communications, and that they should ask a few job-related questions of the interviewer.

APA CODE: 2.11
INDEX NUMBER: 03
answer: b
TP-MASTERY 4

Edit the following for sentence structure:

> Erikson's psychosocial theory emphasizes not only developmental stages but also the role of the ego.

a. leave as is

b. Erikson's psychosocial theory not only emphasizes developmental stages but also the role of the ego.

c. Erikson's psychosocial theory emphasizes not only developmental stages but also the role of the ego, as well.

d. Erikson's psychosocial theory emphasizes not only developmental stages but neither the role of the ego.

APA CODE: 2.11
INDEX NUMBER: 04
answer: a
TP-FAMILIARIZATION

Which of the following should be used in scientific writing?
a. rhyming
b. poetic expressions
c. sexist language
d. none of the above

APA CODE: 2.12
INDEX NUMBER: 01
answer: d
TP-PRACTICE

Edit the following for the use of nonsexist language:

Accumulating evidence suggests that a supervisor will be more effective if he allows his workers to participate in decision making in a meaningful way.

a. leave as is

b. Accumulating evidence suggests that a supervisor will be more effective if he or she allows workers to participate in decision making in a meaningful way.

c. Accumulating evidence suggests that a supervisor who allows workers to participate in decision making in a meaningful way will be more effective.

d. Both b and c are correct.

APA CODE: 2.13 &
Table 2.1
INDEX NUMBER: 02
answer: d
TP-MASTERY 1

Edit the following for the use of nonsexist language:

A telephone operator must decode numerous messages daily from voices she has never previously heard.

a. leave as is

b. A telephone operator must decode numerous messages daily from male or female voices she has never previously heard.

c. A telephone operator must decode numerous messages daily from voices he has never previously heard.

d. A telephone operator must decode numerous messages daily from voices the operator has never previously heard.

APA CODE: 2.13 &
Table 2.1
INDEX NUMBER: 03
answer: d
TP-MASTERY 2

Edit the following for the use of nonsexist language:

Before an experienced computer programmer attempts a particular solution, he tries to relate the problem structure to other problems he has solved successfully.

a. leave as is

b. Before an experienced computer programmer attempts a particular solution, he/she tries to relate the problem structure to other problems he/she has solved successfully.

c. Before experienced computer programmers attempt a particular solution, they try to relate the problem structure to other problems they have solved successfully.

d. Before an experienced computer programmer attempts a particular solution, the programmer (he or she) tries to relate the problem structure to other problems he (or she if she really is experienced) has solved successfully.

APA CODE: 2.13 &
Table 2.1
INDEX NUMBER: 04
answer: c
TP-MASTERY 3

Edit the following for the use of nonsexist language:

They predicted that men would be selected more frequently as partners for the cognitive tasks and that females would be chosen more frequently for the interpersonal tasks.

a. leave as is

b. They predicted that males would be selected more frequently as partners for the cognitive tasks and that nonmales would be chosen more frequently for the interpersonal tasks.

c. They predicted that men would be selected more frequently as partners for the cognitive tasks and that women would be chosen more frequently for the interpersonal tasks.

d. They predicted that guys would be selected more frequently as partners for the cognitive tasks and that girls would be chosen more frequently for the interpersonal tasks.

APA CODE: 2.13 &
Table 2.1
INDEX NUMBER: 05
answer: c
TP-MASTERY 4

Edit the following for the use of nonsexist language:

It has been suggested that the major factor giving man a performance advantage over other primates on many cognitive tasks is that the tasks have been selected and administered by other men.

a. leave as is

b. It has been suggested that the major factor giving the species of man a performance advantage over other primates on many cognitive tasks is that the tasks have been selected and administered by men of the same species.

c. It has been suggested that the major factor giving human beings a performance advantage over other primates on many cognitive tasks is that the tasks have been selected and administered by other human beings.

d. It has been suggested that the major factor giving human beings (men or women) a performance advantage over other primates on many cognitive tasks is that the tasks have been selected and administered by other human beings.

APA CODE: 2.13 &
Table 2.1
INDEX NUMBER: 06
answer: c
TP-FAMILIARIZATION

Edit the following for the use of nonsexist language:

> The data in Table 2 are the proportion of male participants who selected the competitive action over the cooperative one on each trial and, similarly, the proportion of female participants who were willing to act aggressively on each trial.

a. leave as is

b. The data in Table 2 are the proportion of male and female participants who selected the competitive action over the cooperative one on each trial.

c. The data in Table 2 are the proportion of male participants who selected the competitive action over the cooperative one on each trial and the proportion of female participants who were willing to act aggressively on each trial.

d. The data in Table 2 are the proportion of males who selected the competitive action over the cooperative one on each trial and, similarly, the proportion of females who were willing to act in typically male fashion (aggressively) on each trial.

APA CODE: 2.13 &
Table 2.1
INDEX NUMBER: 07
answer: b
TP-PRACTICE

Edit the following for language that shows consideration of the reader:

> The relative frequency of testing for AIDS was assessed in normal and homosexual populations.

a. leave as is

b. The relative frequency of testing for AIDS was assessed in sexually normal (heterosexual) and sexually abnormal (homosexual) populations.

c. The relative frequency of testing for AIDS was assessed in heterosexual as well as in gay and lesbian populations.

d. The relative frequency of testing for AIDS was assessed in straight and deviant populations.

APA CODE: 2.14
INDEX NUMBER: 08
answer: c
TP-MASTERY 1

Edit the following for avoiding ethnic bias:

> Black and White participants were asked to rate the attractiveness of Black and White models pictured in black-and-white photographs.

a. leave as is

b. Black (Negro) and White participants were asked to rate the attractiveness of Black (Negro) and White models pictured in black-and-white photographs.

c. Negro and Caucasian participants were asked to rate the attractiveness of Negro and Caucasian models pictured in black-and-white photographs.

d. Black and Caucasian participants were asked to rate the attractiveness of Black and Caucasian models pictured in black-and-white photographs.

APA CODE: 2.15
INDEX NUMBER: 01
answer: a
TP-MASTERY 2

Edit the following for avoiding ethnic bias:

In each age group, the American citizens who were foreigners performed better on the American history test than did the Americans.

a. leave as is

b. In each age group, the American citizens who were foreigners performed better on the American history test than did the American citizens who were native-born.

c. In each age group, the naturalized American citizens performed better on the American history test than did the native-born American citizens.

d. In each age group, the foreigners who became American citizens performed better on the American history test than did the Americans.

APA CODE: 2.15
INDEX NUMBER: 02
answer: c
TP-MASTERY 3

Edit the following for avoiding ethnic bias:

Participation in ethnic celebrations was compared for oriental immigrants and their first-, second-, and third-generation counterparts of the same cohort.

a. leave as is

b. Participation in ethnic celebrations was compared for immigrants from oriental countries and their first-, second-, and third-generation counterparts of the same cohort.

c. Participation in ethnic celebrations was compared for oriental immigrants and first-, second-, and third-generation orientals of the same cohort.

d. Participation in ethnic celebrations was compared for Asian immigrants and for first-, second-, and third-generation Asian Americans of the same cohort.

APA CODE: 2.15
INDEX NUMBER: 03
answer: d
TP-MASTERY 4

Edit the following for avoiding ethnic bias:

Because of their cultural deprivation, children in Third World countries have fewer opportunities to develop our moral values.

a. leave as is

b. Because of cultural differences, children in Third World countries may develop moral values different from those of children in Western countries.

c. Because of their cultural deprivation, children in Third World countries may not develop higher moral values.

d. Because of their cultural experiences, children in Third World countries have fewer opportunities to develop our moral values.

APA CODE: 2.15
INDEX NUMBER: 04
answer: b
TP-FAMILIARIZATION

In choosing nouns referring to ethnic groups, one should use

    a.   the most acceptable current terms.
    b.   the standard terms of the media.
    c.   anthropological terms.
    d.   none of the above.

APA CODE: 2.15
INDEX NUMBER: 05
answer: a
TP-PRACTICE

End a complete declarative sentence with a

    a.   prepositional clause followed by a question mark.
    b.   semicolon.
    c.   period.
    d.   comma.

APA CODE: 3.01
INDEX NUMBER: 01
answer: c
TP-MASTERY 1

Edit the following for punctuation:

Blind sleepers also show a cyclical pattern of sleep stages, they do not, however, display eye movements (Schwartz et al., 1978).

    a.   leave as is

    b.   Blind sleepers also show a cyclical pattern of sleep stages: They do not, however, display eye movements (Schwartz et al., 1978).

    c.   Blind sleepers also show a cyclical pattern of sleep stages. They do not, however, display eye movements (Schwartz et al., 1978).

    d.   Blind sleepers also show a cyclical pattern of sleep stages--They do not, however, display eye movements (Schwartz et al., 1978).

APA CODE: 3.01
INDEX NUMBER: 02
answer: c
TP-MASTERY 2

Edit the following for punctuation:

Optimal-level theories of motivation follow a homeostatic model. Opponent-process theories were advanced to account for addiction and other phenomena.

    a.   leave as is

    b.   Optimal-level theories of motivation follow a homeostatic model, opponent-process theories were advanced to account for addiction and other phenomena.

    c.   Optimal-level theories of motivation follow a homeostatic model-- Opponent-process theories were advanced to account for addiction and other phenomena.

    d.   Optimal-level theories of motivation follow a homeostatic model; Opponent-process theories were advanced to account for addiction and other phenomena.

APA CODE: 3.01
INDEX NUMBER: 03
answer: a
TP-MASTERY 3

Edit the following for punctuation:

> The confederate always sat to the experimenter's immediate left and the experimenter began the discussion by asking the confederate to evaluate the therapist's degree of empathy.

a.   leave as is

b.   The confederate always sat to the experimenter's immediate left; and the experimenter began the discussion by asking the confederate to evaluate the therapist's degree of empathy.

c.   The confederate always sat to the experimenter's immediate left, the experimenter began the discussion by asking the confederate to evaluate the therapist's degree of empathy.

d.   The confederate always sat to the experimenter's immediate left. The experimenter began the discussion by asking the confederate to evaluate the therapist's degree of empathy.

APA CODE: 3.01
INDEX NUMBER: 04
answer: d
TP-PRACTICE

Edit the following for punctuation:

> According to Piaget, the four stages of intellectual development are the sensorimotor stage, the preoperational stage, the concrete-operational stage, and the formal-operational stage.

a.   leave as is

b.   According to Piaget, the four stages of intellectual development are the sensorimotor stage, the preoperational stage, the concrete-operational stage and the formal-operational stage.

c.   According to Piaget, the four stages of intellectual development are the sensorimotor stage; the preoperational stage; the concrete-operational stage; and the formal-operational stage.

d.   According to Piaget, the four stages of intellectual development are the sensorimotor stage--the preoperational stage--the concrete-operational stage--and the formal-operational stage.

APA CODE: 3.02
INDEX NUMBER: 01
answer: a
TP-MASTERY 4

Edit the following for punctuation:

The participants were introduced to each of the trainers, but they were not allowed to choose their own trainer.

a. leave as is

b. The participants were introduced to each of the trainers but they were not allowed to choose their own trainer.

c. The participants were introduced to each of the trainers; but they were not allowed to choose their own trainer.

d. The participants were introduced to each of the trainers. But they were not allowed to choose their own trainer.

APA CODE: 3.02
INDEX NUMBER: 02
answer: a
TP-MASTERY 1

Edit the following for punctuation:

Damage to the left temporal cortex may impair language comprehension; whereas damage to the left frontal cortex may impair language production.

a. leave as is

b. Damage to the left temporal cortex may impair language comprehension. Whereas damage to the left frontal cortex may impair language production.

c. Damage to the left temporal cortex may impair language comprehension, whereas damage to the left frontal cortex may impair language production.

d. Damage to the left temporal cortex may impair language comprehension--whereas damage to the left frontal cortex may impair language production.

APA CODE: 3.02
INDEX NUMBER: 03
answer: c
TP-MASTERY 2

Edit the following for correct punctuation:

The floor was covered with cedar shavings and paper was available for shredding and nest building.

a. The sentence is correct as it stands.
b. Put a semicolon after *shavings*.
c. Put a comma after *shavings*.
d. Put a comma after *floor*.

APA CODE: 3.02
INDEX NUMBER: 04
answer: c
TP-MASTERY 3

Use a comma
a. before *and* and *or* in a series of three or more items.
b. between the two parts of a compound predicate.
c. to separate two independent clauses joined by a conjunction.
d. in all of the above instances.
e. in instances a and c above.

APA CODE: 3.02
INDEX NUMBER: 05
answer: e
TP-MASTERY 4

Which of the following phrases is correctly punctuated?

    a.   the study, by Jones Davis and Stewart (1972)

    b.   the study by Jones, Davis, and Stewart (1972)

    c.   the study by Jones, Davis, and Stewart, (1972)

    d.   the study by Jones, Davis and Stewart (1972)

    e.   the study by Jones Davis and Stewart (1972)

APA CODE: 3.02
INDEX NUMBER: 06
answer: b
TP-FAMILIARIZATION

Use a semicolon
    a.   to set off a nonessential or nonrestrictive clause.
    b.   to separate two independent clauses that are not joined by a conjunction.
    c.   in references between place of publication and publisher.
    d.   to do all of the above.

APA CODE: 3.03
INDEX NUMBER: 01
answer: b
TP-PRACTICE

What punctuation should follow *volunteers* in the example below?

    The participants in the first study were unpaid volunteers those in the second study were paid for their participation.

    a.   comma
    b.   colon
    c.   dash
    d.   semicolon

APA CODE: 3.03
INDEX NUMBER: 02
answer: d
TP-MASTERY 1

Edit the following for punctuation:

    Decay theory attributes forgetting to the passage of time, interference theory attributes it to other activities.

    a.   leave as is

    b.   Decay theory attributes forgetting to the passage of time: Interference theory attributes it to other activities.

    c.   Decay theory attributes forgetting to the passage of time; interference theory attributes it to other activities.

    d.   Decay theory attributes forgetting to the passage of time; and interference theory attributes it to other activities.

APA CODE: 3.03
INDEX NUMBER: 03
answer: c
TP-MASTERY 2

Edit the following for punctuation:

    Thus, the light status for the three trials in the four conditions was on, off, on: off, on, off: on, on, on: or off, off, off.

    a.   leave as is

    b.   Thus, the light status for the three trials in the four conditions was on, off, on, off, on, off, on, on, on, or off, off, off.

    c.   Thus the light status for the three trials in the four conditions was on, off, and on, or off, on, and off, or on, on, and on, or off, off, and off.

    d.   Thus, the light status for the three trials in the four conditions was on, off, on; off, on, off; on, on, on; or off, off, off.

APA CODE: 3.03
INDEX NUMBER: 04
answer: d
TP-MASTERY 3

Edit the following for punctuation:

From shortest to longest wavelength, the colors of the visible spectrum appear in the following order: blue-purple, blue, blue-green, green, yellow-green, yellow, orange, and red.

a.   leave as is

b.   From shortest to longest wavelength, the colors of the visible spectrum appear in the following order--blue-purple, blue, blue-green, green, yellow-green, yellow, orange, and red.

c.   From shortest to longest wavelength, the colors of the visible spectrum appear in the following order: Blue-purple, blue, blue-green, green, yellow-green, yellow, orange, and red.

d.   From shortest to longest wavelength, the colors of the visible spectrum appear in the following order ... blue-purple, blue, blue-green, green, yellow-green, yellow, orange, and red.

APA CODE: 3.04
INDEX NUMBER: 01
answer: a
TP-MASTERY 4

Edit the following for punctuation:

The James-Lange theory of emotion states that our emotional experience is caused by our awareness of our bodily reaction to some stimulus: Schachter and Singer (1962) proposed that a cognitive evaluation mediates between the bodily reaction and the subjective emotion.

a.   leave as is

b.   The James-Lange theory of emotion states that our emotional experience is caused by our awareness of our bodily reaction to some stimulus. Schachter and Singer (1962) proposed that a cognitive evaluation mediates between the bodily reaction and the subjective emotion.

c.   The James-Lange theory of emotion states that our emotional experience is caused by our awareness of our bodily reaction to some stimulus--Schachter and Singer (1962) proposed that a cognitive evaluation mediates between the bodily reaction and the subjective emotion.

d.   The James-Lange theory of emotion states that our emotional experience is caused by our awareness of our bodily reaction to some stimulus. And Schachter and Singer (1962) proposed that a cognitive evaluation mediates between the bodily reaction and the subjective emotion.

APA CODE: 3.04
INDEX NUMBER: 02
answer: b
TP-FAMILIARIZATION

Edit the following for the punctuation of a reference entry:

> Strunk, W., Jr., & White, E. B. (1979). *The elements of style* (3rd ed.). New York.
> Macmillan.

a. leave as is

b. Strunk, W., Jr., & White, E. B. (1979). *The elements of style* (3rd ed.). New York:
   Macmillan.

c. Strunk, W., Jr., & White, E. B. (1979). *The elements of style* (3rd ed.). New York,
   Macmillan.

d. Strunk, W., Jr., & White, E. B. (1979). *The elements of style* (3rd ed.). New York/
   Macmillan.

APA CODE: 3.04
INDEX NUMBER: 03
answer: b
TP-FAMILIARIZATION

Edit the following for the punctuation of ratios:

> Moving from the lowest subordinate level of the organization to the highest
> executive level, the ratios of men to women were 1.2 to 1, 2 to 1, 6 to 1, and
> 14 to 1, respectively.

a. leave as is

b. Moving from the lowest subordinate level of the organization to the highest
   executive level, the ratios of men/women were 1.2/1, 2/1, 6/1, and 14/1,
   respectively.

c. Moving from the lowest subordinate level of the organization to the highest
   executive level, the ratios of men:women were 1.2:1, 2:1, 6:1, and 14:1, respectively.

d. Moving from the lowest subordinate level of the organization to the highest
   executive level, the ratios of men-women were 1.2-1, 2-1, 6-1, and 14-1,
   respectively.

APA CODE: 3.04
INDEX NUMBER: 04
answer: c
TP-PRACTICE

Edit the following for punctuation:

> Human beings also undergo conditioning procedures that develop taste aversions ... bacteria in the food or an unrelated event such as chemotherapy may cause severe nausea following the ingestion of a novel, distinctively flavored food.

a. leave as is

b. Human beings also undergo conditioning procedures that develop taste aversions: Bacteria in the food or an unrelated event such as chemotherapy may cause severe nausea following the ingestion of a novel, distinctively flavored food.

c. Human beings also undergo conditioning procedures that develop taste aversions: bacteria in the food or an unrelated event such as chemotherapy may cause severe nausea following the ingestion of a novel, distinctively flavored food.

d. Human beings also undergo conditioning procedures that develop taste aversions-- Bacteria in the food or an unrelated event such as chemotherapy may cause severe nausea following the ingestion of a novel, distinctively flavored food.

APA CODE: 3.04
INDEX NUMBER: 05
answer: b
TP-MASTERY 1

Which of the following examples is correctly punctuated?

a. They have agreed on the outcome, informed participants perform better than uninformed participants.

b. They have agreed on the outcome; Informed participants perform better than uninformed participants.

c. They have agreed on the outcome: Informed participants perform better than uninformed participants.

d. None of the above is correct.

APA CODE: 3.04
INDEX NUMBER: 06
answer: c
TP-MASTERY 2

Which sentence is correct?

a. The digits were shown in the following order: 3, 2, 4, 1.

b. The digits were shown in the following order, 3, 2, 4, 1.

c. The digits were shown in the following order; 3, 2, 4, 1.

d. The digits were shown in the following order--3, 2, 4, 1.

APA CODE: 3.04
INDEX NUMBER: 07
answer: a
TP-MASTERY 3

The dash is used
a. to indicate a sudden interruption in the continuity of a sentence.
b. in APA articles only with permission of the technical editor.
c. frequently in APA articles in the statistical section.
d. by Type A psychologists.

APA CODE: 3.05
INDEX NUMBER: 01
answer: a
TP-MASTERY 4

When is the dash used?
a. to extend a thought
b. instead of commas to set off restrictive clauses
c. never in APA articles
d. to indicate a sudden interruption in the continuity of a sentence

APA CODE: 3.05
INDEX NUMBER: 02
answer: d
TP-FAMILIARIZATION

Edit the following for punctuation:

The children: none of whom had previously heard the story: listened as a master storyteller told the story.

a. leave as is

b. The children; none of whom had previously heard the story; listened as a master storyteller told the story.

c. The children ... none of whom had previously heard the story ... listened as a master storyteller told the story.

d. The children--none of whom had previously heard the story--listened as a master storyteller told the story.

APA CODE: 3.05
INDEX NUMBER: 03
answer: d
TP-PRACTICE

Edit the following for punctuation:

The book--that the client selected to read aloud--was given to the client as a reward for completing the task.

a. leave as is

b. The book that the client selected to read aloud was given to the client as a reward for completing the task.

c. The book, that the client selected to read aloud, was given to the client as a reward for completing the task.

d. The book (that the client selected to read aloud) was given to the client as a reward for completing the task.

APA CODE: 3.05
INDEX NUMBER: 04
answer: b
TP-MASTERY 1

Edit the following for punctuation:

The stimuli were six songs--matched for length, complexity of melody; and familiarity of lyrics.

a. leave as is

b. The stimuli were six songs: matched for length, complexity of melody, and familiarity of lyrics.

c. The stimuli were six songs ... matched for length, complexity of melody, and familiarity of lyrics.

d. The stimuli were six songs matched for length, complexity of melody, and familiarity of lyrics.

APA CODE: 3.05
INDEX NUMBER: 05
answer: d
TP-MASTERY 2

Edit the following for punctuation:

The 4 participants--2 in the vicarious condition, 1 in the direct condition, and 1 in the control condition--who recognized the confederate as a fellow student were excused from the second part of the experiment.

a.   leave as is

b.   The 4 participants, 2 in the vicarious condition, 1 in the direct condition, and 1 in the control condition, who recognized the confederate as a fellow student were excused from the second part of the experiment.

c.   The 4 participants: 2 in the vicarious condition, 1 in the direct condition, and 1 in the control condition: who recognized the confederate as a fellow student were excused from the second part of the experiment.

d.   The 4 participants ... 2 in the vicarious condition, 1 in the direct condition, and 1 in the control condition ... who recognized the confederate as a fellow student were excused from the second part of the experiment.

APA CODE: 3.05
INDEX NUMBER: 06
answer: a
TP-MASTERY 3

Edit the following for punctuation:

Harlow's (1959) article, *Love in Infant Monkeys*, made the case for the role of contact comfort in infant development.

a.   leave as is

b.   Harlow's (1959) article, titled Love in Infant Monkeys, made the case for the role of contact comfort in infant development.

c.   Harlow's (1959) article, 'Love in Infant Monkeys,' made the case for the role of contact comfort in infant development.

d.   Harlow's (1959) article, "Love in Infant Monkeys," made the case for the role of contact comfort in infant development.

APA CODE: 3.06
INDEX NUMBER: 01
answer: d
TP-MASTERY 4

Edit the following for the correct way to report verbatim instructions:

The participants were instructed to COMPLETE EACH SENTENCE BASED ON YOUR OWN FEELINGS AT THIS MOMENT.

a.   leave as is

b.   The participants were instructed to *complete each sentence based on your own feelings at this moment.*

c.   The participants were instructed to "complete each sentence based on your own feelings at this moment."

d.   The participants were instructed to 'complete each sentence based on your own feelings at this moment.'

APA CODE: 3.06
INDEX NUMBER: 02
answer: c
TP-FAMILIARIZATION

Edit the following for punctuation of the anchor points on a rating scale:

The respondents ranked each of the 30 characteristics on a scale ranging from "most like my mother" (1) to "most like my father" (5).

a. leave as is

b. The respondents ranked each of the 30 characteristics on a scale ranging from MOST LIKE MY MOTHER (1) to MOST LIKE MY FATHER (5).

c. The respondents ranked each of the 30 characteristics on a scale ranging from: most like my mother (1) to: most like my father (5).

d. The respondents ranked each of the 30 characteristics on a scale ranging from *most like my mother* (1) to *most like my father* (5).

APA CODE: 3.06
INDEX NUMBER: 03
answer: d
TP-PRACTICE

Edit the following for highlighting key terms:

According to Freud, the *latent dream* is censored by the defense mechanisms and replaced by a less threatening *manifest dream*.

a. leave as is

b. According to Freud, the "latent dream" is censored by the defense mechanisms and replaced by a less threatening "manifest dream."

c. According to Freud, the 'latent dream' is censored by the defense mechanisms and replaced by a less threatening 'manifest dream.'

d. According to Freud, the LATENT DREAM is censored by the defense mechanisms and replaced by a less threatening MANIFEST DREAM.

APA CODE: 3.06
INDEX NUMBER: 04
answer: a
TP-MASTERY 1

Edit the following for the correct way to identify an ironic, coined, or invented expression:

In Selfridge's (1959) pandemonium model of pattern recognition, feature detectors are represented by demons in the sensory system who shout to the next level of analysis when their feature is present in the stimulus.

a. leave as is

b. In Selfridge's (1959) pandemonium model of pattern recognition, feature detectors are represented by DEMONS in the sensory system who SHOUT to the next level of analysis when their feature is present in the stimulus.

c. In Selfridge's (1959) pandemonium model of pattern recognition, feature detectors are represented by *demons* in the sensory system who *shout* to the next level of analysis when their feature is present in the stimulus.

d. In Selfridge's (1959) pandemonium model of pattern recognition, feature detectors are represented by "demons" in the sensory system who "shout" to the next level of analysis when their feature is present in the stimulus.

APA CODE: 3.06
INDEX NUMBER: 05
answer: d
TP-MASTERY 2

When using slang or a coined phrase, set the expression off with
    a. double quotation marks the first time the expression is used.
    b. double quotation marks every time it is used.
    c. dashes every time it is used.
    d. single quotation marks the first time it is used.

APA CODE: 3.06
INDEX NUMBER: 07
answer: a
TP-MASTERY 3

Use double quotation marks
    a. every time an invented expression is used.
    b. only the first time an invented expression is introduced.
    c. to introduce a technical or key term.
    d. Answers b and c are correct.

APA CODE: 3.06
INDEX NUMBER: 08
answer: b
TO-MASTERY 4

When quoting long sections of material (e.g., verbatim instructions to participants of more than 40 words),
    a. set the quote off with double quotation marks.
    b. indent and use a block format without any quotation marks.
    c. use a single quotation mark at the beginning and the end of the quotation.
    d. use double quotation marks and single-spacing.

APA CODES: 3.06 &
3.34
INDEX NUMBER: 09
answer: b
TP-FAMILIARIZATION

Punctuation is used incorrectly in which example?

    a. The results were significant (see Figure 5).

    b. Smith and Jones, 1970, reported results similar to those of Walker (1976).

    c. The GSR of rodents is unreliable (Adams & Baker, 1957).

    d. "When sea turtles were studied, the effect was not seen" (p. 276).

APA CODE: 3.07
INDEX NUMBER: 01
answer: b
TP-PRACTICE

Edit the following for the punctuation of a reference citation in text:

Masters and Johnson, 1966, found a similarity in the phases of the sexual response of men and women.

    a. leave as is

    b. Masters and Johnson, in 1966, found a similarity in the phases of the sexual response of men and women.

    c. Masters and Johnson, 1966, found a similarity in the phases of the sexual response of men and women.

    d. Masters and Johnson (1966) found a similarity in the phases of the sexual response of men and women.

APA CODE: 3.07
INDEX NUMBER: 02
answer: d
TP-MASTERY 1

Edit the following for punctuation:

Scores were higher when participants were tested in the same environment as the one in which they learned (the effect of environmental similarity is reflected in the interaction of study environment and test environment).

a. leave as is

b. Scores were higher when participants were tested in the same environment as the one in which they learned. (The effect of environmental similarity is reflected in the interaction of study environment and test environment.)

c. Scores were higher when participants were tested in the same environment as the one in which they learned. (The effect of environmental similarity is reflected in the interaction of study environment and test environment).

d. Scores were higher when participants were tested in the same environment as the one in which they learned (The effect of environmental similarity is reflected in the interaction of study environment and test environment.).

APA CODE: 3.07
INDEX NUMBER: 03
answer: b
TP-MASTERY 2

Edit the following for punctuation:

The length of utterances increases dramatically between the ages of 18 and 60 months. See Figure 1.

a. leave as is

b. The length of utterances increases dramatically between the ages of 18 and 60 months (see Figure 1).

c. The length of utterances increases dramatically between the ages of 18 and 60 months (see Figure 1.).

d. The length of utterances increases dramatically between the ages of 18 and 60 months, see Figure 1.

APA CODE: 3.07
INDEX NUMBER: 04
answer: b
TP-MASTERY 3

Edit the following for punctuation:

Individuals with Type A personalities are more likely to develop coronary heart disease, CHD, than are those with Type B personalities.

a. leave as is

b. Individuals with Type A personalities are more likely to develop coronary heart disease, "CHD," than are those with Type B personalities.

c. Individuals with Type A personalities are more likely to develop coronary heart disease--CHD--than are those with Type B personalities.

d. Individuals with Type A personalities are more likely to develop coronary heart disease (CHD) than are those with Type B personalities.

APA CODE: 3.07
INDEX NUMBER: 05
answer: d
TP-MASTERY 4

Edit the following for the punctuation of a series:

> Theories of work motivation that emphasize the cognitive effects of information include *a* expectancy theory, *b* equity theory, and *c* goal-setting theory.

a.   leave as is

b.   Theories of work motivation that emphasize the cognitive effects of information include (a) expectancy theory, (b) equity theory, and (c) goal-setting theory.

c.   Theories of work motivation that emphasize the cognitive effects of information include a) expectancy theory, b) equity theory, and c) goal-setting theory.

d.   Theories of work motivation that emphasize the cognitive effects of information include: a. expectancy theory, b. equity theory, and c. goal-setting theory.

APA CODE: 3.07
INDEX NUMBER: 06
answer: b
TP-FAMILIARIZATION

Edit the following for quotation from a source:

> According to Hebb (1949), the phase sequence for a familiar event is well organized, so "it runs its course promptly, leaving the field for less well-established sequences" [p. 229].

a.   leave as is

b.   According to Hebb (1949), the phase sequence for a familiar event is well organized, so "it runs its course promptly, leaving the field for less well-established sequences," p. 229.

c.   According to Hebb (1949), the phase sequence for a familiar event is well organized, so "it runs its course promptly, leaving the field for less well-established sequences (p. 229)".

d.   According to Hebb (1949), the phase sequence for a familiar event is well organized, so "it runs its course promptly, leaving the field for less well-established sequences" (p. 229).

APA CODE: 3.07
INDEX NUMBER: 07
answer: d
TP-PRACTICE

Edit the following for punctuation:

Clients on the waiting list who were assigned to the delayed-treatment condition (whose mean age and educational level (see Table 2) did not differ from those assigned to the immediate-treatment condition) were asked to return in 6 weeks.

a. leave as is

b. Clients on the waiting list who were assigned to the delayed-treatment condition [whose mean age and educational level (see Table 2) did not differ from those assigned to the immediate-treatment condition] were asked to return in 6 weeks.

c. Clients on the waiting list who were assigned to the delayed-treatment condition (whose mean age and educational level [see Table 2] did not differ from those assigned to the immediate-treatment condition) were asked to return in 6 weeks.

d. Clients on the waiting list who were assigned to the delayed-treatment condition (whose mean age and educational level, see Table 2, did not differ from those assigned to the immediate-treatment condition) were asked to return in 6 weeks.

APA CODE: 3.08
INDEX NUMBER: 01
answer: c
TP-MASTERY 1

Edit the following for punctuation:

One possibility (as Winer, 1971, suggested) is to pool the error terms.

a. leave as is

b. One possibility (as Winer (1971) suggested) is to pool the error terms.

c. One possibility (as Winer [1971] suggested) is to pool the error terms.

d. One possibility [as Winer (1971) suggested] is to pool the error terms.

e. One possibility (as Winer [1971], suggested) is to pool the error terms.

APA CODE: 3.08
INDEX NUMBER: 02
answer: a
TP-MASTERY 2

The standard spelling reference for APA journals is
a. the most recent edition of *Merriam-Webster's Collegiate Dictionary*.
b. the *British-American Speller*.
c. the *Random House Dictionary*.
d. any of the above.

APA CODE: 3.10
INDEX NUMBER: 01
answer: a
TP-MASTERY 3

Regarding spelling,
a. the standard spelling reference is the most recent edition of *Merriam-Webster's Collegiate Dictionary*.
b. APA accepts all the spelling choices listed in popular English dictionaries.
c. APA has no standard and leaves the matter up to the individual journal editors.
d. British spelling is preferred.

APA CODE: 3.10
INDEX NUMBER: 02
answer: a
TP-MASTERY 4

Which of the following examples should not be hyphenated?
a. role-playing technique
b. super-ordinate variable
c. six-trial problem
d. high-anxiety group
e. all of the above

APA CODE: 3.11
INDEX NUMBER: 01
answer: b
TP-FAMILIARIZATION

Which of the following examples needs a hyphen?
   a.   a posteriori test
   b.   Type II error
   c.   12th grade students
   d.   unbiased

APA CODE: 3.11 &
Table 3.1
INDEX NUMBER: 02
answer: c
TP-PRACTICE

Of the following examples, which represents correct hyphenation?
   a.   randomly-assigned participants
   b.   higher-scoring students
   c.   self-report technique
   d.   all the above

APA CODE: 3.11
INDEX NUMBER: 03
answer: c
TP-MASTERY 1

Which of the following words with a prefix require a hyphen?
   a.   compounds in which the base word is an abbreviation (e.g., pre-UCS)
   b.   *self* compounds (e.g., self-esteem)
   c.   words that could be misunderstood or misread (e.g., un-ionized)
   d.   all of the above
   e.   none of the above

APA CODE: 3.11 &
Table 3.2
INDEX NUMBER: 04
answer: d
TP-MASTERY 2 & 4

Identify the example with incorrect use of capitalization:

   a.   The conclusion is obvious: forgiveness is not granted to the stronger partner in an inequitable relationship.

   b.   Familiar tasks appear to accelerate the acquaintanceship process in groups of strangers.

   c.   Schizophrenia is sometimes associated with visual creativity.

   d.   The brain stem is the "on switch" of consciousness.

APA CODE: 3.12
INDEX NUMBER: 01
answer: a
TP-MASTERY 3

From the alternatives below, select the one that correctly uses capitalization:

   a.   few significant differences were found.

   b.   However, one important observation was made: Participatory followers do not like to be led by authoritarian leaders.

   c.   Authoritarian followers behaved in a curious way: they acted in a participatory manner with participatory leaders.

   d.   these results were reported by Black and Walker (1986).

APA CODE: 3.12
INDEX NUMBER: 02
answer: b
TP-MASTERY 4

In titles of books and articles, initial letters are capitalized in
   a.   major words when titles appear in regular text.
   b.   words of four letters or more when titles appear in regular text.
   c.   the second word in a hyphenated compound when titles appear in regular text.
   d.   major words and words of four letters or more when titles appear in reference lists.
   e.   all of the above except d.

APA CODE: 3.13
INDEX NUMBER: 01
answer: e
TP-FAMILIARIZATION

Which of the examples contains incorrect capitalization?

   a.   During Trial 5, Group B performed at criterion.

   b.   Column 5, Row 3

   c.   The animals ate Purina Lab Chow after tail-pinch administration.

   d.   In his book, *History of Psychology*, the author describes Small's first use of the white rat.

APA CODES: 3.13–
3.15
INDEX NUMBER: 02
answer: b
TP-PRACTICE

Do not capitalize

    a. names of laws, theories, and hypotheses.
    b. trade and brand names.
    c. references to a specific department within a specific university.
    d. all of the above.
    e. b and c of the above.

APA CODE: 3.14
INDEX NUMBER: 01
answer: a
TP-MASTERY 1

Which of the following examples shows the wrong way to capitalize proper nouns?

    a. All psychology departments are reviewing their instructional effectiveness.

    b. Lennox (1988) also has a theory of self-monitoring.

    c. Dolphins are pro-Skinnerian.

    d. The eustachian tube was inserted.

    e. None of the above is incorrect.

APA CODE: 3.14
INDEX NUMBER: 02
answer: e
TP-MASTERY 2

Which noun is incorrectly capitalized in the following example?

Bem's Theory of Self-Perception suggests that a woman will like a stranger more after she dances with him.

    a. Theory
    b. Self
    c. Perception
    d. Bem's
    e. All of the above are incorrect except d.

APA CODE: 3.14
INDEX NUMBER: 03
answer: e
TP-MASTERY 3

From the following choices, select the sentence with the correct use of italics:

    a. She published her results in the *Journal of Interpersonal Relations and Social Behavior*.

    b. She published *her* results in the Journal of Interpersonal Relations and Social Behavior.

    c. When the *participants* read the nonsense syllable gux, they had to soothe their fearful partners.

    d. *Albino rabbits*, oryctolagus cuniculus, were given unconditional positive regard in both experimental groups.

APA CODE: 3.19
INDEX NUMBER: 01
answer: a
TP-FAMILIARIZATION

Which word in the following sentence should be underlined?

Snails were much faster when allowed to bathe ad lib in the acetylcholine solution.

    a. acetylcholine
    b. ad lib
    c. snails
    d. bathe
    e. none of the above

APA CODE: 3.19
INDEX NUMBER: 02
answer: e
TP-PRACTICE

Select the alternative that corrects the error of abbreviation in the following sentence.

The TAT was given to all LH women after they watched 30 hours of TV commercials.

a. The Thematic Apperception Test was given

b. to all left-handed women after

c. they watched 30 hr of

d. TV commercials

e. a, b, and c

APA CODE: 3.20
INDEX NUMBER: 01
answer: e
TP-MASTERY 1

Edit the following for the use of abbreviations to describe a procedural sequence:

All the men read about (R), danced with (D), or smelled (S) potential romantic partners. The bachelor group received one of four romantic interest arousal sequences: RDS, SDR, RSD, or SRD.

a. leave as is

b. read about, danced with, smelled; smelled, danced with, read about; read about, smelled, danced with; or smelled, read about, danced with.

c. read, danced, smelled; smelled, danced, read; read, smelled, danced; or smelled, read, danced.

d. read about then danced with then smelled; smelled then danced with then read about; read about then smelled then danced with; or smelled then read about then danced with.

APA CODE: 3.20
INDEX NUMBER: 02
answer: a
TP-MASTERY 2

Edit the following for correct use of abbreviations:

Three kinds of scene identification tasks were given to the police officers: a murder scene, a robbery scene, and an assault scene. The identification tasks were given in either an MS-RS-AS or AS-RS-MS sequence.

a. Define the abbreviations earlier by putting them within parentheses following the terms they abbreviated.
b. Use no abbreviations because they are not known by most readers.
c. Make no change because the connection between terms and abbreviations is obvious.
d. Make no change because the writer used standard abbreviations.

APA CODE: 3.21
INDEX NUMBER: 01
answer: a
TP-MASTERY 3

In the following example, which abbreviation should be spelled out when it is first introduced?

After the depressed clients received ECT treatments, changes in central nervous system activity were assessed with an EEG and effects on sleep were measured by observing REM periods.

a. EEG
b. ECT
c. REM
d. all of the above
e. any that do not appear in the latest edition of *Merriam-Webster's Collegiate Dictionary*

APA CODE: 3.22
INDEX NUMBER: 01
answer: e
TP-MASTERY 4

Edit the following for use of abbreviations:

According to Pavlov (1927), the conditioned stimulus (CS) should be delivered about 1 s before the unconditioned stimulus (US).

a. leave as is

b. According to Pavlov (1927), the conditioned stimulus (CS) should be delivered about 1 second before the unconditioned stimulus (US).

c. According to Pavlov (1927), the conditioned stimulus (CS) should be delivered about 1 sec. before the unconditioned stimulus (US).

d. According to Pavlov (1927), the CS should be delivered about 1 s before the US.

APA CODE: 3.23
INDEX NUMBER: 01
answer: a
TP-FAMILIARIZATION

Which Latin abbreviation is used incorrectly in the following example?

When management styles were compared (authoritarian vs. participatory), it was found that authoritarian managers, i.e., those who did not solicit or act on input from subordinates, did not do well in smaller organizations (e.g., corporations with fewer than 100 employees).

a. vs.
b. i.e.
c. e.g.
d. all of the above
e. none of the above

APA CODE: 3.24
INDEX NUMBER: 01
answer: b
TP-PRACTICE

Which Latin abbreviations are used correctly in the following example?

Not all traditional sex role expectancies (e.g., women may cry, men should not cry) transfer into all organizational cultures, i.e., an organization's social environment. Some organizations punish traditional sex role behavior in women but not in men, for example, military organizations, heavy industries, etc.

a. e.g.
b. i.e.
c. etc.
d. all of the above
e. none of the above

APA CODE: 3.24
INDEX NUMBER: 02
answer: a
TP-MASTERY 1

Is the Latin abbreviation *i.e.* used incorrectly in the following example?

Some lonely individuals appear to be shy but are in fact isolated because of social rejection (i.e., are actively avoided and excluded by others).

a. The parentheses should be removed.
b. The Latin abbreviation *i.e.* should be *viz.*
c. The abbreviation *i.e.* should be spelled out as *that is*.
d. In the above example, *i.e.* is used correctly.

APA CODE: 3.24
INDEX NUMBER: 03
answer: d
TP-MASTERY 2

Which abbreviations are used only in parentheses?

    a.   vs., kg, i.e.
    b.   i.e., cf., viz.
    c.   e.g., etc., p.
    d.   none of the above
    e.   all of the above

APA CODE: 3.24
INDEX NUMBER: 04
answer: b
TP-MASTERY 3

Latin abbreviations, except *et al.*, should

    a.   be spelled out each time they are used.
    b.   not be used.
    c.   be used only in parenthetical material.
    d.   be spelled out the first time they are used.

APA CODE: 3.24
INDEX NUMBER: 05
answer: c
TP-MASTERY 4

The headings of a manuscript

    a.   reveal the logical organization of the paper to the reader.
    b.   should be at the same level for topics of equal importance.
    c.   need not be numbered.
    d.   All of the above are correct.

APA CODE: 3.30
INDEX NUMBER: 01
answer: d
TP-FAMILIARIZATION

Edit the following by selecting the correct format:

    Scenario and settings. The same action scenario was described in the context of eight different settings designed to represent the eight physical-social conditions of the experiment.

    a.   leave as is

    b.   *Scenario and settings*: The same action scenario was described in the context of eight different settings designed to represent the eight physical-social conditions of the experiment.

    c.   *Scenario and settings.* The same action scenario was described in the context of eight different settings designed to represent the eight physical-social conditions of the experiment.

    d.   *Scenario and Settings.* The same action scenario was described in the context of eight different settings designed to represent the eight physical-social conditions of the experiment.

APA CODE: 3.31
INDEX NUMBER: 01
answer: c
TP-MASTERY 1

Articles in APA journals use

    a.   centered uppercase headings only.
    b.   centered, underlined, uppercase headings only.
    c.   flush left lowercase headings only.
    d.   a and c.
    e.   as many as five levels of headings.

APA CODE: 3.31
INDEX NUMBER: 02
answer: e
TP-MASTERY 2

Level 5 (centered uppercase) headings are used

    a.   only when the article requires five levels of headings.
    b.   in short articles where one level of heading is sufficient.
    c.   after any other type of heading in single-experiment papers.
    d.   only in multiexperiment papers.

APA CODE: 3.32
INDEX NUMBER: 01
answer: a
TP-MASTERY 3

In articles in which one level of heading is sufficient, use

    a.   a centered uppercase heading (level 5).
    b.   a centered uppercase and lowercase heading (level 1).
    c.   any type (level) of heading.
    d.   none of the above.

APA CODE: 3.32
INDEX NUMBER: 02
answer: b
TP-MASTERY 4

Edit the following two levels of headings:

Amphibian Phobias

Fear of Forest Newts

a.   leave as is

b.

Amphibian Phobias

Fear of Forest Newts

c.

Amphibian Phobias

FEAR OF FOREST NEWTS

d.

Amphibian Phobias

Fear of Forest Newts

APA CODE: 3.32
INDEX NUMBER: 03
answer: d
TP-PRACTICE

Which example is correct for an article in which four levels of headings are required?

a.

A History of Psychology

Early Laboratories

Harvard Laboratories

    James's basement.

b.

A HISTORY OF PSYCHOLOGY

Early Laboratories

Harvard Laboratories

    James's Basement.

c.

A HISTORY OF PSYCHOLOGY

Early Laboratories

Harvard Laboratories

    James's basement.

d.

A HISTORY OF PSYCHOLOGY

Early Laboratories

Harvard Laboratories

James's Basement

APA CODE: 3.32
INDEX NUMBER: 04
answer: a
TP-FAMILIARIZATION

Edit the following for the presentation of a series:

> The participants were divided into three groups: (1) Experts, who had completed at least four courses in computer programming; (2) Intermediates, who had completed one course in computer programming; and (3) Novices, who had no experience in computer programming.

a. leave as is

b. The participants were divided into three groups: (a) Experts, who had completed at least four courses in computer programming, (b) Intermediates, who had completed one course in computer programming, and (c) Novices, who had no experience in computer programming.

c. The participants were divided into three groups: a) experts, who had completed at least four courses in computer programming, b) intermediates, who had completed one course in computer programming, and c) novices, who had no experience in computer programming.

d. The participants were divided into three groups: (a) experts, who had completed at least four courses in computer programming; (b) intermediates, who had completed one course in computer programming; and (c) novices, who had no experience in computer programming.

APA CODE: 3.33
INDEX NUMBER: 01
answer: d
TP-PRACTICE

Within a paragraph or sentence, identify elements in a series by
a. arabic numerals in parentheses.
b. arabic numerals underlined.
c. lowercase letters in parentheses.
d. lowercase letters followed by a colon.

APA CODE: 3.33
INDEX NUMBER: 02
answer: c
TP-MASTERY 1

When quoting,
a. provide the author's name in the text.
b. provide the year and page citation in the text.
c. include a complete reference in the reference list.
d. do only a and c.
e. do a, b, and c.

APA CODE: 3.34
INDEX NUMBER: 01
answer: e
TP-MASTERY 2

Identify the error in the following quotation:

> Zwycewicz (1976) concluded the following:
>
> "Children appear to employ the same schemata as adults. Like adults, they are predisposed to structure intragroup relations with an ordering schema more readily than with a grouping schema. Thus, their readiness to arrange inanimate stimuli along a vertical dimension as opposed to a horizontal dimension is seen as well with social stimuli." (p. 61)

a. There are no errors.
b. The quote should not be in block form.
c. The quote does not need quotation marks.
d. There is no need to cite the page number.

APA CODES: 3.34 &
3.39
INDEX NUMBER: 02
answer: c
TP-MASTERY 3

Edit the following for a quotation of a source:

Zwycewicz (1976) concluded that "children appear to employ the same schemata as adults. Like adults, they are predisposed to structure intragroup relations with an ordering schema more readily than with a grouping schema."

a. leave as is
b. The quote should be in block form.
c. A page number should be cited.
d. Quotation marks are not necessary.

APA CODES: 3.34 & 3.39
INDEX NUMBER: 03
answer: c
TP-MASTERY 4

Identify the error in the following quotation:

The author speculated that "negative exemplars within the self-concept are more confidently known than affirmative exemplars" (Brinthaup, 1983).

a. The quote is correctly cited.
b. The quote should be in block form.
c. Quotation marks are not necessary.
d. A page number should be cited.

APA CODES: 3.34 & 3.39
INDEX NUMBER: 04
answer: d
TP-FAMILIARIZATION

Direct quotations
a. must follow the wording, spelling, and interior punctuation of the original source even if incorrect. Errors in the original source are indicated with [*sic*].
b. must follow the wording and interior punctuation of the original source, but any spelling errors should be corrected.
c. should follow the original source but minor changes in wording, spelling, and interior punctuation are permissible.
d. None of the above is correct.

APA CODE: 3.35
INDEX NUMBER: 01
answer: a
TP-PRACTICE

When citing the source of a direct quotation,
a. it is not necessary to give source information in text as it will be given in the reference list.
b. the citation may be enclosed in parentheses and is always placed immediately after the quotation mark.
c. the citation is enclosed in parentheses after the final period of the quotation if the quoted passage is set off in a block and not put in quotation marks.
d. b and c are correct.

APA CODE: 3.39
INDEX NUMBER: 01
answer: c
TP-MASTERY 1

At the end of a block quote,
a. cite the quoted source in parentheses after the final punctuation mark.
b. cite the quoted source in parentheses before the final punctuation mark.
c. use a footnote with a superscript number and cite the quoted source in the footnote.
d. None of the above is correct.

APA CODE: 3.39
INDEX NUMBER: 02
answer: a
TP-MASTERY 2

Any direct, short quotation (less than 500 words) of text from an APA journal must
a. be accompanied by a reference citation.
b. include a page number.
c. be used only with the permission of the copyright owner.
d. be footnoted if copyrighted.
e. Answers a and b are correct.

APA CODE: 3.41
INDEX NUMBER: 01
answer: e
TP-MASTERY 3

From the examples below, identify the correct form of citation:

    a.   According to McMahon (1988), math ability is acquired.

    b.   Individual differences in memory have been found (Gelfand, 1987).

    c.   In 1988, Scarano found that androgynous women respond to self-worth dilemmas differently than do stereotypic women.

    d.   Lavin (1986) observed that TV serves as a surrogate parent for some young adults. Lavin found that "soap addicts" have limited parental contact.

    e.   All of the above are correct.

APA CODE: 3.94
INDEX NUMBER: 01
answer: e
TP-MASTERY 4

Edit the following for the citation of a reference in text:

Gazzaniga, 1967, flashed pictures to the right or left visual field of each patient whose corpus callosum had been surgically severed.

    a.   leave as is

    b.   Gazzaniga/1967 flashed pictures to the right or left visual field of each patient whose corpus callosum had been surgically severed.

    c.   Gazzaniga (Gazzaniga, 1967) flashed pictures to the right or left visual field of each patient whose corpus callosum had been surgically severed.

    d.   Gazzaniga (1967) flashed pictures to the right or left visual field of each patient whose corpus callosum had been surgically severed.

APA CODE: 3.94
INDEX NUMBER: 02
answer: d
TP-FAMILIARIZATION

Edit the following for the citation of a reference in text:

Women are often motivated by a fear of success rather than by a need to achieve because of the negative consequences they experience when they succeed in areas that are traditionally male dominated (Horner, 1970).

    a.   leave as is

    b.   Women are often motivated by a fear of success rather than by a need to achieve because of the negative consequences they experience when they succeed in areas that are traditionally male dominated--Horner, 1970.

    c.   Women are often motivated by a fear of success rather than by a need to achieve because of the negative consequences they experience when they succeed in areas that are traditionally male dominated (Horner: 1970).

    d.   Women are often motivated by a fear of success rather than by a need to achieve because of the negative consequences they experience when they succeed in areas that are traditionally male dominated: Horner (1970).

APA CODE: 3.94
INDEX NUMBER: 03
answer: a
TP-PRACTICE

Edit the following for the citation of a reference in text:

> Milgram (1963) was interested in the degree to which people would obey an authority. A much higher percentage of the participants in Milgram's (1963) experiment obeyed the authority than was predicted by various groups of judges, including psychiatrists.

a. leave as is

b. Milgram (1963) was interested in the degree to which people would obey an authority. A much higher percentage of the participants in Milgram's experiment obeyed the authority than was predicted by various groups of judges, including psychiatrists.

c. Milgram (1963) was interested in the degree to which people would obey an authority. A much higher percentage of the participants in Milgram's (ibid.) experiment obeyed the authority than was predicted by various groups of judges, including psychiatrists.

d. Milgram (1963) was interested in the degree to which people would obey an authority. A much higher percentage of the participants in Milgram's (see Milgram, 1963) experiment obeyed the authority than was predicted by various groups of judges, including psychiatrists.

APA CODE: 3.94
INDEX NUMBER: 04
answer: b
TP-MASTERY 1

From the examples below, identify the correct forms of citation:

a. According to Wagner (1988), depressed people reveal inappropriately.

b. Individual differences in memory have been found (Gelfand, 1987).

c. In 1988, Scarano and Walker found that androgynous women respond to self-worth dilemmas differently than do stereotypic women.

d. Lavin (1986) observed that TV serves as a surrogate parent for some young adults. Lavin found that "soap addicts" spend more time watching TV than being with their parents.

e. All of the above are correct.

APA CODE: 3.94
INDEX NUMBER: 05
answer: e
TP-MASTERY 2

When a work has more than two authors and fewer than six authors, cite
a. all of the authors every time the reference occurs in text.
b. all of the authors the first time the reference occurs in text; use the surname of the first author followed by *et al.* in subsequent citations.
c. the surname of the first author followed by *et al.* every time the reference occurs in text.
d. none of the above.

APA CODE: 3.95
INDEX NUMBER: 01
answer: b
TP-MASTERY 3

Edit the following for the citation of a reference in text:

> Some researchers have recognized that people may not follow mathematical rules in judging the probability of events (Tversky & Kahneman, 1973). Tversky et al. reported evidence that people rely on an availability heuristic in making probability judgments.

a. leave as is

b. Some researchers have recognized that people may not follow mathematical rules in judging the probability of events (Tversky & Kahneman, 1973). Tversky & Kahneman reported evidence that people rely on an availability heuristic in making probability judgments.

c. Some researchers have recognized that people may not follow mathematical rules in judging the probability of events (Tversky & Kahneman, 1973). Tversky and Kahneman reported evidence that people rely on an availability heuristic in making probability judgments.

d. Some researchers have recognized that people may not follow mathematical rules in judging the probability of events (Tversky & Kahneman, 1973). Tversky/ Kahneman reported evidence that people rely on an availability heuristic in making probability judgments.

APA CODE: 3.95
INDEX NUMBER: 02
answer: c
TP-MASTERY 4

Edit the following for the citation of a reference in text:

> In one of the earliest studies (Anand, Chhina, & Singh, 1961), researchers presented a variety of stimuli to a yogi as he meditated. Anand, Chhina, and Singh reported no disruption of the yogi's alpha wave--as indicated by EEG recordings--by a tuning fork or a hand clap.

a. leave as is

b. In one of the earliest studies (Anand, Chhina, & Singh, 1961), researchers presented a variety of stimuli to a yogi as he meditated. Anand, Chhina, et al. reported no disruption of the yogi's alpha wave--as indicated by EEG recordings --by a tuning fork or a hand clap.

c. In one of the earliest studies (Anand, Chhina, & Singh, 1961), researchers presented a variety of stimuli to a yogi as he meditated. Anand *et al.* reported no disruption of the yogi's alpha wave--as indicated by EEG recordings--by a tuning fork or a hand clap.

d. In one of the earliest studies (Anand, Chhina, & Singh, 1961), researchers presented a variety of stimuli to a yogi as he meditated. Anand et al. reported no disruption of the yogi's alpha wave--as indicated by EEG recordings--by a tuning fork or a hand clap.

APA CODE: 3.95
INDEX NUMBER: 03
answer: d
TP-FAMILIARIZATION

Edit the following for the citation of a reference in text:

> Another possibility is that differences in IQ scores between Blacks and Whites are mediated by differences in family size. Family size has been shown to be related to IQ score (Zajonc, Markus, & Markus, 1979).

a. leave as is

b. Another possibility is that differences in IQ scores between Blacks and Whites are mediated by differences in family size. Family size has been shown to be related to IQ score (Zajonc & Markus & Markus, 1979).

c. Another possibility is that differences in IQ scores between Blacks and Whites are mediated by differences in family size. Family size has been shown to be related to IQ score (Zajonc, Markus, Markus, 1979).

d. Another possibility is that differences in IQ scores between Blacks and Whites are mediated by differences in family size. Family size has been shown to be related to IQ score (Zajonc, Markus, and Markus, 1979).

APA CODE: 3.95
INDEX NUMBER: 04
answer: a
TP-PRACTICE

Edit the following for the citation of a reference in text:

Vroom & Yetton (1973) took a more practical approach to leadership and decision making.

    a.   leave as is

    b.   Vroom/Yetton (1973) took a more practical approach to leadership and decision making.

    c.   Vroom, and Yetton (1973) took a more practical approach to leadership and decision making.

    d.   Vroom and Yetton (1973) took a more practical approach to leadership and decision making.

APA CODE: 3.95
INDEX NUMBER: 05
answer: d
TP-MASTERY 1

Edit the following for the citation of a reference in text:

Briddell, Rimm, Caddy, Krawitz, Scholis, and Wunderlin (1978) showed that some of the inhibition-releasing effects of alcohol are due to expectations aroused by drinking rather than to the chemical effects on bodily functions.

    a.   leave as is

    b.   Briddell & Rimm & Caddy & Krawitz & Scholis, & Wunderlin (1978) showed that some of the inhibition-releasing effects of alcohol are due to expectations aroused by drinking rather than to the chemical effects on bodily functions.

    c.   Briddell et al. (1978) showed that some of the inhibition-releasing effects of alcohol are due to expectations aroused by drinking rather than to the chemical effects on bodily functions.

    d.   Briddell, et al. (1978) showed that some of the inhibition-releasing effects of alcohol are due to expectations aroused by drinking rather than to the chemical effects on bodily functions.

APA CODE: 3.95
INDEX NUMBER: 06
answer: c
TP-MASTERY 2

When a reference source is cited in the text,
    a.   each author's surname must be cited every time a reference occurs in the text when there are two authors of a single work.
    b.   every author's surname is used only the first time a reference is made when a work has more than two and less than six authors.
    c.   only the first author's surname is used followed by an *et al.* every time the reference is made when a work has six or more authors.
    d.   All of the above are correct.
    e.   Only b and c are correct.

APA CODE: 3.95
INDEX NUMBER: 07
answer: d
TP-MASTERY 3

When a work has two authors, cite
    a.   only one name every time the reference occurs in text.
    b.   both names the first time the reference occurs in text and only one thereafter.
    c.   both names every time the reference occurs in text.
    d.   None of the above is correct.

APA CODE: 3.95
INDEX NUMBER: 08
answer: c
TP-MASTERY 4

When a publication has no author,

    a.   the text citation must have the entire title of the publication.
    b.   the text citation should use the publisher's name.
    c.   no citation is necessary.
    d.   None of the above is true.

APA CODE: 3.97
INDEX NUMBER: 01
answer: d
TP-FAMILIARIZATION

Choose the correct citation:

    a.   (Dorrow & O'Neal, 1979; Mullaney, 1978; Tapers, 1981)

    b.   (Zalichin, 1978, 1979, 1980)

    c.   (Mullaney, 1978; Dorrow & O'Neal, 1979; Tapers, 1981)

    d.   b and c

    e.   a and b

APA CODE: 3.99
INDEX NUMBER: 01
answer: e
TP-PRACTICE

Order the citations of two or more works within the same parentheses in order of their

    a.   appearance in the reference list.
    b.   importance.
    c.   dates of publication.
    d.   None of the above is correct.

APA CODE: 3.99
INDEX NUMBER: 02
answer: a
TP-MASTERY 1

Edit the following for the citation of references in text:

    A nativist (e.g., J. J. Gibson, 1950; J. J. Gibson, 1966; S. G. Gibson, 1979) would try to identify the invariants in the stimulus situation that accounted for a particular perceptual experience.

    a.   leave as is

    b.   A nativist (e.g., J. J. Gibson, 1950, J. J. Gibson, 1966; S. G. Gibson, 1979) would try to identify the invariants in the stimulus situation that accounted for a particular perceptual experience.

    c.   A nativist (e.g., J. J. Gibson, 1950; 1966; S. G. Gibson, 1979) would try to identify the invariants in the stimulus situation that accounted for a particular perceptual experience.

    d.   A nativist (e.g., J. J. Gibson, 1950, 1966; S. G. Gibson, 1979) would try to identify the invariants in the stimulus situation that accounted for a particular perceptual experience.

APA CODE: 3.98
INDEX NUMBER: 03
answer: d
TP-MASTERY 2

Edit the following for the citation of references in text:

Others (e.g., Hoffman, 1975, 1975, 1976) have taken a developmental approach to the study of altruism.

a. leave as is

b. Others (e.g., Hoffman, 1975a, b, 1976) have taken a developmental approach to the study of altruism.

c. Others (e.g., Hoffman, 1975a, 1975b, 1976) have taken a developmental approach to the study of altruism.

d. Others (e.g., Hoffman, 1975a/b, 1976) have taken a developmental approach to the study of altruism.

APA CODE: 3.99
INDEX NUMBER: 04
answer: c
TP-MASTERY 3

Edit the following for the citation of references in text:

Many phobias have been treated successfully with systematic desensitization (Hekmat, Lubitz, & Deal, 1984; Land & Lazovik, 1963; Paul, 1966; Wolpe, 1958).

a. leave as is

b. Many phobias have been treated successfully with systematic desensitization (Hekmat, Lubitz, & Deal, 1984; Paul, 1966; Land & Lazovik, 1963; Wolpe, 1958).

c. Many phobias have been treated successfully with systematic desensitization (Wolpe, 1958; Land & Lazovik, 1963; Paul, 1966; Hekmat, Lubitz, & Deal, 1984).

d. Many phobias have been treated successfully with systematic desensitization (Paul, 1966; Wolpe, 1958; Land & Lazovik, 1963; Hekmat, Lubitz, & Deal, 1984).

APA CODE: 3.99
INDEX NUMBER: 05
answer: a
TP-MASTERY 4

Edit the following for the citation of references in text:

Personality changes may also occur later in life (Neugarten, 1973; Neugarten & Hagestad, 1976; Neugarten, 1977).

a. leave as is

b. Personality changes may also occur later in life (Neugarten, 1973, 1977; Neugarten & Hagestad, 1976).

c. Personality changes may also occur later in life (Neugarten, 1973, 1977; & Hagestad, 1976).

d. Personality changes may also occur later in life (Neugarten, 1973, Neugarten & Hagestad, 1976; ibid., 1977).

APA CODE: 3.99
INDEX NUMBER: 06
answer: b
TP-FAMILIARIZATION

Edit the following for the citation of references in text:

Biofeedback training may not affect alpha-wave regulation (Lynch, Paskewitz, & Orne, 1974, Miller, 1974, Plotkin & Cohen, 1976).

a.   leave as is

b.   Biofeedback training may not affect alpha-wave regulation (Lynch, Paskewitz, & Orne, 1974; Miller, 1974; Plotkin & Cohen, 1976).

c.   Biofeedback training may not affect alpha-wave regulation (Lynch/Paskewitz/Orne: 1974; Miller: 1974; Plotkin/Cohen: 1976).

d.   Biofeedback training may not affect alpha-wave regulation (Lynch, Paskewitz, & Orne, 1974: Miller, 1974: Plotkin & Cohen, 1976).

APA CODE: 3.99
INDEX NUMBER: 07
answer: b
TP-PRACTICE

Edit the following for the citation of a specific part of a source:

Rogers's theory developed out of his experiences as a psychotherapist. He was impressed by the extent to which his clients spoke in terms of the self (Rogers, 1959, pages 200-201).

a.   leave as is

b.   Rogers's theory developed out of his experiences as a psychotherapist. He was impressed by the extent to which his clients spoke in terms of the self (Rogers, 1959, p. 200 201).

c.   Rogers's theory developed out of his experiences as a psychotherapist. He was impressed by the extent to which his clients spoke in terms of the self (Rogers, 1959, pp. 200-201).

d.   Rogers's theory developed out of his experiences as a psychotherapist. He was impressed by the extent to which his clients spoke in terms of the self (Rogers, 1959, *200-201*).

APA CODE: 3.101
INDEX NUMBER: 01
answer: c
TP-MASTERY 1

Edit the following for the citation of a quotation in text:

Although literary style certainly affects readers, "the elegance of presentation is of no importance as a measure of whether the theory will prove an empirically useful tool" (Hall & Linzey, 1957).

a. leave as is

b. Although literary style certainly affects readers, "the elegance of presentation is of no importance as a measure of whether the theory will prove an empirically useful tool" (Hall & Linzey, 1957, p. 551).

c. Although literary style certainly affects readers, "the elegance of presentation is of no importance as a measure of whether the theory will prove an empirically useful tool" (Hall & Linzey, 1957, chap. 14).

d. Although literary style certainly affects readers, "(Hall & Linzey, 1957, p. 551) the elegance of presentation is of no importance as a measure of whether the theory will prove an empirically useful tool."

APA CODE: 3.101
INDEX NUMBER: 02
answer: b
TP-MASTERY 2

Edit the following for the citation of a specific part of a reference in text:

Cook and Campbell (1979, 2) considered two other criteria, statistical conclusion validity and construct validity.

a. leave as is

b. Cook and Campbell (1979, Ch. 2) considered two other criteria, statistical conclusion validity and construct validity.

c. Cook and Campbell (1979, Ch. #2) considered two other criteria, statistical conclusion validity and construct validity.

d. Cook and Campbell (1979, chap. 2) considered two other criteria, statistical conclusion validity and construct validity.

APA CODE: 3.101
INDEX NUMBER: 03
answer: d
TP-MASTERY 3

Edit the following for the citation of a specific part of a reference in text:

Ecphory "is the process by which retrieval information is brought into interaction with stored information" (Tulving, 1983) [p. 178].

a. leave as is

b. Ecphory "is the process by which retrieval information is brought into interaction with stored information (p. 178)" (Tulving, 1983).

c. Ecphory "is the process by which retrieval information is brought into interaction with stored information" (Tulving, 1983, p. 178).

d. Ecphory "is the process by which retrieval information is brought into interaction with stored information" (Tulving, 1983).

APA CODE: 3.101
INDEX NUMBER: 04
answer: c
TP-MASTERY 4

When citing a specific part of a source, be sure to give

    a.   the authors' names.
    b.   the year of publication.
    c.   a page number if a quotation is cited.
    d.   all of the above.

APA CODE: 3.101
INDEX NUMBER: 05
answer: d
TP-FAMILIARIZATION

When citing a direct quotation from a source, be sure to give

    a.   the authors' names.
    b.   the year of publication.
    c.   the page number.
    d.   all of the above.
    e.   the authors' names and the year of publication.

APA CODE: 3.101
INDEX NUMBER: 06
answer: d
TP-PRACTICE

Cite personal communications

    a.   in the text.
    b.   in the reference list.
    c.   Do not cite personal communications.
    d.   Do a and b.

APA CODE: 3.102
INDEX NUMBER: 01
answer: a
TP-MASTERY 1

A reference list

    a.   cites all works supportive of or contradictory to the text.
    b.   is a synonym for bibliography.
    c.   should include only the references cited anywhere in the article.
    d.   should never be used in short articles.

APA CODE: 4.01
INDEX NUMBER: 01
answer: c
TP-MASTERY 2

Each entry in the reference list must be

    a.   relevant to other entries.
    b.   cited in text also.
    c.   published in a credible journal.
    d.   all of the above.

APA CODE: 4.01
INDEX NUMBER: 02
answer: b
TP-MASTERY 3

Reference entries

    a.   may consist of the author's name only, if the bibliography is totally complete.
    b.   may contain only the author's name and title of publication, if the bibliography is totally complete.
    c.   should be complete and correct.
    d.   a or b

APA CODE: 4.02
INDEX NUMBER: 01
answer: c
TP-MASTERY 4

Who has the responsibility to ensure that references are accurate and complete?

    a.   an editor
    b.   a proofreader
    c.   a printer
    d.   an author

APA CODE: 4.02
INDEX NUMBER: 02
answer: d
TP-FAMILIARIZATION

If no author is given for a source, put the source in the correct order in the reference list by

    a.   moving the title to the author position and alphabetizing by the first significant word of the title.
    b.   beginning the entry with the word *Anonymous* and alphabetizing as if this were the author's name.
    c.   moving the journal title or publishing house to the author position and alphabetizing by the first significant word of the name.
    d.   Do none of the above.

APA CODE: 4.04
INDEX NUMBER: 01
answer: a
TP-PRACTICE

Edit the following for ordering the references in a reference list. Choose the sequence of numbers that indicates the correct order of the four references. (*Note:* The numbers are not part of APA style but are used here for brevity.)

1. Tulving, E., & Pearlstone, Z. (1966). Availability versus accessibility of information in memory for words. *Journal of Verbal Learning and Verbal Behavior, 5,* 381-391.

2. Tulving, E., & Thomson, D. M. (1973). Encoding specificity and retrieval processes in episodic memory. *Psychological Review, 80,* 352-373.

3. Craik, F. I. M., & Tulving, E. (1975). Depth of processing and the retention of words in episodic memory. *Journal of Experimental Psychology: General, 104,* 268-294.

4. Tulving, E. (1983). *Elements of episodic memory.* New York: Oxford University Press.

a. leave as is (i.e., 1, 2, 3, 4)
b. 1, 3, 4, 2
c. 3, 4, 1, 2
d. 4, 3, 1, 2

APA CODE: 4.04
INDEX NUMBER: 02
answer: c
TP-MASTERY 1

Edit the following for ordering the references in a reference list. Choose the sequence of numbers that indicates the correct order of the four references. (*Note:* The numbers are not part of APA style but are used here for brevity.)

1. Bandura, A. (1973). *Aggression: A social learning analysis.* Englewood Cliffs, NJ: Prentice Hall.

2. Bandura, A., & Menlove, F. L. (1968). Factors determining vicarious extinction and avoidance behavior through symbolic modeling. *Journal of Personality and Social Psychology, 8,* 99-108.

3. Bandura, A. (1965). Influence of models' reinforcement contingencies on the acquisition of imitative responses. *Journal of Personality and Social Psychology, 1,* 589-595.

4. Bandura, A., & Walters, R. H. (1963). *Social learning and personality development.* New York: Holt, Rinehart & Winston.

a. leave as is (i.e., 1, 2, 3, 4)
b. 1, 3, 2, 4
c. 3, 1, 2, 4
d. 4, 3, 2, 1

APA CODE: 4.04
INDEX NUMBER: 03
answer: c
TP-MASTERY 2

Edit the following for ordering the references in a reference list. Choose the sequence of numbers that indicates the correct order of the four references. (*Note:* The numbers are not part of APA style but are used here for brevity.)

1. Miller, G. A. (1956b). The magical number seven plus or minus two: Some limits on our capacity for processing information. *Psychological Review, 63,* 81-97.

2. Miller, G. A. (1956a). Human memory and the storage of information. *IRE Transactions on Information Theory, IT-2,* 129-137.

3. Miller, G. A., Galanter, E., & Pribram, K. H. (1960). *Plans and the structure of behavior.* New York: Holt, Rinehart & Winston.

4. Miller, G. A., & Selfridge, J. (1950). Verbal context and the recall of meaningful material. *American Journal of Psychology, 63,* 176-185.

a. leave as is (i.e., 1, 2, 3, 4)
b. 4, 1, 2, 3
c. 2, 3, 1, 4
d. 2, 1, 3, 4

APA CODE: 4.04
INDEX NUMBER: 04
answer: d
TP-MASTERY 3

Edit the following for ordering the references in a reference list. Choose the sequence of numbers that indicates the correct order of the four references. (*Note:* The numbers are not part of APA style but are used here for brevity.)

1. McKenzie, B., & Over, R. (1983). Young infants fail to imitate facial and manual gestures. *Infant Behavior and Development, 6,* 85 96.

2. Martin, G. B., & Clark, R. D. (1982). Distress crying in neonates: Species and peer specificity. *Developmental Psychology, 18,* 3-9.

3. Maurer, D., & Salapatek, P. (1976). Developmental changes in the scanning of faces by young infants. *Child Development, 47,* 523-527.

4. Meltzoff, A. N., & Moore, M. K. (1977). Imitation of facial and manual gestures by human neonates. *Science, 198,* 75-78.

a. leave as is (i.e., 1, 2, 3, 4)
b. 3, 4, 2, 1
c. 3, 2, 4, 1
d. 2, 3, 1, 4

APA CODE: 4.04
INDEX NUMBER: 05
answer: d
TP-MASTERY 4

Edit the following for ordering the references in a reference list. Choose the sequence of numbers that indicates the correct order of the four references. (*Note:* The numbers are not part of APA style but are used here for brevity.)

1. Lazarus, R. S. (1969). *Psychological stress and the coping process.* New York: McGraw-Hill.

2. Lazarus, A. A. (1977). Has behavior therapy outlived its usefulness? *American Psychologist, 32,* 550-554.

3. Smith, M. L., & Glass, G. V. (1977). Meta-analysis of psychotherapy outcome studies. *American Psychologist, 32,* 752-760.

4. Smith, D. (1982). Trends in counseling and psychotherapy. *American Psychologist, 37,* 802-809.

a. leave as is (i.e., 1, 2, 3, 4)
b. 2, 1, 4, 3
c. 2, 3, 1, 4
d. 4, 3, 2, 1

APA CODE: 4.04
INDEX NUMBER: 06
answer: b
TP-FAMILIARIZATION

In a reference list, when ordering several works by the same first author,
a. place single-author entries before multiple-author entries.
b. do not repeat the first author's name after the first entry.
c. you may order them alphabetically by the name of the journal.
d. All of the above are correct.

APA CODE: 4.04
INDEX NUMBER: 07
answer: a
TP-PRACTICE

The general rule to follow in alphabetizing surnames that contain articles and prepositions (e.g., DeVries, von Helmholtz) is to
a. always treat the prefix as part of the surname.
b. always treat the prefix as part of the middle name.
c. treat the prefix as part of the surname if it is commonly used that way or as part of the middle name if it is not customarily used.
d. None of the above is correct.

APA CODE: 4.04
INDEX NUMBER: 08
answer: c
TP-MASTERY 1

A reference list entry should have
a. the author's surname and initials in inverted order (e.g., McMahon, P. M.).
b. the title of the article, page number, ISBN code, and book title.
c. the author's surname only.
d. only b and c.

APA CODES: 4.07–4.15
INDEX NUMBER: 01
answer: a
TP-MASTERY 2

Edit the following for the application of APA reference style:

> Brickman, P., Coates, D., & Janoff-Bulman, R. (1978). Lottery Winners and Accident
>
> Victims: Is Happiness Relative? *Journal of Personality and Social Psychology,*
>
> *36,* 917-927.

a.   leave as is

b.   Brickman, P., Coates, D., & Janoff-Bulman, R. (1978). *Lottery Winners and Accident*

> *Victims: Is Happiness Relative? Journal of Personality and Social Psychology,*
>
> *36,* 917-927.

c.   Brickman, P., Coates, D., & Janoff-Bulman, R. (1978). Lottery winners and accident

> victims: Is happiness relative? *Journal of Personality and Social Psychology, 36,*
>
> 917-927.

d.   Brickman, P., Coates, D., & Janoff-Bulman, R. (1978). "Lottery Winners and Accident

> Victims: Is Happiness Relative?" *Journal of Personality and Social Psychology,*
>
> *36,* 917-927.

APA CODE: 4.16A
INDEX NUMBER: 02
answer: c
TP-MASTERY 3

Edit the following for the application of APA reference style:

> Bower, G. H. (1970). Analysis of a mnemonic device. *American Scientist, 58,* 496-
>
> 510.

a.   leave as is

b.   Bower, G. H. (1970). Analysis of a mnemonic device. *AMERICAN SCIENTIST, 58,*

> 496-510.

c.   Bower, G. H. (1970). Analysis of a mnemonic device. AMERICAN SCIENTIST, *58,*

> 496-510.

d.   Bower, G. H. (1970). Analysis of a mnemonic device. *"American Scientist,"* 58, 496-

> 510.

APA CODE: 4.16A
INDEX NUMBER: 03
answer: a
TP-MASTERY 4

Edit the following for the application of APA reference style:

> Olds, J., & Milner, P. Positive reinforcement produced by electrical stimulation of septal areas and other regions of rat brains. *Journal of Comparative and Physiological Psychology*, (1954), 47, 419-427.

a. leave as is

b. Olds, J., & Milner, P. Positive reinforcement produced by electrical stimulation of septal areas and other regions of rat brains. *Journal of Comparative and Physiological Psychology*, 1954, 47, 419-427.

c. Olds, J., & Milner, P. 1954. Positive reinforcement produced by electrical stimulation of septal areas and other regions of rat brains. *Journal of Comparative and Physiological Psychology*, 47, 419-427.

d. Olds, J., & Milner, P. (1954). Positive reinforcement produced by electrical stimulation of septal areas and other regions of rat brains. *Journal of Comparative and Physiological Psychology*, 47, 419-427.

APA CODE: 4.16A
INDEX NUMBER: 04
answer: d
TP-FAMILIARIZATION

Edit the following for the application of APA reference style:

> Lovaas, O. I., Schaeffer, B., and Simmons, J. Q. (1965). Building social behavior in autistic children by use of electric shock. *Journal of Experimental Research in Personality*, 1, 99-109.

a. leave as is

b. Lovaas, O. I., Schaeffer, B., & Simmons, J. Q. (1965). Building social behavior in autistic children by use of electric shock. *Journal of Experimental Research in Personality*, 1, 99-109.

c. Lovaas, O. I., et al. (1965). Building social behavior in autistic children by use of electric shock. *Journal of Experimental Research in Personality*, 1, 99-109.

d. Lovaas, O. I., Schaeffer, B., Simmons, J. Q. (1965). Building social behavior in autistic children by use of electric shock. *Journal of Experimental Research in Personality*, 1, 99-109.

APA CODE: 4.16A
INDEX NUMBER: 05
answer: b
TP-PRACTICE

Edit the following for the application of APA reference style:

> Eagly, A. H., and Carli, L. L. *1981*. "Sex of researchers and sex-typed communications as determinants of sex differences in influenceability: A meta-analysis of social influence studies." *Psychological Bulletin, 90,* 1-20.

a. leave as is

b. Eagly, A. H., & Carli, L. L. (1981). Sex of researchers and sex-typed communications as determinants of sex differences in influenceability: A meta-analysis of social influence studies. *Psychological Bulletin, 90,* 1-20.

c. Eagly, A. H., & Carli, L. L. *1981.* Sex of Researchers and Sex-Typed Communications as Determinants of Sex Differences in Influenceability: A Meta-Analysis of Social Influence Studies. *Psychological Bulletin, 90,* 1-20.

d. Eagly, A. H., and Carli, L. L. (1981). *Sex of researchers and sex-typed communications as determinants of sex differences in influenceability: A meta-analysis of social influence studies.* Psychological Bulletin, *90,* 1-20.

APA CODE: 4.16A
INDEX NUMBER: 06
answer: b
TP-MASTERY 1

Edit the following for the application of APA reference style:

> Feldman-Summers, S., Gordon, P. E., & Meagher, J. R. (1979). The impact of rape on sexual satisfaction. *Journal of Abnormal Psychology, 88,* 101-105.

a. leave as is

b. Feldman-Summers, S., Gordon, P. E., & Meagher, J. R. (1979). "The Impact of Rape on Sexual Satisfaction." *JOURNAL OF ABNORMAL PSYCHOLOGY,* 88, 101-105.

c. Feldman-Summers, S., Gordon, P. E., & Meagher, J. R. (1979, *88,* 101-105). The impact of rape on sexual satisfaction. *Journal of Abnormal Psychology.*

d. Feldman-Summers, S., Gordon, P. E., and Meagher, J. R. (1979). "The impact of rape on sexual satisfaction." *Journal of Abnormal Psychology, 88,* 101-105.

APA CODE: 4.16A
INDEX NUMBER: 07
answer: a
TP-MASTERY 2

Edit the following for the application of APA reference style:

> Bronfenbrenner, U. (1970). *Two worlds of childhood: U.S. and U.S.S.R.* New York: Russell Sage Foundation.

a. leave as is

b. Bronfenbrenner, U. *Two worlds of childhood: U.S. and U.S.S.R.* New York: Russell Sage Foundation. (1970).

c. Bronfenbrenner, U. (1970). "Two worlds of childhood: U.S. and U.S.S.R." New York: Russell Sage Foundation.

d. Bronfenbrenner, U. (1970). *Two Worlds of Childhood: U.S. and U.S.S.R.* Russell Sage Foundation: New York.

APA CODE: 4.16B
INDEX NUMBER: 08
answer: a
TP-MASTERY 3

Edit the following for the application of APA reference style:

Deaux, Kay. (1976). *The behavior of women and men*. Brooks/Cole: Monterey, CA.

a. leave as is

b. Deaux, Kay. (1976). *The Behavior of Women and Men*. Monterey, CA: Brooks/Cole.

c. Deaux, K. "The Behavior of Women and Men." Monterey, CA: Brooks/Cole, 1976.

d. Deaux, K. (1976). *The behavior of women and men*. Monterey, CA: Brooks/Cole.

APA CODE: 4.16B
INDEX NUMBER: 09
answer: d
TP-MASTERY 4

Edit the following for the application of APA reference style:

Hilgard, E. R., & Bower, G. H. (1975). *Theories of learning, fourth ed.* Englewood
Cliffs, NJ: Prentice Hall.

a. leave as is

b. Hilgard, E. R., & Bower, G. H. (1975). *Theories of learning, 4th ed.* Englewood
Cliffs, NJ: Prentice Hall.

c. Hilgard, E. R., & Bower, G. H. (1975). *Theories of learning* (4th ed.). Englewood
Cliffs, NJ: Prentice Hall.

d. Hilgard, E. R., & Bower, G. H. (1975, 4th ed.). *Theories of learning*. Englewood
Cliffs, NJ: Prentice Hall.

APA CODE: 4.16B
INDEX NUMBER: 10
answer: c
TP-FAMILIARIZATION

Edit the following for the application of APA reference style:

Roveé-Collier, C. (1984). "The ontogeny of learning and memory in human
infancy." In Kail, R., and Spear, N. E. (Eds.), *Comparative perspectives on the
development of memory* (pp. 103-134). Hillsdale, NJ: Erlbaum.

a. leave as is

b. Roveé-Collier, C. (1984). *The ontogeny of learning and memory in human infancy*.
In R. Kail & N. E. Spear (Eds.), "Comparative Perspectives on the
Development of Memory (pp. 103-134)." Hillsdale, NJ: Erlbaum.

c. Roveé-Collier, C. (1984). The ontogeny of learning and memory in human infancy.
In R. Kail & N. E. Spear (Eds.), *Comparative perspectives on the development
of memory* (pp. 103-134). Hillsdale, NJ: Erlbaum.

d. Roveé-Collier, C. (1984). The ontogeny of learning and memory in human infancy.
In Kail, R., & Spear, N. E. (Editors), *Comparative perspectives on the
development of memory* (pp. 103-134). Hillsdale, NJ: Erlbaum.

APA CODE: 4.16B
INDEX NUMBER: 11
answer: c
TP-PRACTICE

Edit the following for the application of APA electronic reference style:

VandenBos, G., Knapp, S., & Doe, J. (2001). Role of reference elements in the selection of resources by psychology undergraduates. *Journal of Bibliographic Research, 5,* 117-123 (electronic version).

a. VandenBos, G., Knapp, S., & Doe, J. (2001). Role of reference elements in the selection of resources by psychology undergraduates [Electronic version]. *Journal of Bibliographic Research, 5,* 117-123.

b. VandenBos, G., Knapp, S., & Doe, J. (2001). Role of reference elements in the selection of resources by psychology undergraduates (electronic version). *Journal of Bibliographic Research, 5,* 117-123.

c. VandenBos, G., Knapp, S., & Doe, J. (2001). Role of reference elements in the selection of resources by psychology undergraduates [electronic version]. *Journal of Bibliographic Research, 5,* 117-123.

d. VandenBos, G., Knapp, S., & Doe, J. (2001). Role of reference elements in the selection of resources by psychology undergraduates. *Journal of Bibliographic Research, 5,* 117-123 [Electronic version].

APA CODE: 4.16l
INDEX NUMBER: 01
answer: a
TP-MASTERY 4

Edit the following for the application of APA electronic reference style:

VandenBos, G., Knapp, S., & Doe, J. (2001, October 13). Role of reference elements in the selection of resources by psychology undergraduates. *Journal of Bibliographic Research, 5,* 117-123. Retrieved online from http://jbr.org/articles.html

a. leave as is

b. VandenBos, G., Knapp, S., & Doe, J. (2001). Role of reference elements in the selection of resources by psychology undergraduates. *Journal of Bibliographic Research, 5,* 117-123. Retrieved October 13, 2001, from http://jbr.org/articles.html

c. VandenBos, G., Knapp, S., & Doe, J. (2001, October 31). Role of reference elements in the selection of resources by psychology undergraduates [Retrieved from http://jbr.org/articles.html]. *Journal of Bibliographic Research, 5,* 117-123.

d. VandenBos, G., Knapp, S., & Doe, J. (2001). Role of reference elements in the selection of resources by psychology undergraduates. *Journal of Bibliographic Research, 5,* 117-123 [retrieved October 13, 2001, from http://jbr.org/articles.html].

APA CODE: 4.16l
INDEX NUMBER: 02
answer: b
TP-MASTERY 4

In entries in the reference list
a. periods are used to separate major elements (e.g., names of authors, dates, titles).
b. a comma is used to separate the name of a periodical from volume and page number information.
c. a colon is used in references for books, reports, proceedings, films, and audiotapes to separate the place of publication from the publisher's name.
d. punctuation may vary in format according to the type of source.
e. All of the above are correct.

APA CODES: 4.07–4.15
INDEX NUMBER: 12
answer: e
TP-MASTERY 1

The paper on which your article is printed should be

    a.   onionskin, to save filing space.
    b.   erasable bond for ease of correcting.
    c.   heavy, nonerasable, white bond for durability.
    d.   legal-size paper.

APA CODE: 5.01
INDEX NUMBER: 01
answer: c
TP-MASTERY 2

A manuscript should be printed on

    a.   erasable white bond paper.
    b.   heavy, white nonerasable bond paper.
    c.   white onionskin paper.
    d.   any professional-looking paper.

APA CODE: 5.01
INDEX NUMBER: 02
answer: b
TP-MASTERY 3

Use a typeface that is

    a.   dark
    b.   clear.
    c.   readable.
    d.   all of the above.

APA CODE: 5.02
INDEX NUMBER: 01
answer: d
TP-MASTERY 4

When typing a paper,

    a.   double-space after headings and between paragraphs and reference list citations; single-space elsewhere.
    b.   double-space throughout the paper.
    c.   single-space between lines of table headings.
    d.   double-space everything except triple-space after major headings.

APA CODE: 5.03
INDEX NUMBER: 01
answer: b
TP-FAMILIARIZATION

Which kind of spacing should not be used anywhere in a manuscript?

    a.   single-spacing
    b.   double double-spacing
    c.   triple-spacing
    d.   all of the above

APA CODE: 5.03
INDEX NUMBER: 02
answer: d
TP-PRACTICE

Edit the following for line spacing:

Experiment 1

Method

  Participants. The participants were 44 sets of parents who were bringing their firstborn infant children to a well-baby clinic in a university hospital. The ages of the parents ranged from 19 to 38.

a. leave as is

b.

Experiment 1

Method

  Participants. The participants were 44 sets of parents who were bringing their firstborn infant children to a well-baby clinic in a university hospital. The ages of the parents ranged from 19 to 38.

c.

Experiment 1

Method

  Participants. The participants were 44 sets of parents who were bringing their firstborn infant children to a well-baby clinic in a university hospital. The ages of the parents ranged from 19 to 38.

d.

Experiment 1

Method

  Participants. The participants were 44 sets of parents who were bringing their firstborn infant children to a well-baby clinic in a university hospital. The ages of the parents ranged from 19 to 38.

APA CODE: 5.03
INDEX NUMBER: 03
answer: c
TP-MASTERY 1

Edit the following by selecting the correct spacing arrangement:

> Effects of Academic Stress on Interpersonal Relationships
> of Male and Female Students
>
> Whatever the academic standards of a college or university, there always seem to be students who do not meet the standards.

a.   leave as is

b.

> Effects of Academic Stress on Interpersonal Relationships
> of Male and Female Students
>
>
> Whatever the academic standards of a college or university, there always seem to be students who do not meet the standards.

c.

> Effects of Academic Stress on Interpersonal Relationships
> of Male and Female Students
> Whatever the academic standards of a college or university, there always seem to be students who do not meet the standards.

d.

> Effects of Academic Stress on Interpersonal Relationships
> of Male and Female Students
>
>
> Whatever the academic standards of a college or university, there always seem to be students who do not meet the standards.

APA CODE: 5.03
INDEX NUMBER: 04
answer: a
TP-MASTERY 2

Edit the following by selecting the correct spacing arrangement:

Naturalistic Observation of the Duration and Distribution
of Sleep Across the Life Span

Although individual differences within each age group are certainly recognized, our society has general notions about the sleep patterns--duration and distribution--of people at different ages.

a.   leave as is

b.

Naturalistic Observation of the Duration and Distribution

of Sleep Across the Life Span

Although individual differences within each age group are certainly

recognized, our society has general notions about the sleep patterns--duration and

distribution--of people at different ages.

c.

Naturalistic Observation of the Duration and Distribution
of Sleep Across the Life Span

Although individual differences within each age group are certainly

recognized, our society has general notions about the sleep patterns--duration and

distribution--of people at different ages.

d.

Naturalistic Observation of the Duration and Distribution

of Sleep Across the Life Span

Although individual differences within each age group are certainly

recognized, our society has general notions about the sleep patterns--duration and

distribution--of people at different ages.

APA CODE: 5.03
INDEX NUMBER: 05
answer: d
TP-MASTERY 3

Edit the following by selecting the correct spacing arrangement:

Survey Methods

Telephone Survey

    In urban environments, many respondents screen their calls or record them on answering machines. Simple random sampling is not easily done because direct contact with the respondent is difficult to achieve.

a.   leave as is

b.

Survey Methods

Telephone Survey

    In urban environments, many respondents screen their calls or record them on answering machines. Simple random sampling is not easily done because direct contact with the respondent is difficult to achieve.

c.

Survey Methods

Telephone Survey

    In urban environments, many respondents screen their calls or record them on answering machines. Simple random sampling is not easily done because direct contact with the respondent is difficult to achieve.

d.

Survey Methods

Telephone Survey

    In urban environments, many respondents screen their calls or record them on answering machines. Simple random sampling is not easily done because direct contact with the respondent is difficult to achieve.

APA CODE: 5.03
INDEX NUMBER: 06
answer: c
TP-MASTERY 4

Edit the following by selecting the correct spacing and margin arrangement:

The mating and social behaviors of many species change dramatically when they are removed from their natural environments, whether to be domesti cated or to be exhibited in zoos.

a. leave as is

b. The mating and social behaviors of many species change dramatically when they are removed from their natural environments, whether to be domesticated or to be exhibited in zoos.

c. The mating and social behaviors of many species change dramatically when they are removed from their natural environments, whether to be domesticated or to be exhibited in zoos.

d. The mating and social behaviors of many species change dramatically when they are removed from their natural environments, whether to be domesticated or to be exhibited in zoos.

APA CODE: 5.04
INDEX NUMBER: 01
answer: b
TP-FAMILIARIZATION

The right margin should
a. have divided words to achieve an even margin.
b. not have divided words and may be uneven.
c. have a 1-in. (2.54-cm) space rather than a 2-in. (5.08-cm) space.
d. have divided or undivided words to achieve a clean line.

APA CODE: 5.04
INDEX NUMBER: 02
answer: b
TP-PRACTICE

Margin size
a. depends on the style of the typeface on the typewriter.
b. should always be 1 in. (2.54 cm) at the top, bottom, and sides of the paper.
c. depends on what section of the paper is being typed.
d. should be 2 in. (5.08 cm) at the top and bottom and 1/2 in. (1.27 cm) at the left and right sides.

APA CODE: 5.04
INDEX NUMBER: 03
answer: b
TP-MASTERY 1

Identify the numbering error in the following example of the first page of text of a manuscript that has a title page and an abstract page:

Slug Love

3

a. The numbering is correct.
b. The first text page is numbered with a 1.
c. A number is not put on the first page.
d. Page numbers are typed flush with the left margin.

APA CODES: 5.05 &
5.06
INDEX NUMBER: 01
answer: a
TP-MASTERY 2

Edit the following for numbering of an abstract page:

Firefly Helplessness

1

a. leave as is
b. Change the page number 1 to the number 2.
c. The page number is correct, but it should not be typed flush with the right margin.
d. The page number is correct, but the short title should not appear on the abstract page.

APA CODES: 5.05 &
5.06
INDEX NUMBER: 02
answer: b
TP-MASTERY 3

Concerning page numbers,
  a. number your pages consecutively starting with the title page.
  b. place the numbers in the center of each page at the top margin.
  c. if a page is inserted after numbering is complete, number the inserted page with an *a* (e.g., 6a).
  d. pages used for figures are not numbered.
  e. a and d are correct.

APA CODE: 5.06
INDEX NUMBER: 01
answer: e
TP-MASTERY 4

Corrections should be
  a. written in the margins of the manuscript.
  b. made by covering the error with correction tape, paper, or fluid and then typing the correction on top.
  c. typed on separate half pages and attached to the pages to be corrected.
  d. made in the word-processing file and printed out.
  e. b and d.

APA CODE: 5.07
INDEX NUMBER: 01
answer: e
TP-FAMILIARIZATION

When correcting typing errors,
  a. retype the page if any errors are made.
  b. correct neatly using correction paper, fluid, or tape to cover the error and then type the correction.
  c. correct the word-processing file and make a clean printout.
  d. type an insert on a slip and attach it to the page with one staple.
  e. b and c.

APA CODE: 5.07
INDEX NUMBER: 02
answer: e
TP-PRACTICE

Indentation at paragraphs
  a. is not necessary if there is triple-spaced typing between paragraphs.
  b. should be at least 10 spaces.
  c. is not necessary if block-style typing format is used for the entire page.
  d. is required in all but a few instances.

APA CODE: 5.08
INDEX NUMBER: 03
answer: d
TP-MASTERY 1

The typing instruction "type in capital and lowercase letters" means
  a. capitalize only the first letters of important words.
  b. type it twice, once in capitals and once in lowercase letters.
  c. type all of the letters of important words in capital letters.
  d. type the headings in all capital letters and the body of the text in lowercase letters.

APA CODE: 5.09
INDEX NUMBER: 01
answer: a
TP-MASTERY 2

A heading that is flush left
  a. should be typed in uppercase and lowercase letters.
  b. need not be underlined.
  c. may be typed in all uppercase letters or all lowercase letters depending on the heading's level.
  d. must end with a period.

APA CODE: 5.10
INDEX NUMBER: 01
answer: a
TP-MASTERY 3

One space should follow
  a. colons used in the text.
  b. all punctuation marks at the end of sentences.
  c. periods that separate parts of a reference.
  d. all of the above.
  e. none of the above.

APA CODE: 5.11
INDEX NUMBER: 01
answer: d
TP-MASTERY 4

One space should follow
  a. semicolons.
  b. colons in two-part titles.
  c. periods in the initials of personal names.
  d. all of the above.
  e. none of the above.

APA CODE: 5.11
INDEX NUMBER: 02
answer: d
TP-FAMILIARIZATION

In most cases, space once after all of the following punctuation marks except
  a. periods in a reference citation.
  b. periods ending a sentence.
  c. internal periods in abbreviations.
  d. colons.

APA CODE: 5.11
INDEX NUMBER: 03
answer: c
TP-PRACTICE

Put no space after
   a. the colon in ratios.
   b. periods in the initials of personal names.
   c. periods that separate parts of a reference.
   d. all of the above.
   e. none of the above.

APA CODE: 5.11
INDEX NUMBER: 04
answer: a
TP-MASTERY 1

Edit the following for the spacing of punctuation:

Some therapists select the method of treatment on a case--by--case basis.

   a. leave as is

   b. Some therapists select the method of treatment on a case by case basis.

   c. Some therapists select the method of treatment on a case-by-case basis.

   d. Some therapists select the method of treatment on a case - by - case basis.

APA CODES: 5.11 &
3.11
INDEX NUMBER: 05
answer: c
TP-MASTERY 2

Edit the following for spacing and punctuation:

Physical and psychological measures of the members of the medical emergency staff--nurses and doctors--were taken immediately and 48 hr after the crisis.

   a. leave as is

   b. Physical and psychological measures of the members of the medical emergency staff - nurses and doctors - were taken immediately and 48 hr after the crisis.

   c. Physical and psychological measures of the members of the medical emergency staff-nurses and doctors-were taken immediately and 48 hr after the crisis.

   d. Physical and psychological measures of the members of the medical emergency staff: nurses and doctors--were taken immediately and 48 hr after the crisis.

APA CODES: 5.11 &
3.05
INDEX NUMBER: 06
answer: a
TP-MASTERY 3

Edit the following for spacing and punctuation:

> When the applicant's ethnic origin was stated explicitly, ethnic origin did affect selection (see Table 1,) but when ethnic origin was not stated explicitly, it did not affect selection (see Table 2) (The interviewers represented a variety of ethnic origins).

a. leave as is

b. When the applicant's ethnic origin was stated explicitly, ethnic origin did affect selection, (see Table 1), but when ethnic origin was not stated explicitly, it did not affect selection, (see Table 2). (The interviewers represented a variety of ethnic origins.).

c. When the applicant's ethnic origin was stated explicitly, ethnic origin did affect selection (see Table 1), but when ethnic origin was not stated explicitly, it did not affect selection (see Table 2). (The interviewers represented a variety of ethnic origins.)

d. When the applicant's ethnic origin was stated explicitly, ethnic origin did affect selection, (see Table 1), but when ethnic origin was not stated explicitly, it did not affect selection, (see Table 2). (The interviewers represented a variety of ethnic origins).

APA CODE: 5.11
INDEX NUMBER: 07
answer: c
TP-MASTERY 4

Edit the following for the spacing of punctuation:

We conducted field observations to determine whether people would respond differently to men and women performing the same activities with a same-sex partner: throwing a football, holding hands, and whispering in the partner's ear. The response measures were length of gaze and facial expression as recorded by two independent judges.

a.   leave as is

b.   We conducted field observations to determine whether people would respond differently to men and women performing the same activities with a same - sex partner: throwing a football, holding hands, and whispering in the partner's ear. The response measures were length of gaze and facial expression as recorded by two independent judges.

c.   We conducted field observations to determine whether people would respond differently to men and women performing the same activities with a same--sex partner: throwing a football,holding hands,and whispering in the partner's ear. The response measures were length of gaze and facial expression as recorded by two independent judges.

d.   We conducted field observations to determine whether people would respond differently to men and women performing the same activities with a same-sex partner: throwing a football, holding hands, and whispering in the partner's ear. The response measures were length of gaze and facial expression as recorded by two independent judges.

e.   We conducted field observations to determine whether people would respond differently to men and women performing the same activities with a same -- sex partner: throwing a football, holding hands, and whispering in the partner's ear. The response measures were length of gaze and facial expression as recorded by two independent judges.

APA CODES: 5.11
and 3.11
INDEX NUMBER: 08
answer: a
TP-EXTRA

Edit the following for the spacing of punctuation:

> The four groups went through one of four training sequences before final testing: practice, practice, practice; practice, model, practice; model, practice, model; or model, model, model. The practice and model sessions all lasted 90 s, and the model's hit: miss ratio was approximately 9: 1.

a. leave as is

b. The four groups went through one of four training sequences before final testing: practice, practice, practice; practice, model, practice; model, practice, model; or model, model, model. The practice and model sessions all lasted 90 s, and the model's hit:miss ratio was approximately 9:1.

c. The four groups went through one of four training sequences before final testing: practice, practice, practice; practice, model, practice; model, practice, model; or model, model, model. The practice and model sessions all lasted 90 s, and the model's hit : miss ratio was approximately 9 : 1.

d. The four groups went through one of four training sequences before final testing: practice, practice, practice; practice, model, practice; model, practice, model; or model, model, model. The practice and model sessions all lasted 90 s, and the model's hit : miss ratio was approximately 9 : 1.

e. The four groups went through one of four training sequences before final testing:practice, practice, practice; practice, model, practice; model, practice, model; or model, model, model. The practice and model sessions all lasted 90 s, and the model's hit:miss ratio was approximately 9:1.

APA CODE: 5.11
INDEX NUMBER: 09
answer: b
TP-EXTRA

Edit the following for the presentation of a series:

> The researchers attempted to determine the relation between the age of the mother at the child's birth and (1) the child's intellectual development, (2) the child's social development, and (3) the mother's personal adjustment.

a. leave as is

b. The researchers attempted to determine the relation between the age of the mother at the child's birth and (a) the child's intellectual development, (b) the child's social development, and (c) the mother's personal adjustment.

c. The researchers attempted to determine the relation between the age of the mother at the child's birth and (*a*) the child's intellectual development, (*b*) the child's social development, and (c) the mother's personal adjustment.

d. The researchers attempted to determine the relation between the age of the mother at the child's birth and (A) the child's intellectual development, (B) the child's social development, and (C) the mother's personal adjustment.

APA CODES: 5.12 & 3.33
INDEX NUMBER: 01
answer: b
TP-FAMILIARIZATION

Edit the following for typing a title page:

COOPERATIVE AND COMPETITIVE PROCESSES IN ACADEMIC WORK

Harold Gelfand and Charles J. Walker

St. Bonaventure University

a. leave as is

b.

Cooperative and Competitive Processes in Academic Work

Harold Gelfand and Charles J. Walker

St. Bonaventure University

c.

Cooperative and Competitive Processes in Academic Work

Harold Gelfand and Charles J. Walker

St. Bonaventure University

d.

Cooperative and Competitive Processes in Academic Work

Harold Gelfand	Charles J. Walker
St. Bonaventure University	St. Bonaventure University

APA CODE: 5.15
INDEX NUMBER: 01
answer: b
TP-PRACTICE

Edit the following for typing a reference entry:

>Muñoz, R. F., Glish, M., Soo-Hoo, T., & Robertson, J. (1982). The San Francisco mood survey project: Preliminary work toward the prevention of depression. *American Journal of Community Psychology, 10,* 317-330.

a. leave as is

b. Muñoz, R. F., Glish, M., Soo-Hoo, T., & Robertson, J. (1982). The San Francisco mood survey project: Preliminary work toward the prevention of depression. *American Journal of Community Psychology, 10,* 317-330.

c. Muñoz, R. F., Glish, M., Soo-Hoo, T., & Robertson, J. (1982). The San Francisco mood survey project: Preliminary work toward the prevention of depression. *American Journal of Community Psychology, 10,* 317-330.

d. Muñoz, R. F., Glish, M., Soo-Hoo, T., & Robertson, J. (1982). The San Francisco mood survey project: Preliminary work toward the prevention of depression. *American Journal of Community Psychology, 10,* 317-330.

APA CODE: 5.18
INDEX NUMBER: 01
answer: a
TP-MASTERY 1

Edit the following for the typing of a reference list:

1. Garcia, J. (1981). The logic and limits of mental aptitude testing. *American Psychologist, 36,* 1172-1180.

2. Kamin, L. (1974). *The science and politics of I.Q.* Hillsdale, NJ: Erlbaum.

a. leave as is

b. Garcia, J. (1981). The logic and limits of mental aptitude testing. *American Psychologist, 36,* 1172-1180.

Kamin, L. (1974). *The science and politics of I.Q.* Hillsdale, NJ: Erlbaum.

c. Garcia, J. (1981). The logic and limits of mental aptitude testing. *American Psychologist, 36,* 1172-1180.

Kamin, L. (1974). *The science and politics of I.Q.* Hillsdale, NJ: Erlbaum.

d. Garcia, J. (1981). The logic and limits of mental aptitude testing. *American Psychologist, 36,* 1172-1180.

Kamin, L. (1974). *The science and politics of I.Q.* Hillsdale, NJ: Erlbaum.

APA CODE: 5.18
INDEX NUMBER: 02
answer: b
TP-MASTERY 2

Edit the following for the typing of a reference list:

REFERENCES

Baron, J. B., & Sternberg, R. J. (1987). *Teaching thinking skills: Theory and practice.* San Francisco: Freeman.

Nickerson, R. S., Perkins, D. N., & Smith, E. E. (1985). *The teaching of thinking.* Hillsdale, NJ: Erlbaum.

a. leave as is

b.

References

   Baron, J. B., & Sternberg, R. J. (1987). *Teaching thinking skills: Theory and practice.* San Francisco: Freeman.

   Nickerson, R. S., Perkins, D. N., & Smith, E. E. (1985). *The teaching of thinking.* Hillsdale, NJ: Erlbaum.

c.

References

Baron, J. B., & Sternberg, R. J. (1987). *Teaching thinking skills: Theory and practice.* San Francisco: Freeman.

Nickerson, R. S., Perkins, D. N., & Smith, E. E. (1985). *The teaching of thinking.* Hillsdale, NJ: Erlbaum.

d.

References

Baron, J. B., & Sternberg, R. J. (1987). *Teaching thinking skills: Theory and practice.* San Francisco: Freeman.

Nickerson, R. S., Perkins, D. N., & Smith, E. E. (1985). *The teaching of thinking.* Hillsdale, NJ: Erlbaum.

APA CODE: 5.18
INDEX NUMBER: 03
answer: c
TP-MASTERY 3

When typing a reference list,
   a. begin it after the last word of the Discussion section on the same page.
   b. type each reference with the first line indented and all of the remaining lines flush left.
   c. head and section with the word *References* even if you cite only one source.
   d. indent all lines of each reference except the first line at least five spaces.

APA CODE: 5.18
INDEX NUMBER: 04
answer: d
TP-MASTERY 4

Edit the following for the typing of the reference list:

REFERENCES

Estes, W. K. (1950). Toward a statistical theory of learning. *Psychological Review,*
57, 94-107.

Tolman, E. C. (1948). Cognitive maps in rats and men. *Psychological Review, 55,*
189-208.

a.　leave as is

b.

REFERENCES

Estes, W. K. (1950). Toward a statistical theory of learning. *Psychological Review,*
57, 94-107.
Tolman, E. C. (1948). Cognitive maps in rats and men. *Psychological Review, 55,*
189-208.

c.

References

Estes, W. K. (1950). Toward a statistical theory of learning. *Psychological Review,*
57, 94-107.
Tolman, E. C. (1948). Cognitive maps in rats and men. *Psychological Review, 55,*
189-208.

d.

REFERENCES

Estes, W. K. (1950). Toward a statistical theory of learning. *Psychological Review,*

57, 94-107.

Tolman, E. C. (1948). Cognitive maps in rats and men. *Psychological Review, 55,*

189-208.

e.

References

Estes, W. K. (1950). Toward a statistical theory of learning. *Psychological Review,*

57, 94-107.

Tolman, E. C. (1948). Cognitive maps in rats and men. *Psychological Review, 55,*

189-208.

APA CODE: 5.18
INDEX NUMBER: 05
answer: e
TP-EXTRA

RESEARCH REPORT MASTER TEST FILE

In contrast to empirical or theoretical articles, review articles
   a.   define and clarify a problem.
   b.   summarize previous investigations.
   c.   identify relations, contradictions, or inconsistencies in the literature.
   d.   suggest steps for future research.
   e.   do all of the above.

APA CODE: 1.04
INDEX NUMBER: 01
answer: e
RR-FAMILIARIZATION

A report of an empirical study usually includes an introduction and sections called Method, Results, and
   a.   Statistics.
   b.   Bibliography.
   c.   Discussion.
   d.   Statement of the Problem.

APA CODE: 1.04
INDEX NUMBER: 02
answer: c
RR-PRACTiCE

A report of an empirical study usually includes an introduction and sections called Method, _____, and Discussion.
   a.   Results
   b.   Bibliography
   c.   Statement of the Problem
   d.   Conclusion

APA CODE: 1.04
INDEX NUMBER: 03
answer: a
RR-MASTERY 1

When writing a report of original research, the sections should be arranged by
   a.   order of importance.
   b.   relation to each other.
   c.   chronology in the experiment.
   d.   none of the above.

APA CODE: 1.04
INDEX NUMBER: 04
answer: c
RR-MASTERY 2

A research report usually includes an introduction and sections called _____, Results, and Discussion.
   a.   Method
   b.   Bibliography
   c.   Statement of the Problem
   d.   Hypotheses

APA CODE: 1.04
INDEX NUMBER: 05
answer: a
RR-MASTERY 3

Which of the following must identify the specific variables investigated and the relation between them?
   a.   the first sentence of the introduction section
   b.   the conclusion of the Discussion section
   c.   the title of the report
   d.   the first table that is cited

APA CODE: 1.06
INDEX NUMBER: 01
answer: c
RR-MASTERY 4 &
FAMILIARIZATION

The abstract of an article should
   a.   offer a brief evaluation of the material in the body of the manuscript.
   b.   be a concise and specific report on the content of the article.
   c.   be written in the passive voice whenever possible.
   d.   do all of the above.

APA CODE: 1.07
INDEX NUMBER: 01
answer: b
RR-PRACTICE

The abstract of an article should be
   a.   a specific and concise summary of the entire report.
   b.   about 25 to 50 words.
   c.   an evaluation of the research report.
   d.   all of the above.

APA CODE: 1.07
INDEX NUMBER: 02
answer: a
RR-MASTERY 1

The abstract of an article should contain
   a.   statements of the problem, method, results, and conclusions.
   b.   raw data statements with conclusions.
   c.   conclusions not found in the text of the report.
   d. F values, degrees of freedom, and probability levels.

APA CODE: 1.07
INDEX NUMBER: 03
answer: a
RR-MASTERY 2

A poorly written abstract is not self-contained. Which of the sentences below violates the criterion of being self-contained?

    a.   The DSM treatment group was superior to the control group.

    b.   Salt-sensitive clients are more reactive than are non-salt-sensitive clients.

    c.   According to Smith (1990), "male-dominant sexual activity is seen in cultures where rape receives little or no punishment" (p. 221).

    d.   all of the above
    e.   a and c of the above

APA CODE: 1.07
INDEX NUMBER: 04
answer: e
RR-MASTERY 3

Abstracts of empirical studies are between 100 and 120 words and contain
    a.   a one-sentence statement of the problem.
    b.   pertinent details from the Method section.
    c.   all statistical findings, degrees of freedom, F or t values, and significance levels.
    d.   all of the above.
    e.   a and b of the above.

APA CODE: 1.07
INDEX NUMBER: 05
answer: e
RR-MASTERY 4

An abstract for a research report should be about
    a.   100 to 120 words.
    b.   75 to 100 words.
    c.   100 to 150 words.
    d.   150 to 200 words.

APA CODE: 1.07
INDEX NUMBER: 06
answer: a
RR-FAMILIARIZATION

What question should the introduction section of a research report attempt to answer?
    a.   What are the theoretical implications of the current research?
    b.   What is the point of the study?
    c.   What is the logical link between the problem and the research design?
    d.   All of the above are correct.
    e.   Only a and c of the above are correct.

APA CODE: 1.08
INDEX NUMBER: 01
answer: d
RR-PRACTICE

The introduction section of a research report should
    a.   include a thorough historical review of the literature.
    b.   define all of the terms that would be unintelligible to a reader with no previous exposure to the field.
    c.   present the specific problem to be explored and describe the research strategy.
    d.   be clearly labeled.

APA CODE: 1.08
INDEX NUMBER: 02
answer: c
RR-MASTERY 1

When closing the introduction section, questions to bear in mind include the following:
    a.   What variables did I plan to manipulate?
    b.   What was the rationale for each of my hypotheses?
    c.   What statistical tests were used?
    d.   all of the above.
    e.   a and b.

APA CODE: 1.08
INDEX NUMBER: 03
answer: e
RR-MASTERY 2

When citing references in the introduction,
    a.   avoid exhaustive historical reviews.
    b.   cite select studies pertinent to the problem issue.
    c.   refer the reader to reviews if they are available.
    d.   do all of the above.
    e.   do only a and b.

APA CODE: 1.08
INDEX NUMBER: 04
answer: d
RR-MASTERY 3

Before writing the introduction, questions to bear in mind include the following:
    a.   What is the point of the study?
    b.   How does the study relate to past research?
    c.   What are the theoretical implications of the study?
    d.   How will the study's hypotheses be derived from the literature?
    e.   all of the above.

APA CODE: 1.08
INDEX NUMBER: 05
answer: e
RR-MASTERY 4

Conventionality and expediency dictate that the Method section should be written

    a.   as a unified whole.

    b.   in subsections.

    c.   without reference notes.

    d.   Answers a and c are correct.

    e.   None of the above is correct.

APA CODE: 1.09
INDEX NUMBER: 01
answer: b
RR-FAMILIARIZATION

The Method section should

    a.   include enough detail to make replication of the experiment possible for the reader.

    b.   briefly describe the method to the reader, omitting details about subjects and apparatus.

    c.   fully describe all statistical testing procedures used.

    d.   explain why the study was done.

APA CODE: 1.09
INDEX NUMBER: 02
answer: a
RR-PRACTICE

When animals are the subjects in a study, it is not usually necessary to report

    a.   the name of the supplier.

    b.   details of their treatment and handling.

    c.   their age, sex, and weight.

    d.   the cost of maintaining them.

APA CODE: 1.09
INDEX NUMBER: 03
answer: d
RR-MASTERY 1

When describing participants in your research, you should

    a.   give major demographic characteristics.

    b.   state how they were selected.

    c.   report if they were provided incentives to participate.

    d.   do all of the above.

APA CODE: 1.09
INDEX NUMBER: 04
answer: d
RR-MASTERY 2

The Method section should be described in enough detail to

    a.   permit a reader to evaluate the reality of your hypotheses.

    b.   permit an experienced investigator to replicate your study.

    c.   allow a perfect duplication of your investigation.

    d.   allow an editor to judge the external validity of your study.

APA CODE: 1.09
INDEX NUMBER: 05
answer: b
RR-MASTERY 3

The usual subsections of the Method section include

    a.   introduction, procedures, and design.

    b.   procedures, procedure tests, and subjects.

    c.   subjects, apparatus, and procedure.

    d.   none of the above.

APA CODE: 1.09
INDEX NUMBER: 06
answer: c
RR-MASTERY 4

When describing human participants, you should state

    a.   the number of participants who did not complete the experiment.

    b.   the total number of participants.

    c.   the number of participants assigned to each experimental condition.

    d.   all of the above.

    e.   b and c of the above.

APA CODE: 1.09
INDEX NUMBER: 07
answer: d
RR-FAMILIARIZATION

In reporting your data

    a.   refer to tables of raw data to be exact.

    b.   include figures that represent data described fully in the text.

    c.   include figures or tables that supplement but are not redundant with data descriptions in the text.

    d.   use many figures and tables because they communicate your results best.

APA CODE: 1.10
INDEX NUMBER: 01
answer: c
RR-PRACTICE

Results are sometimes difficult to read and understand; therefore, it is useful to

    a.   start a Results section by stating your main findings and then reporting each data analysis in detail.

    b.   introduce the reader to statistical theory before you report the results of even basic statistical analyses.

    c.   let the statistics drive the logic of your Results section, not the logic you developed in your introduction (i.e., your hypotheses).

    d.   report raw data, descriptive statistics, and the results of inferential analyses.

APA CODE: 1.10
INDEX NUMBER: 02
answer: a
RR-MASTERY 1

When reporting statistics, include

    a.   information about the magnitude or value of the test (e.g., t tests or F tests).

    b.   information about degrees of freedom.

    c.   descriptive statistics.

    d.   all of the above.

APA CODE: 1.10
INDEX NUMBER: 03
answer: d
RR-MASTERY 2

In the Results section, you should

    a.   summarize data collected.
    b.   discuss the statistical treatment of data.
    c.   discuss the implications of the findings.
    d.   do all of the above.
    e.   do a and b of the above.

APA CODE: 1.10
INDEX NUMBER: 04
answer: e
RR-MASTERY 3

An analysis of variance on your 2 × 2 design has revealed two main effects without an interaction effect (fewer errors were made with easy tasks, and 6-month-olds did better than 1-month-olds in all tasks). In planning your Results section, the best alternative from among the possibilities is to include

    a.   no figure.
    b.   one figure to show the main effect of age.
    c.   a simple table showing the main effect means.
    d.   both a table and a figure.

APA CODE: 1.10
INDEX NUMBER: 05
answer: a
RR-MASTERY 4

In reporting tests of significance,

    a.   give the exact value of the test (F or t value).
    b.   state the relevant degrees of freedom.
    c.   indicate the probability level.
    d.   describe the direction of an effect.
    e.   do all of the above.

APA CODE: 1.10
INDEX NUMBER: 06
answer: e
RR-FAMILIARIZATION

Tables and figures should

    a.   not be referred to in the text.
    b.   not be used for data that can be easily presented in a few lines of text.
    c.   only be used to represent data that are fully described in the text.
    d.   only be used to show inferential statistics.

APA CODE: 1.10
INDEX NUMBER: 07
answer: b
RR-PRACTICE

Speculation is permitted in the Discussion section if it is

    a.   faithful to the intuition of the authors.
    b.   related closely and logically to empirical data or theory.
    c.   expressed verbosely and eloquently.
    d.   none of the above.

APA CODE: 1.11
INDEX NUMBER: 01
answer: b
RR-MASTERY 1

The Discussion section is a part of the report in which you are

    a.   free to discuss theory independent of your results.
    b.   free to interpret your results and to discuss their implications.
    c.   permitted to develop literature support for your hypotheses.
    d.   encouraged to emphasize the flaws of your study.

APA CODE: 1.11
INDEX NUMBER: 02
answer: b
RR-MASTERY 2

Speculation can be used in the Discussion section when it

    a.   bravely goes beyond empirical data and the theory being tested.
    b.   is expressed concisely.
    c.   is identified as speculation.
    d.   does all of the above.
    e.   does b and c of the above.

APA CODE: 1.11
INDEX NUMBER: 03
answer: e
RR-MASTERY 3

The Discussion section should begin with

    a.   a statement regarding implications for future research.
    b.   a statement of the support or nonsupport of your original hypothesis.
    c.   a reformulation of the important points of the paper.
    d.   an analysis of the flaws in your study.

APA CODE: 1.11
INDEX NUMBER: 04
answer: b
RR-MASTERY 4

If your study is simple and your Discussion section is brief and straightforward, you can

    a.   discuss the flaws of the study at length.
    b.   spend most of your time discussing the next study you plan to do.
    c.   combine the Results and Discussion sections.
    d.   discuss the negative findings, listing all of the possible causes.
    e.   do all of the above.

APA CODE: 1.11
INDEX NUMBER: 05
answer: c
RR-FAMILIARIZATION

Speculation is in order in the Discussion section when it is
- a. identified as speculation.
- b. logically related to empirical data or the theory being tested.
- c. expressed concisely.
- d. all of the above.
- e. none of the above.

APA CODE: 1.11
INDEX NUMBER: 06
answer: d
RR-PRACTICE

In a paper that integrates several experiments, you should
- a. not try to relate the experiments to each other.
- b. have only one Results section for all of the experiments.
- c. make it at least twice as long as a one-experiment study.
- d. include a comprehensive general discussion of all of the work.

APA CODE: 1.12
INDEX NUMBER: 01
answer: d
RR-MASTERY 1

In a paper that integrates several experiments, you should
- a. not try to relate the experiments to each other.
- b. have only one Results section for all of the experiments.
- c. include a comprehensive general discussion of all the work.
- d. make it at least twice as long as a one-experiment study.

APA CODE: 1.12
INDEX NUMBER: 02
answer: c
RR-MASTERY 2

Consistency of verb tense helps to smooth expression. Select the preferred match of paper section with verb tense from the choices below:
- a. conclusion: present tense
- b. literature review: present tense
- c. Results: past tense
- d. Method: past tense
- e. all of the above except b

APA CODE: 2.02
INDEX NUMBER: 01
answer: e
RR-MASTERY 2 & 3

On the basis of verb tense, in which part of a report is the following text segment likely to appear?

College students judged time differently than did college faculty. Faculty were

more accurate in judging the amount of time required to do academic tasks.

- a. Method
- b. hypotheses
- c. Discussion
- d. conclusion

APA CODE: 2.02
INDEX NUMBER: 02
answer: c
RR-MASTERY 4

On the basis of verb tense, in which part of a report is the following text segment likely to appear?

College students judge time differently than do college faculty. Faculty are more

accurate in judging the amount of time required to do academic tasks.

- a. Method
- b. a review of the literature in an introduction
- c. a conclusion in a Discussion
- d. Results

APA CODE: 2.02
INDEX NUMBER: 03
answer: c
RR-FAMILIARIZATION

What causes the following segment of a student's research report to lack smoothness of expression?

According to the research of Savin-Williams (1988), how gay men publicly

revealed their sexual preference is correlated with the stability of their mental

health. He finds that well-adjusted gay men reveal early to trusted others.

- a. intransitive inferences
- b. too much jargon
- c. abrupt changes in verb tense
- d. misplaced modifiers

APA CODE: 2.02
INDEX NUMBER: 04
answer: c
RR-PRACTICE

Past tense is usually appropriate for describing

  a. previous experiments.
  b. an experimental design.
  c. a procedure.
  d. all of the above.

APA CODE: 2.02
INDEX NUMBER: 05
answer: d
RR-MASTERY 1

The present tense is usually appropriate when you are

  a. presenting past research.
  b. describing the demographic details of the subjects.
  c. discussing results and presenting conclusions.
  d. describing the results.
  e. The present tense is never used.

APA CODE: 2.02
INDEX NUMBER: 06
answer: c
RR-MASTERY 3

Informal verb use such as *the participant felt that*, colloquial expressions such as *lab report*, or approximations of quantity such as *in large measure*

  a. have a place in serious scientific writing.
  b. add warmth to dull scientific prose.
  c. reduce word precision and clarity.
  d. can be used to enhance communication.
  e. are more acceptable in written than in oral communication.

APA CODE: 2.04
INDEX NUMBER: 01
answer: c
RR-MASTERY 4

Approximations of quantity such as *a major portion of*, colloquial expressions such as *write-up*, or informal verb use such as *it was her feeling that*

  a. reduce word precision and clarity.
  b. add warmth to dull scientific prose.
  c. have a place in serious scientific writing.
  d. can be used to enhance communication.
  e. are more acceptable in written than in oral communication.

APA CODE: 2.04
INDEX NUMBER: 02
answer: a
RR-FAMILIARIZATION

When a verb concerns the action of the author-experimenter, the

  a. third person and passive voice should be used.
  b. third person and active choice should be used.
  c. the first person, active voice is used.
  d. third person should be used in all scientific writing to ensure objectivity.

APA CODE: 2.04
INDEX NUMBER: 03
answer: c
RR-PRACTICE

Which of the following examples represents correct hyphenation?

  a. *t*-test results
  b. results from *t* tests
  c. 2-, 3-, and 10-min trials
  d. All of the above are correct.

APA CODE: 3.11
INDEX NUMBER: 01
answer: d
RR-MASTERY 1 & 2

Identify the example with incorrect use of capitalization:

  a. The conclusion is obvious: forgiveness is not granted to the stronger partner in an inequitable relationship.

  b. Familiar tasks appear to accelerate the acquaintanceship process in groups of strangers.

  c. Schizophrenia is sometimes associated with visual creativity.

  d. The brain stem is the "on switch" of consciousness.

APA CODE: 3.12
INDEX NUMBER: 01
answer: a
RR-MASTERY 3

In table headings and figure captions,

  a. capitalize only the first word and proper nouns.
  b. capitalize all major words.
  c. do not capitalize any words.
  d. capitalization will depend on the message you wish to convey.

APA CODE: 3.13
INDEX NUMBER: 02
answer: a
RR-MASTERY 4 &
FAMILIARIZATION

Which of the following examples demonstrates correct use of capitalization?

a. Trial 3 and Item 4
b. trial *n* and item *x*
c. chapter 4
d. Table 2 and Figure 3
e. All of the above are correct.

APA CODE: 3.15
INDEX NUMBER: 01
answer: e
RR-MASTERY 2 &
PRACTICE

Edit the following for capitalization:

On the third day of Experiment 2 the children read Chapter 6 of their sex education text.

a. leave as is
b. *Experiment* and *Chapter* do not need to be capitalized.
c. *Chapter* does not require capitalization.
d. The terms *sex* and *education* should be capitalized.

APA CODE: 3.15
INDEX NUMBER: 02
answer: c
RR-MASTERY 1

Edit the following for capitalization of experimental conditions:

The Sex-education and No-sex-education groups were then asked to view a film on the ethics of physical intimacy.

a. leave as is
b. The names of experimental conditions or groups should not be capitalized.
c. All nouns following hyphens should be capitalized.
d. The word *groups* also should be capitalized.

APA CODE: 3.17
INDEX NUMBER: 01
answer: b
RR- MASTERY 3

Edit the following for the capitalization of names of experimental conditions:

Participants in the tobacco-chewing therapy condition and in the no-therapy control condition then each received two wads of chewing tobacco.

a. leave as is
b. The names of experimental conditions should always be capitalized.
c. The names of treatments such as *two wads* should be capitalized.
d. Because *chewing tobacco* is a commercial term, it should be capitalized.

APA CODE: 3.17
INDEX NUMBER: 02
answer: a
RR-MASTERY 4

Names of conditions or groups in an experiment should

a. be capitalized.
b. not be capitalized.
c. not be capitalized unless followed by numerals or letters.
d. be designated by a letter.

APA CODE: 3.17,
3.15
INDEX NUMBER: 03
answer: c
RR-FAMILIARIZATION

Edit the following for capitalization:

When the hermit crabs listened to classical music, they were significantly more likely to retreat back into their shells than when they listened to rock and roll music. However, there was no music x shell interaction effect.

a. leave as is
b. The interaction term *music x shell* should be *Music x Shell*.
c. Statistical terms such as *significantly* should be capitalized.
d. *Interaction effect* should be *Interaction Effect*.

APA CODE: 3.18
INDEX NUMBER: 01
answer: b
RR-PRACTICE

Capitalize

    a. the word *factor* when it is followed by a number (e.g., Factor 6).
    b. effects or variables that do not appear with multiplication signs.
    c. names of conditions or groups in an experiment.
    d. all of the above.
    e. none of the above.

APA CODES: 3.18 & 3.17
INDEX NUMBER: 02
answer: a
RR-MASTERY 1

Edit the following for capitalization of names of variables, factors, or effects:

    All of the manipulated variables were counterbalanced. Fats, carbohydrates, and

    fiber were introduced into the clients' diets in different orders.

    a. leave as is
    b. Names of variables such as *fats*, *carbohydrates*, and *fiber* should be capitalized.
    c. The word *variables* should be capitalized.
    d. The names of variables or effects should be capitalized unless followed by a multiplication sign.

APA CODE: 3.18
INDEX NUMBER: 03
answer: a
RR-MASTERY 2

Capitalize

    a. the word *factor* when it is followed by a number (e.g., Factor 6).
    b. effects or variables that do not appear with multiplication signs.
    c. sources of effect variance, but not sources of error variance.
    d. all of the above.
    e. none of the above.

APA CODE: 3.18
INDEX NUMBER: 04
answer: a
RR-MASTERY 3

Which of the following should not be italicized?

    a. *a priori*

    b. *(1973), 26, 46-77*

    c. $F(1, 53) = 10.03$

    d. *Journal of Experimental Psychology*

APA CODE: 3.19
INDEX NUMBER: 01
answer: a
RR-MASTERY 4

Use italics for

    a. trigonometric terms.
    b. introduction of key terms and labels.
    c. Greek letters.
    d. all of the above.

APA CODE: 3.19
INDEX NUMBER: 02
answer: b
RR-FAMILIARIZATION

According to the APA style rules regarding italics,

    a. only Greek letters used as statistical symbols are italicized.
    b. all letters used as statistical symbols except Greek letters should be italicized.
    c. letters used as statistical symbols are never italicized in print.
    d. a and c of the above are correct.

APA CODE: 3.19
INDEX NUMBER: 03
answer: b
RR-PRACTICE

In general, use abbreviations

    a. if the reader is more familiar with the abbreviation than with the complete word or words being used.
    b. for long technical terms.
    c. if considerable space can be saved and repetition avoided.
    d. Answers a and c of the above are correct.
    e. All of the above are correct.

APA CODE: 3.20
INDEX NUMBER: 01
answer: d
RR-MASTERY 1

Abbreviations appearing in several figures or tables

    a. must be explained in the figure caption or table note for every figure or table in which they are used.
    b. must be explained in the figure caption or table note of only the first figure or table in which they are used.
    c. should only be explained in the text.
    d. need not be explained.

APA CODE: 3.21
INDEX NUMBER: 01
answer: a
RR-MASTERY 2

The abbreviations S, E, and O (for subject, experimenter, and observer, respectively)

    a.   are treated the same as other abbreviations in the text.
    b.   are not used in APA articles.
    c.   should only be used in table notes and figure captions.
    d.   None of the above is correct.

APA CODE: 3.23
INDEX NUMBER: 01
answer: b
RR-MASTERY 3

The abbreviations S, E, and O (for subject, experimenter, and observer, respectively)

    a.   should always be used in articles.
    b.   should only be used in journals that deal with physiological aspects of psychology.
    c.   should be used only in the Method section.
    d.   are not used in APA articles.

APA CODE: 3.23
INDEX NUMBER: 02
answer: d
RR-MASTERY 4

Edit the following by selecting the correct arrangement of headings:

Experiment 1

Method

Stimulus Materials

    Animal sounds.

  a.   leave as is

  b.

Experiment 1

Method

Stimulus Materials

    Animal sounds.

  c.

EXPERIMENT 1

Method

Stimulus Materials

    Animal sounds.

  d.

EXPERIMENT 1

Method

Stimulus Materials

    Animal sounds.

APA CODE: 3.31
INDEX NUMBER: 01
answer: b
RR-FAMILIARIZATION

Edit the following by selecting the correct arrangement of headings:

Method

Subjects

Procedure

Results

Discussion

a.　leave as is

b.

Method

Subjects

Procedure

Results

Discussion

c.

Method

Subjects

Procedure

Results

Discussion

d.

Method

Subjects

Procedure

Results

Discussion

APA CODE: 3.31
INDEX NUMBER: 02
answer: b
RR-PRACTICE

Choose the correct format for the use of three levels of headings:

a.

Experiment 2

Method

Participants

b.

METHOD

Procedure

 Pretraining period.

c.

Method

 Procedure.

Participants

d.

Method

Procedure

 Pretraining period.

APA CODE: 3.32
INDEX NUMBER: 01
answer: d
RR-MASTERY 1

Edit the following by selecting the correct arrangement of headings:

Method

Subjects

Procedure

Results

Discussion

a.   leave as is

b.

Method

Subjects.

Procedure.

Results

Discussion

c.

Method

Subjects

Procedure

Results

Discussion

d.

METHOD

Subjects

Procedure

RESULTS

DISCUSSION

APA CODE: 3.32
INDEX NUMBER: 02
answer: c
RR-MASTERY 2

Edit the following by selecting the correct arrangement of headings:

Results

Pretraining Phase

    Accuracy.

a.   leave as is

b.

RESULTS

Pretraining Phase

    Accuracy.

c.

RESULTS

    Pretraining Phase

      Accuracy.

d.

Results

    Pretraining Phase

      Accuracy.

APA CODE: 3.32
INDEX NUMBER: 03
answer: d
RR-MASTERY 3

Edit the following by selecting the correct arrangement of headings:

Introduction

Method

a.   leave as is

b.

Introduction and Hypotheses

Method

c.

    Introduction

    Method

d.

Introduction

    Method

e.

Method

APA CODE: 3.32
INDEX NUMBER: 04
answer: e
RR-EXTRA

Edit the following by selecting the correct arrangement of headings:

A.   Method

1.   Subjects

2.   Procedure

B.   Results

a.   leave as is

b.

A.   Method

1.   Subjects

2.   Procedure

B.   Results

c.

A.   Method

   1.   *Subjects*

   2.   *Procedure*

B.   Results

d.

Method

Subjects

Procedure

Results

e.

Method

Subjects

Procedure

Results

APA CODE: 3.32
INDEX NUMBER: 05
answer: e
RR-EXTRA

Edit the following by selecting the correct arrangement of headings:

Experiment 1

Method

    Subjects.

    Procedure.

Results and Discussion

Experiment 2

Method

a.   leave as is

b.

Experiment 1

Method

    Subjects.

    Procedure.

Results and Discussion

Experiment 2

    Method.

c.

Experiment 1

Method

    Subjects.

    Procedure.

Results and Discussion

Experiment 2

    Method.

(continued)

d.

Experiment 1

Method

Subjects.

Procedure.

Results and Discussion

Experiment 2

Method.

e.

Experiment 1

Method

Subjects

Procedure

Results and Discussion

Experiment 2

Method

APA CODE: 3.32
INDEX NUMBER: 06
answer: a
RR-EXTRA

Edit the following by selecting the correct arrangement of headings:

Experiment 1

Method

a. leave as is

b.

Experiment 1

Method

c.

EXPERIMENT 1

Method

d.

EXPERIMENT 1

METHOD

e.

EXPERIMENT 1

Method

APA CODE: 3.32
INDEX NUMBER: 07
answer: b
RR-EXTRA

Edit the following by selecting the correct arrangement of headings:

Method

Assessment of Therapy Effectiveness.

    Pretraining phase.

a.   leave as is

b.

METHOD

ASSESSMENT OF THERAPY EFFECTIVENESS

    Pretraining phase.

c.

METHOD

ASSESSMENT OF THERAPY EFFECTIVENESS

    Pretraining phase.

d.

Method

Assessment of Therapy Effectiveness:

    Pretraining phase.

e.

Method

Assessment of Therapy Effectiveness

    Pretraining phase.

APA CODE: 3.32
INDEX NUMBER: 08
answer: e
RR-EXTRA

Edit the following by selecting the correct arrangement of headings:

EXPERIMENTAL EVIDENCE

Experiment 3

Method

Participants

    Demographic characteristics.

Procedure

Results

a.   leave as is

b.

EXPERIMENTAL EVIDENCE

Experiment 3

Method

Participants

    Demographic characteristics.

Procedure

Results

c.

EXPERIMENTAL EVIDENCE

EXPERIMENT 3

Method

Participants

    Demographic characteristics.

Procedure

Results

(continued)

d.

EXPERIMENTAL EVIDENCE

EXPERIMENT 3

Method

Participants

    Demographic characteristics.

Procedure

Results

e.

EXPERIMENTAL EVIDENCE

Experiment 3

Method

Participants

    Demographic characteristics.

Procedure

APA CODE: 3.32
INDEX NUMBER: 09
answer: a
RR-EXTRA

Results

Edit the following by selecting the correct arrangement of headings:

Experiment 1

Method

Apparatus

    Cortical stimulation.

a.   leave as is

b.

EXPERIMENT 1

Method

Apparatus

    Cortical stimulation.

c.

EXPERIMENT 1

Method

Apparatus

    Cortical stimulation.

d.

EXPERIMENT 1

Method

Apparatus

Cortical stimulation.

e.

EXPERIMENT 1

Method

Apparatus

    Cortical Stimulation

APA CODE: 3.32
INDEX NUMBER: 10
answer: a
RR-EXTRA

The general rule on expressing numbers is
    a.   use words to express all numbers.
    b.   use figures to express all numbers.
    c.   use words to express numbers below 10 and figures to express numbers 10 and above.
    d.   use figures to express numbers in tables and graphs and words to express numbers in the text.

APA CODES: 3.42 &
3.43
INDEX NUMBER: 01
answer: c
RR-MASTERY 4

Use numerical figures to express
    a.   any number that begins a sentence.
    b.   common fractions.
    c.   numbers that immediately precede a unit of measurement.
    d.   none of the above.

APA CODE: 3.42
INDEX NUMBER: 02
answer: c
RR-FAMILIARIZATION

Numerical figures should be used at all times for
- a. ages, times, dates, and percentages.
- b. ratios, arithmetical manipulations, and series of four or more numbers.
- c. fractional or decimal quantities, scores and points on a scale, and units of measurement of time.
- d. all of the above.

APA CODE: 3.42
INDEX NUMBER: 03
answer: d
RR-PRACTICE

Edit the following for the expression of numbers:

> Of the companies that participated, twenty-four were service companies, eleven were high-technology companies, and eight were heavy-industry companies.

- a. leave as is
- b. Of the companies that participated, 24 were service companies, eleven were high-technology companies, and eight were heavy-industry companies.
- c. Of the companies that participated, 24 were service companies, 11 were high-technology companies, and eight were heavy-industry companies.
- d. Of the companies that participated, 24 were service companies, 11 were high-technology companies, and 8 were heavy-industry companies.

APA CODE: 3.42
INDEX NUMBER: 04
answer: d
RR-MASTERY 1

Edit the following for the expression of numbers:

> The maze consisted of a series of 18 choice points.

- a. leave as is
- b. The maze consisted of a series of eighteen choice points.
- c. 18 choice points composed the maze.

APA CODE: 3.42
INDEX NUMBER: 05
answer: a
RR-MASTERY 2

Edit the following for the expression of numbers:

> The stimulus presentations were separated by a masking field that lasted for 2 ms.

- a. leave as is
- b. The stimulus presentations were separated by a masking field that lasted for two ms.

APA CODE: 3.42
INDEX NUMBER: 06
answer: a
RR-MASTERY 3

Edit the following for the expression of numbers:

> The number of times the client used *I* in each therapy session is shown in Figure Two.

- a. leave as is
- b. The number of times the client used *I* in each therapy session is shown in Figure II.
- c. The number of times the client used *I* in each therapy session is shown in Figure 2.
- d. The number of times the client used *I* in each therapy session is shown in Figure two.

APA CODE: 3.42
INDEX NUMBER: 07
answer: c
RR-MASTERY 4

Edit the following for the expression of numbers:

> Respondents in each of the age groups were asked to describe what they had eaten for dinner two and four weeks previously.

    a.   leave as is

    b.   Respondents in each of the age groups were asked to describe what they had eaten for dinner 2 and 4 weeks previously.

APA CODE: 3.42
INDEX NUMBER: 08
answer: b
RR-FAMILIARIZATION

Edit the following for the expression of numbers:

> It would be wrong to estimate absentees for the week by taking the number of absentees on Monday and multiplying by 5.

    a.   leave as is

    b.   It would be wrong to estimate absentees for the week by taking the number of absentees on Monday and multiplying by five.

    c.   It would be wrong to estimate absentees for the week by taking the number of absentees on Monday and multiplying by five (5).

APA CODE: 3.42
INDEX NUMBER: 09
answer: a
RR-PRACTICE

Edit the following for the expression of numbers:

> Procedural errors occurred while testing 2 rats in the drug condition and 3 rats in the placebo condition.

    a.   leave as is

    b.   Procedural errors occurred while testing 2.0 rats in the drug condition and 3.0 rats in the placebo condition.

    c.   Procedural errors occurred while testing two rats in the drug condition and three rats in the placebo condition.

    d.   Procedural errors occurred while testing two (2) rats in the drug condition and three (3) rats in the placebo condition.

APA CODE: 3.42
INDEX NUMBER: 10
answer: a
RR-MASTERY 1

Edit the following for the expression of numbers:

> The survey had a sampling error of four %.

    a.   leave as is

    b.   The survey had a sampling error of four percent.

    c.   The survey had a sampling error of 4%.

    d.   The survey had a sampling error of 4 percent.

APA CODE: 3.42
INDEX NUMBER: 11
answer: c
RR-MASTERY 2

Edit the following for the expression of numbers:

> Each critical word was preceded by zero, one, two, or three priming words in the list.

a. leave as is

b. Each critical word was preceded by zero, 1, 2, or 3 priming words in the list.

c. Each critical word was preceded by 0, 1, 2, or 3 priming words in the list.

d. Each critical word was preceded by zero (0), one (1), two (2), or three (3) priming words in the list.

APA CODE: 3.42
INDEX NUMBER: 12
answer: c
RR-MASTERY 3

Edit the following for the expression of numbers:

> The investigation compared the effectiveness of 3 methods for disseminating health information in the local community.

a. leave as is

b. The investigation compared the effectiveness of three methods for disseminating health information in the local community.

c. Both a and b are correct.

APA CODE: 3.43
INDEX NUMBER: 01
answer: b
RR-MASTERY 4

Edit the following for the expression of numbers:

> Eighty nurses volunteered to keep a daily record of their stress levels.

a. leave as is

b. 80 nurses volunteered to keep a daily record of their stress levels.

c. Eighty (80) nurses volunteered to keep a daily record of their stress levels.

APA CODE: 3.43
INDEX NUMBER: 02
answer: a
RR-FAMILIARIZATION

Edit the following for the expression of numbers:

> The authors identify 7 different groups of personality theories.

a. leave as is

b. The authors identify seven different groups of personality theories.

c. Both a and b are correct.

APA CODE: 3.43
INDEX NUMBER: 03
answer: b
RR-PRACTICE

Edit the following for the expression of numbers:

> The 3-dimensional conceptualization allows for 8 possible dyadic relationships.

a. leave as is

b. The 3-dimensional conceptualization allows for eight possible dyadic relationships.

c. The three-dimensional conceptualization allows for eight possible dyadic relationships.

d. The three-dimensional conceptualization allows for 8 possible dyadic relationships.

APA CODE: 3.43
INDEX NUMBER: 04
answer: c
RR-MASTERY 1

Edit the following for the expression of numbers:

> To test the program, schools were sought in which at least one fourth of the students did not finish the year above grade level on the criterion measure.

a. leave as is

b. To test the program, schools were sought in which at least 1/4 of the students did not finish the year above grade level on the criterion measure.

c. To test the program, schools were sought in which at least 1/4th of the students did not finish the year above grade level on the criterion measure.

d. To test the program, schools were sought in which at least one/fourth of the students did not finish the year above grade level on the criterion measure.

APA CODE: 3.43
INDEX NUMBER: 05
answer: a
RR-MASTERY 2

Edit the following for the expression of numbers:

> Each participant evaluated each of the 12 social portraits on each of 6 dimensions.

a. leave as is

b. Each participant evaluated each of the twelve social portraits on each of six dimensions.

c. Each participant evaluated each of the 12 social portraits on each of six dimensions.

d. Each participant evaluated each of the twelve social portraits on each of 6 dimensions.

APA CODES: 3.43 & 3.42
INDEX NUMBER: 06
answer: c
RR-MASTERY 3

Edit the following for the expression of numbers:

> Sixty percent of the victims' closest relatives, but only twenty-eight percent of the victims themselves, showed signs of anxiety and stress on the delayed tests.

a. leave as is

b. Sixty percent of the victims' closest relatives, but only 28% of the victims themselves, showed signs of anxiety and stress on the delayed tests.

c. 60% of the victims' closest relatives, but only 28% of the victims themselves, showed signs of anxiety and stress on the delayed tests.

d. Sixty percent (60%) of the victims' closest relatives, but only 28% of the victims themselves, showed signs of anxiety and stress on the delayed tests.

APA CODES: 3.43 & 3.42
INDEX NUMBER: 07
answer: b
RR-MASTERY 4

Words should be used to express numbers
a. whenever numbers are greater than 20 but less than 200.
b. from zero to nine, not representing a precise measurement and not grouped for comparison with numbers 10 and above.
c. always, except when cardinal numbers have satisfied the requirements of ratio measurement and are grouped for comparison with themselves.
d. as seldom as possible.

APA CODE: 3.43
INDEX NUMBER: 08
answer: b
RR-FAMILIARIZATION

Edit the following for the expression of numbers:

"Large" financial responsibility was defined as responsibility for an annual budget in excess of five million dollars.

a. leave as is

b. "Large" financial responsibility was defined as responsibility for an annual budget in excess of $5 x 10⁶.

c. "Large" financial responsibility was defined as responsibility for an annual budget of $5,000,000.

d. "Large" financial responsibility was defined as responsibility for an annual budget in excess of $5 million.

Edit the following for the expression of numbers:

There were twenty 6-year-olds, eighteen 10-year-olds, and twenty-four 14-year-olds.

a. leave as is

b. There were 20 6-year olds, 18 10-year-olds, and 24 14-year-olds.

c. There were 20 six-year-olds, 18 ten-year-olds, and 24 fourteen-year-olds.

d. There were twenty six-year-olds, eighteen 10-year-olds, and twenty-four 14-year-olds.

Edit the following for the expression of numbers:

Each client was asked to describe his or her actual and ideal selves on 16 5-point rating scales.

a. leave as is

b. Each client was asked to describe his or her actual and ideal selves on 16, 5-point rating scales.

c. Each client was asked to describe his or her actual and ideal selves on sixteen 5-point rating scales.

d. Each client was asked to describe his or her actual and ideal selves on 16 five-point rating scales.

Edit the following for the expression of numbers:

There was 20 4-person teams in each leadership-style condition.

a. leave as is

b. There were twenty four-person teams in each leadership-style condition.

c. There were 20 four-person teams in each leadership-style condition.

d. There were twenty 4-person teams in each leadership-style condition.

Edit the following for the expression of ordinal numbers:

>The sequence of events changed on the fourth trial.

    a.   leave as is

    b.   The sequence of events changed on the 4th trial.

    c.   The sequence of events changed on the IVth trial.

APA CODE: 3.45
INDEX NUMBER: 01
answer: a
RR-MASTERY 4

Edit the following for the expression of ordinal numbers:

>The critical stimuli were placed in the second and 10th positions in each block of trials.

    a.   leave as is

    b.   The critical stimuli were placed in the 2nd and 10th positions in each block of trials.

    c.   The critical stimuli were placed in the second and tenth positions in each block of trials.

APA CODE: 3.45
INDEX NUMBER: 02
answer: b
RR-FAMILIARIZATION

Edit the following for the expression of ordinal numbers:

>The trainees were all in at least their 3rd year of unemployment.

    a.   leave as is

    b.   The trainees were all in at least their third (3rd) year of unemployment.

    c.   The trainees were all in at least their third year of unemployment.

APA CODE: 3.45
INDEX NUMBER: 03
answer: a
RR-PRACTICE

Edit the following for the expression of ordinal numbers:

>The 6th and 12th graders in each of the treatment conditions returned for a 5th session in which the performance measures were taken.

    a.   leave as is

    b.   The sixth and 12th graders in each of the treatment conditions returned for a fifth session in which the performance measures were taken.

    c.   The sixth and twelfth graders in each of the treatment conditions returned for a fifth session in which the performance measures were taken.

    d.   The 6th and 12th graders in each of the treatment conditions returned for a fifth session in which the performance measures were taken.

APA CODE: 3.45
INDEX NUMBER: 04
answer: d
RR-MASTERY 1

Edit the following for the expression of decimal fractions:

>The dots appeared simultaneously on the screen, .5 cm apart.

    a.   leave as is

    b.   The dots appeared simultaneously on the screen, 0.5 cm apart.

    c.   The dots appeared simultaneously on the screen, .50 cm apart.

APA CODE: 3.46
INDEX NUMBER: 01
answer: b
RR-MASTERY 2

Edit the following for the expression of decimal fractions:

The correlation between scores on the two measures of job satisfaction was .84.

a. leave as is

b. The correlation between scores on the two measures of job satisfaction was 0.84.

c. The correlation between scores on the two measures of job satisfaction was

84×10^{-2}.

d. The correlation between scores on the two measures of job satisfaction was .8400.

APA CODE: 3.46
INDEX NUMBER: 02
answer: a
RR-MASTERY 3

Edit the following for the expression of decimal fractions:

The main effect of training condition was significant, $F(3, 150) = 5.28$, $p < 0.01$.

a. leave as is

b. The main effect of training condition was significant, $F(3, 150) = 5.28$, $p < .01$.

c. The main effect of training condition was significant, $F(3, 150) = 5.28$, $p < .010$.

APA CODE: 3.46
INDEX NUMBER: 03
answer: b
RR-MASTERY 4

Edit the following for the expression of decimal fractions:

The containers were made of transparent plastic and weighed .6 kg.

a. leave as is

b. The containers were made of transparent plastic and weighed 0.6 kg.

c. The containers were made of transparent plastic and weighed 6×10^{-1} kg.

d. The containers were made of transparent plastic and weighed 60×10^{-2} kg.

APA CODE: 3.46
INDEX NUMBER: 04
answer: b
RR-FAMILIARIZATION

When using decimal numbers less than one,
a. a zero is always used before the decimal point (0.05).
b. a zero is never used before the decimal point (.05).
c. the author should check with the editor of each specific journal, as this is a highly controversial topic.
d. a zero is used before the decimal point (0.05) except when the number cannot be greater than one (e.g., correlations, proportions, and levels of statistical significance; $r = -.96$, $p < .05$).

APA CODE: 3.46
INDEX NUMBER: 05
answer: d
RR-PRACTICE

When using decimal numbers,
a. a zero is used before the decimal point (0.05) only when the number cannot be greater than one (e.g., correlations, proportions, and levels of significance; $r = -0.96$, $p < 0.05$).
b. a zero is never used before the decimal point (.05).
c. the author should check with the editor of each specific APA journal.
d. a zero is always used before the decimal point (0.05) when numbers can take on values greater than one.

APA CODE: 3.46
INDEX NUMBER: 06
answer: d
RR-MASTERY 1

According to the *Publication Manual of the American Psychological Association*,
a. roman and arabic numbers can be used in equal frequency.
b. arabic numerals should be used wherever possible except when roman numerals are part of an established terminology.
c. roman numerals should never be used.
d. roman numerals should be used wherever possible.

APA CODE: 3.47
INDEX NUMBER: 01
answer: b
RR-MASTERY 2

Edit the following for the expression of numbers:

Experiment I was a normative study to determine the reactions of hospital staff members to different diseases and illnesses.

a. leave as is

b. Experiment One was a normative study to determine the reactions of hospital staff members to different diseases and illnesses.

c. Experiment 1 was a normative study to determine the reactions of hospital staff members to different diseases and illnesses.

d. Experiment one was a normative study to determine the reactions of hospital staff members to different diseases and illnesses.

APA CODES: 3.47 & 3.42
INDEX NUMBER: 02
answer: c
RR-MASTERY 3

Edit the following for the expression of numbers:

The differential treatments were implemented on Trial 2.

a. leave as is

b. The differential treatments were implemented on Trial II.

c. The differential treatments were implemented on Trial Two.

d. The differential treatments were implemented on trial two.

APA CODES: 3.47 & 3.42
INDEX NUMBER: 03
answer: a
RR-MASTERY 4

Edit the following for the expression of numbers:

When the payoff for finding an effective treatment is so high, it is important to minimize Type 2 errors.

a. leave as is

b. When the payoff for finding an effective treatment is so high, it is important to minimize Type II errors.

c. When the payoff for finding an effective treatment is so high, it is important to minimize Type Two errors.

APA CODE: 3.47
INDEX NUMBER: 04
answer: b
RR-FAMILIARIZATION

Edit the following for the expression of numbers:

Days I and IV were baseline days, and Days II and III were teatment days.

a. leave as is

b. Days One and Four were baseline days, and Days Two and Three were treatment days.

c. Days 1 and 4 were baseline days, and Days 2 and 3 were treatment days.

d. Days I and Four were baseline days, and Days II and III were treatment days.

APA CODE: 3.47
INDEX NUMBER: 05
answer: c
RR-PRACTICE

Edit the following for the presentation of numbers:

The interaction of class year and type of organization was not significant, $F(3, 1,590) = 1.85$, $p > .10$.

a.   leave as is

b.   The interaction of class year and type of organization was not significant, $F(3, 1590) = 1.85$, $p > .10$.

c.   The interaction of class year and type of organization was not significant, $F(3, 1590K) = 1.85$, $p > .10$.

APA CODE: 3.48
INDEX NUMBER: 01
answer: b
RR-MASTERY 1

Edit the following for the punctuation of numbers:

A content analysis was performed on 1,480 episodes of soap operas that had been televised in the preceding 5 years.

a.   leave as is

b.   A content analysis was performed on 1480 episodes of soap operas that had been televised in the preceding 5 years.

APA CODE: 3.48
INDEX NUMBER: 02
answer: a
RR-MASTERY 2

Edit the following for the expression of numbers:

The tones were presented at 6,000 Hz for varying durations.

a.   leave as is

b.   The tones were presented at 6000 Hz for varying durations.

c.   The tones were presented at 6×10^3 Hz for varying durations.

APA CODE: 3.48
INDEX NUMBER: 03
answer: b
RR-MASTERY 3

Edit the following for the punctuation of numbers:

We counted the number of times that incumbent and nonincumbent candidates referred to themselves and their opposition in a total of 1663 speeches during the 1984 and 1988 political campaigns.

a.   leave as is

b.   We counted the number of times that incumbent and nonincumbent candidates referred to themselves and their opposition in a total of 1,663 speeches during the 1,984 and 1,988 political campaigns.

c.   We counted the number of times that incumbent and nonincumbent candidates referred to themselves and their opposition in a total of 1,663 speeches during the 1984 and 1988 political campaigns.

APA CODE: 3.48
INDEX NUMBER: 04
answer: c
RR-MASTERY 4

Use commas between groups of three digits in figures of 1,000 or more except when expressing
   a.   page numbers.
   b.   serial numbers.
   c.   degrees of freedom.
   d.   all of the above.

APA CODE: 3.48
INDEX NUMBER: 05
answer: d
RR-FAMILIARIZATION

Which example is the correct way to use commas and spacing when presenting statistics in text?

    a. $F,_{(24, 1000)}$
    b. $F_{(24, 1000)}$
    c. $F(24, 1000)$
    d. $F(24\ 1,000)$

APA CODE: 3.48
INDEX NUMBER: 06
answer: c
RR-PRACTICE

Physical measurements should be reported in

    a.   metric units.
    b.   traditional nonmetric units.
    c.   units of the original measurement.
    d.   physical units.

APA CODE: 3.50
INDEX NUMBER: 01
answer: a
RR-MASTERY 1

Experimenters who use instruments that record measurements in nonmetric units

    a.   should report the measurement as recorded.
    b.   may report the nonmetric units but must also report the SI (metric) equivalents.
    c.   can report either the nonmetric units or the SI (metric) equivalents.
    d.   None of the above is correct.

APA CODE: 3.50
INDEX NUMBER: 02
answer: b
RR-MASTERY 2

The APA policy on the use of metric units in writing states that

    a.   due to the complex nature of the metric system it should only be used for publication in international journals.
    b.   the metric system is used in journals if possible; when not possible, nonmetric units must also be accompanied by their equivalents (in parentheses) in the International System of Units.
    c.   either system, metric or nonmetric, is acceptable.
    d.   the use of nonmetric units is completely unacceptable.

APA CODE: 3.50
INDEX NUMBER: 03
answer: b
RR-MASTERY 3 & 4

Edit the following for the correct use of metric measurement:

Conductance and inductance were measured in siemens (S) and henrys (H), respectively.

    a.   leave as is
    b.   The measurements do not conform to the International System of Units.
    c.   Measurements should not be expressed in metric units in social or behavioral science journals.
    d.   Inductance should be measured in newtons per meter, not in henrys.

APA CODES: 3.50 & 3.52
INDEX NUMBER: 04
answer: a
RR-FAMILIARIZATION

Which of the following metric units is correctly expressed?

    a.   33 cms.
    b.   3 mm.
    c.   13 cm
    d.   3 cms.

APA CODE: 3.51
INDEX NUMBER: 01
answer: c
RR-PRACTICE

Which of the following is correctly expressed?

    a.   13 cms
    b.   313 cm.
    c.   31 cm
    d.   313 cms.

APA CODE: 3.51
INDEX NUMBER: 02
answer: c
RR-MASTERY 1

Spell out the metric unit

    a.   when the unit does not appear with a numeric value.
    b.   when the unit appears with a numeric value.
    c.   in table headings.
    d.   None of the above is correct.

APA CODE: 3.51
INDEX NUMBER: 03
answer: a
RR-MASTERY 2

When you include statistics from another source in a research report, cite the reference

    a.   for less common statistics.
    b.   for statistics used in a controversial way.
    c.   when the statistic itself is the focus of an article.
    d.   all of the above.

APA CODE: 3.55
INDEX NUMBER: 01
answer: d
RR-MASTERY 3

Formulas for statistics should be given
    a.   at all times.
    b.   for common statistics and for a statistic that is used only once in the article.
    c.   for a statistic not yet widely known or for one that is the focus of the article.
    d.   None of the above is correct.

APA CODES: 3.55 &
3.56
INDEX NUMBER: 02
answer: c
RR-MASTERY 4

When you present statistics, cite the reference
    a.   for less common statistics.
    b.   for statistics used in a controversial way.
    c.   when a statistic itself is the focus of an article.
    d.   for all of the above.
    e.   for any statistics and all uses of a statistic.

APA CODE: 3.55
INDEX NUMBER: 03
answer: d
RR-FAMILIARIZATION

Edit the following for the citation of a statistic in text:

A 4 x 3 analysis of variance (Keppel, 1982) was conducted on the preference scores.

    a.   leave as is

    b.   A 4 x 3 analysis of variance (see any standard statistics text) was conducted on the preference scores.

    c.   A 4 x 3 analysis of variance was conducted on the preference scores.

APA CODE: 3.55
INDEX NUMBER: 04
answer: c
RR-PRACTICE

Edit the following for the citation of a statistic in text:

A t test for related means was used to compare the number of targets found by birds in the experimental group with the number found by their yoked partners.

    a.   leave as is

    b.   A t test for related means (Hays, 1963) was used to compare the number of targets found by birds in the experimental group with the number found by their yoked partners.

    c.   A t test for related means (see any standard statistics reference work) was used to compare the number of targets found by birds in the experimental group with the number found by their yoked partners.

APA CODE: 3.55
INDEX NUMBER: 05
answer: a
RR-MASTERY 1

Edit the following for citing the source of a statistic in text:

A one-way analysis of variance (see any standard statistics text) was used to assess the effect of drug dosage.

    a.   leave as is

    b.   A one-way analysis of variance was used to assess the effect of drug dosage.

    c.   A one-way analysis of variance (Winer, 1971) was used to assess the effect of drug dosage.

APA CODE: 3.55
INDEX NUMBER: 06
answer: b
RR-MASTERY 2

Edit the following for citing the source of a statistic in text:

A chi-square test (Ferguson, 1981) was used to compare the preference distributions for girls and boys.

a. leave as is

b. A chi-square test (see any standard statistics text) was used to compare the preference distributions for girls and boys.

c. A chi-square test was used to compare the preference distributions for girls and boys.

Edit the following for the presentation of formulas:

The participants were divided into high and low self-monitors by a median split (Mdn = 50th percentile).

a. leave as is

b. The participants were divided into high and low self-monitors by a median split (Mdn = 50th %ile).

c. The participants were divided into high and low self-monitors by a median split [$Mdn = (n + 1)/2$].

d. The participants were divided into high and low self-monitors by a median split.

Edit the following for the expression of formulas:

The participants were told their mean reaction times (M = total reaction time/ number of trials) after each block of trials.

a. leave as is

b. The participants were told their mean reaction times ($M = \Sigma RT/n$ trials) after each block of trials.

c. The participants were told their mean reaction times [$M = (RT_1 + RT_2 + RT_3 \ldots + RT_n)/n_T$] after each block of trials.

d. The participants were told their mean reaction times after each block of trials.

Edit the following for the presentation of formulas:

The relation between premarital sexual experience and incidence of divorce was evaluated using a chi-square test {$\chi^2 = [\Sigma(\text{Observed} - \text{Expected})/\text{Expected}]$}.

a. leave as is

b. The relationship between premarital sexual experience and incidence of divorce was evaluated using a chi-square test (see Appendix A for formula).

c. The relationship between premarital sexual experience and incidence of divorce was evaluated using a chi-square test.

Edit the following for the presentation of a formula:

The frequencies of heterosexual intercourse per month by heterosexual and bisexual men were compared using a t test.

a. leave as is

b. The frequencies of heterosexual intercourse per month by heterosexual and bisexual men were compared using a t test (t = difference between means/standard error of difference between means).

c. The frequencies of heterosexual intercourse per month by heterosexual and bisexual men were compared using a t test [$t = (M_H - M_B)$/standard error of difference between means].

d. The frequencies of heterosexual intercourse per month by heterosexual and bisexual men were compared using a t test [$(M_H - M_B)/(s_H - {}_B)$].

APA CODE: 3.56
INDEX NUMBER: 04
answer: a
RR-MASTERY 1

Include formulas for
a. new or rare statistics or mathematical expressions.
b. a statistical or mathematical expression essential to a paper.
c. all statistics and mathematical expressions.
d. a and b.
e. none of the above.

APA CODE: 3.56
INDEX NUMBER: 05
answer: d
RR-MASTERY 2

Edit the following for the presentation of statistics:

Suggested starting salary was significantly lower when the applicant was described as a woman (M = $19,600) than when the application was described as a man (M = $22,080), $t(df = 62) = 2.58$, $p < .01$.

a. leave as is

b. Suggesting starting salary was significantly lower when the applicant was described as a woman (M = $19,600) than when the applicant was described as a man (M = $22,080), $t_{62} = 2.58$, $p < .01$.

c. Suggested starting salary was significantly lower when the applicant was described as a woman (M = $19,600) than when the applicant was described as a man (M = $22,080), $t(62) = 2.58$, $p < .01$.

d. Suggested staring salary was significantly lower when the applicant was described as a woman (M = $19,600) than when the applicant was described as a man (M = $22,080), $t = 2.58$, $p < .01$.

APA CODE: 3.57
INDEX NUMBER: 01
answer: c
RR-MASTERY 3

Which of the following is the correct way to present a statistic in text?

a. $t = 2.62(22)$, $p < .01$

b. $t = 2.62(22)$, $p <. 01$

c. $t(22) = 2.62$, $p<. 01$

d. any of the above

e. none of the above

APA CODE: 3.57
INDEX NUMBER: 02
answer: e
RR-MASTERY 4

Which of the following is the correct way to present a statistic in text?

a. $F = 2.62(22)$, $p< .01$

b. $t(22) = 2.62$, $p <. 01$

c. $t = 2.62(22)$, $p<. 01$

d. none of the above

When presenting statistical information in the text, in order to clarify the nature of effects (i.e., mean differences and the direction of mean differences)
a. give only the inferential statistics.
b. always give descriptive and inferential statistics.
c. give inferential and descriptive statistics only when presenting correlational data.
d. give inferential statistics for experiments with more than one independent variable and descriptive statistics for correlational research.

When presenting an inferential statistic in text, give
a. the statistical symbol.
b. degrees of freedom.
c. the probability level.
d. all of the above.
e. none of the above.

Edit the following for the presentation of statistics:

The interaction between depression status of the participant and content of the message had a significant effect on mood judgments (see Table 2), $F(1, 92) = 4.26$, $p < .05$.

a. leave as Is

b. The interaction between depression status of the participant and content of the message had a significant effect on mood judgments (see Table 2), $p < .05$.

c. The interaction between depression status of the participant and content of the message had a significant effect on mood judgments (see Table 2), $F = 4.26$, $p < .05$.

d. The interaction between depression status of the participant and content of the message had a significant effect on mood judgments (see Table 2), $F(1/92)$, $p < .05$.

Edit the following for the presentation of statistics:

The grade distributions of instructors who conducted extra help sessions were significantly different from those of instructors who did not, $\chi_4^2(1{,}208) = 10.25$, $p < .05$.

a. leave as is

b. The grade distributions of instructors who conducted extra help sessions were significantly different from those of instructors who did not, $\chi_{1,208}^2(df = 4) = 10.25$, $p < .05$.

c. The grade distributions of instructors who conducted extra help sessions were significantly different from those of instructors who did not, $\chi^2(4, N = 1{,}208) = 10.25$, $p < .05$.

d. The grade distributions of instructors who conducted extra help sessions were significantly different from those of instructors who did not, $\chi^2 = 10.25$ $(df = 4, N = 1{,}208)$, $p < .05$.

APA CODE: 3.57
INDEX NUMBER: 07
answer: c
RR-MASTERY 3

Edit the following for the presentation of statistics:

The means for the no-treatment, placebo, and drug conditions were 8.8, 7.2, and 4.6, respectively.

a. leave as is

b. The means for the three conditions were 8.8, 7.2, and 4.6.

c. The means for the three conditions were 8.8, 7.2, and 4.6, respectively.

APA CODE: 3.57
INDEX NUMBER: 08
answer: a
RR-MASTERY 4

Edit the following for the presentation of statistics:

The children were divided into two groups on the basis of which hand they used to hold the pen. The mean scores on the orientation task for the two groups were 34 and 142.

a. leave as is

b. The children were divided into two groups on the basis of which hand they used to hold the pen. The mean scores on the orientation task for the left-handed and right-handed groups were 34 and 142, respectively.

c. The children were divided into two groups on the basis of which hand they used to hold the pen. The mean scores on the orientation task for the left-handed and right-handed groups were 34 and 142.

d. The children were divided into two groups on the basis of which hand they used to hold the pen. The means scores on the orientation task for the two groups were 34 and 142, respectively.

APA CODE: 3.57
INDEX NUMBER: 09
answer: b
RR-FAMILIARIZATION

Edit the following for the use of statistical symbols:

In the group therapy condition, 16 percent of the clients did not return for the second session and another 8 percent did not return for the third session.

a. leave as is

b. In the group therapy condition, 16% of the clients did not return for the second session and another eight percent did not return for the third session.

c. In the group therapy condition, 16% of the clients did not return for the second session and another eight % did not return for the third session.

d. In the group therapy condition, 16% of the clients did not return for the second session and another 8% did not return for the third session.

APA CODE: 3.58
INDEX NUMBER: 01
answer: d
RR-PRACTICE

Edit the following for the use of statistical symbols:

We first conducted a pilot study to determine the % of participants who would complete the task with different time limits.

a. leave as is

b. We first conducted a pilot study to determine the percentage of participants who could complete the task with different time limits.

c. We first conducted a pilot study to determine the % age of participants who could complete the task with different time limits.

d. We first conducted a pilot study to determine the percentage (%) of participants who could complete the task with different time limits.

APA CODE: 3.58
INDEX NUMBER: 02
answer: b
RR-MASTERY 1

Edit the following for the presentation of statistics:

The volunteers who appeared for the orientation session (sample size = 120) were then randomly assigned to one of the three conditions.

a. leave as is

b. The volunteers who appeared for the orientation session (N = 120) were then randomly assigned to one of the three conditions.

c. The volunteers who appeared for the orientation session (N = 120) were then randomly assigned to one of the three conditions.

d. The volunteers who appeared for the orientation session (n = 120) were then randomly assigned to one of the three conditions.

APA CODE: 3.58
INDEX NUMBER: 03
answer: c
RR-MASTERY 2

Edit the following for the presentation of statistics:

The applicants in the support condition (n = 18) were given a training course in résumé writing and interview techniques.

a. leave as is

b. The applicants in the support condition (n = 18) were given a training course in résumé writing and interview techniques.

c. The applicants in the support condition (N = 18) were given a training course in résumé writing and interview techniques.

d. The applicants in the support condition (sample size = 18) were given a training course in résumé writing and interview techniques.

APA CODE: 3.58
INDEX NUMBER: 04
answer: a
RR-MASTERY 3

Edit the following for the expression of statistical terms:

The Ms for the alcohol and no-alcohol conditions were 18.4 and 13.6, respectively.

a. leave as is

b. The means for the alcohol and no-alcohol conditions were 18.4 and 13.6, respectively.

c. The MEANS for the alcohol and no-alcohol conditions were 18.4 and 13.6, respectively.

d. The $\overline{X}$s for the alcohol and no-alcohol conditions were 18.4 and 13.6, respectively.

APA CODE: 3.58
INDEX NUMBER: 05
answer: b
RR-MASTERY 4

Edit the following for the presentation of statistical symbols:

Respondents who received feedback after each response hit more targets (mean = 74.4, standard deviation = 9.7) than did those who received feedback after each block of 24 responses (mean = 44.7, standard deviation = 2.3), $t(30)$ = 3.42, p < .01.

a. leave as is

b. Respondents who received feedback after each response hit more targets (M = 74.4, SD = 9.7) than did those who received feedback after each block of 24 responses (M = 44.7, SD = 2.3), t(30) = 3.42, p < .01.

c. Respondents who received feedback after each response hit more targets ($\overline{X}$ = 74.4, SD = 9.7) than did those who received feedback after each block of 24 responses ($\overline{X}$ = 44.7, SD = 2.3), t(30) = 3.42, p < .01.

d. Respondents who received feedback after each response hit more targets (M = 74.4, SD = 9.7) than did those who received feedback after each block of 24 responses (M = 44.7, SD = 2.3), $t(30)$ = 3.42, p < .01.

APA CODE: 3.58
INDEX NUMBER: 06
answer: d
RR-FAMILIARIZATION

Which of the following should be used to designate the number of cases or observations in a total sample?

    a.   *N*
    b.   N
    c.   *n*
    d.   n

APA CODE: 3.58
INDEX NUMBER: 07
answer: a
RR-PRACTICE

Which of the following should be used to designate the number of members in a part of a total sample?

    a.   N
    b.   *n*
    c.   n
    d.   *N*

APA CODE: 3.58
INDEX NUMBER: 08
answer: b
RR-MASTERY 1

A table should be used

    a.   whenever data analyses are involved.
    b.   when an article is more than 1,200 words.
    c.   when it compresses data and allows relationships to be seen that are not readily seen in text.
    d.   for all of the above.

APA CODE: 3.62
INDEX NUMBER: 01
answer: c
RR-MASTERY 2 & 4

Tables should be used for

    a.   any data relevant to the article.
    b.   important data directly related to the content of the article.
    c.   any data presented in the text.
    d.   all of the above.

APA CODE: 3.62
INDEX NUMBER: 02
answer: b
RR-MASTERY 3

Before constructing a table, you should consider that

    a.   rounded-off values display patterns more clearly than precise values.
    b.   readers can compare numbers down a column more easily than across rows.
    c.   data from a 2 × 2 design should be put in a table rather than in the text.
    d.   adding space between columns or rows can make a table easier to read.
    e.   all of the above except c.

APA CODE: 3.62
INDEX NUMBER: 03
answer: e
RR-FAMILIARIZATION

Edit Table 17 for errors in tabular presentation and notes to a table:

Table 17

Mean Mood Scores Before and After Physical Activity

	Mood	
Physical activity	Before	After
Nonaerobic		
Bird watching	3.2	3.7
Bowling	3.0	3.0
Golfing[a]	3.4	2.7
Aerobic		
Cycling	3.3	8.1
Dancing[b]	3.3	8.4
Hill climbing	3.2	8.2
Rowing	3.1	8.0
Running	3.4	7.9
Ski skating	3.1	9.0

Note. Mood was rated on a 10-point scale.

[a]Golfers rode around the course in golf carts. [b]Dancers danced to rock and

roll music.

a.   The mean values are rounded off too much.
b.   There is not enough spacing between columns.
c.   The footnotes are in the wrong sequence.
d.   Roman numerals should be used to number a table.
e.   There are no errors in Table 17.

APA CODES: 3.62 &
3.70
INDEX NUMBER: 04
answer: e
RR-PRACTICE

Edit the table below for tabular presentation:

Table 6

Mean Imaginal Scores of Students Reporting an

Out-of-Body Experience

Condition	Imaginal scores
Visual	7.1
Auditory	4.0

a. Means should be carried out to two decimal places.
b. No standard deviations are given.
c. Results consisting of only two means should be presented in the text, not in a table.
d. b and c

APA CODE: 3.62
INDEX NUMBER: 05
answer: d
RR-MASTERY 1

Edit the following table for tabular presentation:

Table 4

Mean Imaginal Scores of Students Reporting an

Out-of-Body Experience

Condition	Imaginal scores
Visual	7.1
Auditory	4.0

a. Table 4 should be Table IV.
b. Results consisting of only two means should be presented in the text, not in a table.
c. No standard deviations are given.
d. b and c

APA CODE: 3.62
INDEX NUMBER: 06
answer: d
RR-MASTERY 2

Tables should be an integral part of the text, yet be readable alone. To accomplish this end,
a. use extensive footnotes (one third of a page).
b. explain all but the most common statistical abbreviations.
c. cite the table in the text by saying "in the above table."
d. put tables in an appendix.
e. do all of the above.

APA CODE: 3.63
INDEX NUMBER: 01
answer: b
RR-MASTERY 3 & 4

A good table
a. is intelligible without reference to the text.
b. does not need to be discussed in the text.
c. duplicates information in the text.
d. does a and b of the above.

APA CODE: 3.63
INDEX NUMBER: 02
answer: a
RR-FAMILIARIZATION

Tables should be
    a. intelligible without reference to the text.
    b. referred to but not duplicated in the text.
    c. referred to in text by their numbers.
    d. all of the above.

APA CODE: 3.63
INDEX NUMBER: 03
answer: d
RR-MASTERY 1

For all tables within one paper, use
    a. the same terminology.
    b. similar formats.
    c. the same title.
    d. a and b.

APA CODE: 3.64
INDEX NUMBER: 01
answer: d
RR-MASTERY 2 & 3

Tables should be numbered in the order
    a. in which they are first mentioned in the text.
    b. that seems most logical to the author.
    c. that seems most logical to an editor.
    d. of any of the above.

APA CODE: 3.65
INDEX NUMBER: 01
answer: a
RR-MASTERY 4

Tables should be numbered in the order
    a. that puts the longest table first.
    b. in which they are first mentioned in the text.
    c. that seems most logical to the author.
    d. that seems most logical to an editor.

APA CODE: 3.65
INDEX NUMBER: 02
answer: b
RR-FAMILIARIZATION

Of the following possible titles for Table 17 (see p. 229), which would not be clear and explanatory?

    a. *Mood and Exercise*

    b. *Mean Changes in Mood of Subjects Prior to and Following a Variety of*
        Nonaerobic and Aerobic Physical Activities

    c. *A Comparison of Physical Activities*

    d. All of the above titles are poorly written.

APA CODE: 3.66
INDEX NUMBER: 01
answer: d
RR-PRACTICE

Every table should have a title that is
    a. brief.
    b. clear.
    c. explanatory.
    d. all of the above.

APA CODE: 3.66
INDEX NUMBER: 02
answer: d
RR-MASTERY 1

A table title should be
    a. brief (i.e., no more than four to six words).
    b. clear about what data are in the table, yet concise.
    c. detailed about all independent and dependent variables.
    d. a and b are correct.

APA CODE: 3.66
INDEX NUMBER: 03
answer: b
RR-MASTERY 2

Identify a column spanner in Table 17 (see p. 229):
    a. Bird watching
    b. Cycling
    c. Mood
    d. Aerobic

APA CODE: 3.67
INDEX NUMBER: 01
answer: c
RR-PRACTICE

The left-hand column of a table (the *stub*) usually lists
    a. mean values.
    b. the major independent variables.
    c. decked heads.
    d. none of the above.

APA CODE: 3.67
INDEX NUMBER: 02
answer: b
RR-MASTERY 3

The column spanner of a table

    a.   is a thick line used to mark the top of the table.
    b.   is exclusively used to list the dependent variables.
    c.   labels the column head variable.
    d.   should be no more than 20 characters wide.

APA CODE: 3.67
INDEX NUMBER: 03
answer: c
RR-MASTERY 4

The left-hand column of a table (the *stub*) has a heading (the *stubhead*) that usually describes the

    a.   elements in that column.
    b.   dependent variables.
    c.   independent variables.
    d.   data.
    e.   a and c.

APA CODE: 3.67
INDEX NUMBER: 04
answer: e
RR-FAMILIARIZATION
& MASTERY 2

In Table 17 (see p. 229), identify a column heading:

    a.   Nonaerobic
    b.   Ski skating
    c.   Before
    d.   Mood

APA CODE: 3.67
INDEX NUMBER: 05
answer: c
RR-PRACTICE

Which of the following abbreviations need not be explained in table headings?

    a.   abbreviations of technical terms
    b.   standard abbreviations for nontechnical terms
    c.   group names
    d.   none of the above

APA CODE: 3.67
INDEX NUMBER: 06
answer: b
RR-MASTERY 1

The body of a table

    a.   always contains data rounded off to the nearest tenth.
    b.   contains columns of data even if those data can be easily calculated from other columns.
    c.   contains words or numerical data.
    d.   does all of the above.

APA CODE: 3.68
INDEX NUMBER: 01
answer: c
RR-MASTERY 3 & 4

When more than one level of significance is reported in a table,

    a.   each level is represented by a single asterisk.
    b.   one asterisk is used for the lowest level.
    c.   another asterisk is added for each level of significance.
    d.   b and c are correct.

APA CODE: 3.70
INDEX NUMBER: 01
answer: d
RR-FAMILIARIZATION

A specific note to a table

    a.   refers to a particular column or individual entry.
    b.   is indicated by a superscript lowercase letter.
    c.   is placed below the table.
    d.   does all of the above.
    e.   does none of the above.

APA CODE: 3.70
INDEX NUMBER: 02
answer: a
RR-PRACTICE

A specific note to a table

    a.   refers to a particular column or individual entry.
    b.   is indicated by a superscript uppercase letter.
    c.   is placed within the body of the table.
    d.   does none of the above.

APA CODE: 3.70
INDEX NUMBER: 03
answer: a
RR-MASTERY 1

In the word-processed manuscript, all rules used in a table should be

    a.   drawn with the underline key.
    b.   drawn with the table border function.
    c.   used only to clarify division.
    d.   all of the above.

APA CODE: 3.71
INDEX NUMBER: 01
answer: d
RR-MASTERY 2

When ruling tables,

    a.   almost never use vertical rules.
    b.   use both horizontal and vertical rules.
    c.   you may substitute appropriately positioned white space for rules.
    d.   do a and c.
    e.   do all of the above.

APA CODE: 3.71
INDEX NUMBER: 02
answer: d
RR-MASTERY 3

When ruling tables, use

    a.   horizontal rules only.
    b.   vertical rules only.
    c.   both horizontal and vertical rules.
    d.   well-positioned white space rather than horizontal rules.
    e.   b and d.

APA CODE: 3.71
INDEX NUMBER: 03
answer: a
RR-MASTERY 4

Tables, including titles and headings, should be

    a.   triple-spaced.
    b.   double-spaced.
    c.   single-spaced.
    d.   any of the above.

APA CODE: 3.74
INDEX NUMBER: 01
answer: b
RR-FAMILIARIZATION
& PRACTICE

When inspecting a newly constructed table, what question should you *not* ask yourself?

    a.   Should this table be vertically displayed?
    b.   Is the table necessary?
    c.   Does every column have a heading?
    d.   Is it double-spaced?
    e.   all of the above

APA CODE: 3.74
INDEX NUMBER: 02
answer: a
RR-MASTERY 1

The word *figure* refers to

    a.   halftones.
    b.   graphs and charts.
    c.   illustrations.
    d.   all of the above.

APA CODE: 3.75
INDEX NUMBER: 01
answer: d
RR-FAMILIARIZATION
& MASTERY 2

The word *figure* is used to refer to

    a.   tables of data.
    b.   graphs and charts.
    c.   statistical symbols.
    d.   all of the above.

APA CODE: 3.75
INDEX NUMBER: 02
answer: b
RR-MASTERY 3

What factors weigh against using a figure?

    a.   It duplicates the text.
    b.   It complements text and reduces lengthy discussions.
    c.   It will be expensive to make.
    d.   Answers a and c are correct.
    e.   Answers a and b are correct.

APA CODE: 3.75
INDEX NUMBER: 03
answer: d
RR-MASTERY 1

A figure is not necessary if it

    a.   augments text.
    b.   duplicates text.
    c.   eliminates lengthy discussion from the text.
    d.   does none of the above.

APA CODES: 3.75 &
3.76
INDEX NUMBER: 04
answer: b
RR-MASTERY 2

A good figure

    a.   conveys only essential facts.
    b.   is easy to understand.
    c.   is prepared in the same style as similar figures in the same article.
    d.   does all of the above.

APA CODE: 3.76
INDEX NUMBER: 01
answer: d
RR-PRACTICE &
MASTERY 4

What type of graph is useful to represent the intersection of two variables?

    a.   bar
    b.   scatter
    c.   line
    d.   circle

APA CODE: 3.77
INDEX NUMBER: 02
answer: b
RR-MASTERY 3

If a graph could be misinterpreted because the origin of the coordinates is not zero,

    a.   do not include the graph in the research report.
    b.   break the axes with a double slash.
    c.   specify the origin in the notes to the table.
    d.   separate the axes by at least 1 cm.

APA CODE: 3.77
INDEX NUMBER: 03
answer: b
RR-MASTERY 4

What kind of graph (a type of figure) is useful to show a continuous change across time?

    a.   bar
    b.   circle
    c.   line
    d.   pie
    e.   scatter

APA CODE: 3.77
INDEX NUMBER: 04
answer: c
RR-FAMILIARIZATION

What kind of graph (a type of figure) is useful to show a continuous change across time?

    a.   line
    b.   circle
    c.   pie
    d.   bar
    e.   scatter

APA CODE: 3.77
INDEX NUMBER: 05
answer: a
RR-PRACTICE

What kind of figure is easy and inexpensive to prepare and reproduce?

    a.   photograph
    b.   line art
    c.   halftone
    d.   color
    e.   laser

APA CODES: 3.78 &
3.80
INDEX NUMBER: 01
answer: b
RR-MASTERY 1

A figure legend should be positioned

    a.   within the figure.
    b.   to the left of the figure.
    c.   below the figure.
    d.   above the figure.

APA CODE: 3.79
INDEX NUMBER: 01
answer: a
RR-MASTERY 2

What kind of lettering should not be used when lettering a figure?

    a.   careful freehand
    b.   professional
    c.   typewritten
    d.   dry-transfer or stencil
    e.   a and c

APA CODE: 3.80
INDEX NUMBER: 01
answer: e
RR-MASTERY 3

From the following examples, select the correct way to refer to a figure in text:

    a.   see the figure above

    b.   see the figure on page 14

    c.   see Figure 2

    d.   see Figure 2 above on page 14

APA CODE: 3.83
INDEX NUMBER: 01
answer: c
RR-FAMILIARIZATION
& MASTERY 4

Edit the following for numbering of figures. Assume that this is the first time the figures are presented.

Results

        The predicted social facilitation effects were observed. As can be seen in Figure 2, a videocamera increased errors with the difficult task and decreased errors with the easy task. As can be seen in Figure 1, the presence of an evaluative audience produced the same pattern of results.

    a.   leave as is
    b.   Figure 2 should be Figure II.
    c.   Figure 2 should be Figure Two.
    d.   Figure 2 should be Figure 1 and vice versa.

APA CODE: 3.83
INDEX NUMBER: 02
answer: d
RR-PRACTICE

Select the figure caption that does not explain its figure effectively:

a. *Figure 1.* Videocamera effects.

b. *Figure 4.* Varimax rotation of factors.

c. *Figure 2.* Outpatient and inpatient contrasts.

d. All of the above captions are too brief and not sufficiently explanatory.

APA CODE: 3.84
INDEX NUMBER: 01
answer: d
RR-MASTERY 1

Figure captions
a. serve as the explanation and as the title of the figure.
b. should describe the contents of the figure in a brief sentence or phrase.
c. should be typed on a separate sheet for submission to a journal.
d. do all of the above.

APA CODE: 3.84
INDEX NUMBER: 02
answer: d
RR-MASTERY 2

A good figure caption
a. describes the figure in detail no matter how lengthy it becomes.
b. should refer the reader to a place in the text for explanation of the figure.
c. is concise but explanatory.
d. does none of the above.

APA CODE: 3.84
INDEX NUMBER: 03
answer: c
RR-MASTERY 3

Table notes
a. are placed below the bottom rule of a table.
b. explain table data or provide additional information.
c. acknowledge the source of a reprinted table.
d. do all of the above.
e. do none of the above.

APA CODE: 3.88
INDEX NUMBER: 01
answer: d
RR-MASTERY 4

Which of the following is the correct ordering of manuscript subsections?
a. title page, introduction, abstract
b. References, appendixes, author identification notes
c. Method, Discussion, Results
d. figures, figure captions, tables
e. Discussion, footnotes, References

APA CODE: 5.05
INDEX NUMBER: 01
answer: b
RR-FAMILIARIZATION

Where should figures be placed in a submitted manuscript?
a. at the end
b. at the beginning
c. in an appropriate place in text
d. None of the above is correct.

APA CODE: 5.05
INDEX NUMBER: 02
answer: a
RR-PRACTICE

Which part of a research report should not always begin on a new page?
a. abstract
b. References
c. Method
d. author identification notes
e. a and b

APA CODE: 5.05
INDEX NUMBER: 03
answer: c
RR-MASTERY 1

Which of the following is the correct ordering of manuscript sections in a research report?
a. title page, abstract, introduction
b. Method, Results, Discussion
c. References, tables, footnotes
d. a and b

APA CODE: 5.05
INDEX NUMBER: 04
answer: d
RR-MASTERY 2

Which of the following is the correct ordering of manuscript sections in a research report?
a. Method, Results, tables, Discussion
b. References, tables, figure captions, figures
c. author notes, figures, figure captions, tables
d. none of the above

APA CODE: 5.05
INDEX NUMBER: 05
answer: b
RR-MASTERY 3

Which of the following should be placed on a separate page of a manuscript?

- a. the abstract
- b. appendixes
- c. figure captions
- d. all of the above
- e. none of the above

APA CODE: 5.05
INDEX NUMBER: 06
answer: d
RR-MASTERY 4

If the title of your manuscript is *Effects of Deviant Revealing on the Mood States of the Chronically Happy*, and your running head is REVELATION AND HAPPINESS, what short title should you use?

- a. Effects of Deviant
- b. Revelation and Happiness
- c. Deviant Revealing and the Mood of the Chronically Happy
- d. Chronic Revealing

APA CODE: 5.06
INDEX NUMBER: 01
answer: a
RR-FAMILIARIZATION

Edit the following for typing statistical and mathematical copy:

> The students who planned to keep their textbooks wrote on a significantly greater number of their pages (M = 182.4, SD = 6.2) than did the students who planned to sell their textbooks (M = 128.6, SD = 1.7), $t($ 46 $)$ = 3.27, $p<.01$.

- a. leave as is
- b. The students who planned to keep their textbooks wrote on a significantly greater number of their pages (M = 182.4, SD = 6.2) than did the students who planned to sell their textbooks (M = 128.6, SD = 1.7), $t(46)$ = 3.27, $p < .01$.
- c. The students who planned to keep their textbooks wrote on a significantly greater number of their pages (M = 182.4, SD = 6.2) than did the students who planned to sell their textbooks (M = 128.6, SD = 1.7), $t(46)=3.27, p<.01$.
- d. The students who planned to keep their textbooks wrote on a significantly greater number of their pages (M = 182.4, SD = 6.2) than did the students who planned to sell their textbooks (M = 128.6, SD = 1.7), t (46) = 3.27, $p<.01$.

APA CODES: 5.14 &
3.59
INDEX NUMBER: 01
answer: b
RR-PRACTICE

Edit the following for the typing of statistical copy:

> The problem-solving scores (see Table 3) yielded no significant effect due to the sex of the participant, F (1,152)=1.49, $p > .20$.

- a. leave as is
- b. The problem-solving scores (see Table 3) yielded no significant effect due to the sex of the participant, $F(1,152)$ = 1.49, $p>.20$.
- c. The problem-solving scores (see Table 3) yielded no significant effect due to the sex of the participant, $F(1,152)=1.49$, $p>.20$.
- d. The problem-solving scores (see Table 3) yielded no significant effect due to the sex of the participant, $F(1, 152)$ = 1.49, $p > .20$.

APA CODES: 5.14 &
3.59
INDEX NUMBER: 02
answer: d
RR-MASTERY 1

Edit the following for typing statistical and mathematical copy:

A 2 x 2 x 3 (Sex of Participant x Sex of Target x Activity Profile) analysis of variance was performed on the attractiveness scores.

a. leave as is

b. A 2x2x3 (Sex of Participant x Sex of Target x Activity Profile) analysis of variance was performed on the attractiveness scores.

c. A 2X2X3 (Sex of Participant X Sex of Target X Activity Profile) analysis of variance was performed on the attractiveness scores.

d. A 2 X 2 X 3 (Sex of Participant X Sex of Target X Activity Profile) analysis of variance was performed on the attractiveness scores.

APA CODES: 5.14 & 3.59
INDEX NUMBER: 03
answer: a
RR-MASTERY 2

Edit the following for typing statistical and mathematical copy:

The students' use of the computer for word processing was independent of their knowledge of computer programming, $Chi^2(1, N=86) = 1.23, p > .25$.

a. leave as is

b. The students' use of the computer for word processing was independent of their knowledge of computer programming, $\chi^2(1, N = 86) = 1.23, p > .25$.

c. The students' use of the computer for word processing was independent of their knowledge of computer programming, $\chi^2(1, N=86) = 1.23, p > .25$.

d. The students' use of the computer for word processing was independent of their knowledge of computer programming, $X^2(1, N = 86)=1.23, p>.25$.

APA CODES: 5.14 & 3.58
INDEX NUMBER: 05
answer: b
RR-MASTERY 3 & 4

Edit the following for typing the title page:

EFFECTIVENESS OF TRAINING METHODS FOR MASTERING APA STYLE

Harold Gelfand and Charles J. Walker

St. Bonaventure University

a.   leave as is

b.

Effectiveness of Training Methods for Mastering APA Style

Harold Gelfand and Charles J. Walker

St. Bonaventure University

c.

Effectiveness of Training Methods for Mastering APA Style

Harold Gelfand and Charles J. Walker

St. Bonaventure University

d.

Effectiveness of Training Methods for Mastering APA Style

Harold Gelfand   Charles J. Walker

St. Bonaventure University   St. Bonaventure University

APA CODE: 5.15
INDEX NUMBER: 01
answer: b
RR-FAMILIARIZATION

A running head to be used in a research report should be typed
a.   centered at the bottom of the title page in all uppercase letters.
b.   flush left at the top of the title page.
c.   centered at the bottom of the title page in uppercase and lowercase letters.
d.   flush right at the bottom of the title page.

APA CODE: 5.15
INDEX NUMBER: 02
answer: a
RR-PRACTICE &
MASTERY 2

The title page includes the title,
a.   author, and abstract.
b.   author and institutional affiliation, short title, and the page number 1.
c.   author and institutional affiliation, running head, short title, and the page number 1.
d.   author and institutional affiliation, and abstract.

APA CODE: 5.15
INDEX NUMBER: 03
answer: c
RR-MASTERY 1

The title page of a manuscript includes the
a.   author's name.
b.   author's institutional affiliation.
c.   running head.
d.   short title.
e.   All of the above are included.

APA CODE: 5.15
INDEX NUMBER: 04
answer: e
RR-MASTERY 3

The abstract should be typed as
a.   a single paragraph in block format.
b.   one or more paragraphs with the first line indented.
c.   a single paragraph with the first line indented.
d.   more than one paragraph with space between paragraphs.

APA CODE: 5.16
INDEX NUMBER: 01
answer: a
RR-MASTERY 4

The abstract should
a.   appear on the same page above the title and introduction.
b.   be single-spaced and set within larger margins.
c.   begin on page 2.
d.   be no longer than 3% of the text.

APA CODE: 5.16
INDEX NUMBER: 02
answer: c
RR-FAMILIARIZATION

In the text of a manuscript, cite each table by
- a. writing instructions in the margin.
- b. putting a clear break in the text with the instruction "Insert Table _____ about here" set off by lines above and below.
- c. typing instructions in brackets.
- d. using the word *Table* and an arabic numeral.

APA CODE: 5.21
INDEX NUMBER: 01
answer: d
RR-PRACTICE

Choose the correct statement about the placing of a table in a manuscript:
- a. Type the table in full exactly in the place in the text where it should be printed.
- b. Type the table on the back of the page that first refers to it.
- c. Try to type all of the tables on the same page.
- d. Type each table on a separate page.

APA CODE: 5.21
INDEX NUMBER: 02
answer: d
RR-MASTERY 1

Table numbers and titles should be typed
- a. centered in uppercase and lowercase letters.
- b. single-spaced at the top of the table.
- c. flush with the left margin in uppercase and lowercase letters.
- d. according to a and b.

APA CODE: 5.21
INDEX NUMBER: 03
answer: c
RR-MASTERY 2 & 4

Edit the following for placement of a table in text:

Insert Table 99 about here

- a. leave as is
- b. A table insert should not be centered.
- c. The lines above and below the insert should be dotted.
- d. "Insert" instructions should be more precise. The word *about* should be deleted.
- e. It is not necessary to indicate table placement other than by citing it in text.

APA CODE: 5.21
INDEX NUMBER: 04
answer: e
RR-MASTERY 3

Edit the following figure caption:

Figure Caption

Figure 1. Clam Foot Extensions Before and After Escape Conditioning.

- a. leave as is
- b. The heading should be flush left.
- c. The caption should be indented five spaces.
- d. Only the first word and proper names should be capitalized in a figure caption.

APA CODE: 5.22
INDEX NUMBER: 01
answer: d
RR-EXTRA

With regard to the original manuscript, the author should
- a. retain it.
- b. submit it to the journal editors with the other copies.
- c. do either a or b.
- d. do none of the above.

APA CODE: 5.25
INDEX NUMBER: 01
answer: b
RR-EXTRA

The cover letter submitted with a manuscript should include
- a. verification that treatment of subjects was in compliance with APA ethical standards.
- b. the title and length of the manuscript.
- c. information about any closely related manuscripts.
- d. all of the above.
- e. none of the above.

APA CODE: 5.26
INDEX NUMBER: 01
answer: d
RR-EXTRA

The package in which the manuscript is mailed to an editor should include
- a. the original manuscript.
- b. the number of photocopies required by the journal.
- c. letters of permission to reproduce any copyrighted material.
- d. all of the above.
- e. none of the above.

APA CODE: 5.27
INDEX NUMBER: 01
answer: d
RR-EXTRA

While a manuscript is under consideration, inform the editor of
    a.   substantive corrections needed.
    b.   change of address.
    c.   revisions that could be made.
    d.   a and b.
    e.   none of the above.

APA CODE: 5.29
INDEX NUMBER: 01
answer: d
RR-EXTRA

Correspondence about copyediting and other production matters should be sent to
    a.   the journal editor.
    b.   the production editor.
    c.   the printer.
    d.   none of the above.

APA CODE: 7.03
INDEX NUMBER: 01
answer: b
RR-EXTRA

When reviewing the copyedited manuscript,
    a.   use a black pencil.
    b.   answer editor's queries and indicate changes in the margin or on the tags.
    c.   detail long responses or changes in a cover letter.
    d.   do all of the above.
    e.   do none of the above.

APA CODE: 7.03
INDEX NUMBER: 02
answer: d
RR-EXTRA

Limit changes on printed proofs to
    a.   corrections of printer's errors.
    b.   updates of reference citations.
    c.   textual revisions.
    d.   all of the above.
    e.   a and b.

APA CODE: 7.06
INDEX NUMBER: 01
answer: e
RR-EXTRA

A change made on a printed proof for a reason other than to achieve agreement with the manuscript
    a.   is not acceptable under any circumstances.
    b.   is considered an author's alteration and charged to the author.
    c.   must be resubmitted as if it were a new manuscript.
    d.   none of the above.

APA CODE: 7.07
INDEX NUMBER: 01
answer: b
RR-EXTRA

When checking a printed proof, write any special instructions or questions
    a.   in the side margins.
    b.   at the top of the page.
    c.   at the bottom of the page.
    d.   in an accompanying letter.

APA CODE: 7.07
INDEX NUMBER: 02
answer: d
RR-EXTRA

When you find an error on a printed proof,
    a.   make two marks, one in the text and one in the margin.
    b.   make one mark in the margin; do not mark the text.
    c.   make one mark in the text; do not write in the margin.
    d.   do none of the above.

APA CODE: 7.07
INDEX NUMBER: 03
answer: a
RR-EXTRA

Authors who publish articles in APA journals
    a.   are permitted to reproduce their own articles for personal use without obtaining permission from APA.
    b.   are permitted to reproduce their own articles for any purpose without obtaining permission from APA.
    c.   must obtain permission from APA to reproduce their own articles for any purpose.
    d.   none of the above

APA CODE: 7.09
INDEX NUMBER: 01
answer: a
RR-EXTRA

The author should retain data, instructions, details of procedure, and analyses for a minimum of
    a.   2 years after an article has been published.
    b.   5 years after an article has been published.
    c.   10 years after an article has been submitted.
    d.   10 years after an article has been published.

APA CODE: 7.10
INDEX NUMBER: 01
answer: b
RR-EXTRA

When an article carries two receipt dates, publication lag is calculated from the date of receipt for

    a.   the original manuscript.
    b.   the revision.
    c.   either a or b.
    d.   none of the above.

APA CODE: 8.03
INDEX NUMBER: 01
answer: b
RR-EXTRA

According to APA's policy of duplicate publication, an author must not submit a manuscript to an APA primary journal that

    a.   has been published in whole or in substantial part in any readily available work.
    b.   has been rejected by another journal.
    c.   is an elaboration of a dissertation thesis by the same author.
    d.   none of the above

APA CODE: 8.05
INDEX NUMBER: 01
answer: a
RR-EXTRA

An author

    a.   can submit the same manuscript for concurrent consideration by two or more journals as long as he or she withdraws the manuscript from consideration in other journals once it is accepted by a particular journal.
    b.   must not submit the same manuscript for concurrent consideration by two or more journals.
    c.   can submit a manuscript that has been rejected by one journal to another journal.
    d.   none of the above
    e.   b and c

APA CODE: 8.05
INDEX NUMBER: 02
answer: e
RR-EXTRA

The best way for an author to become familiar with each journal's specific context and any special instructions is to

    a.   write the editor of the journal for information.
    b.   examine the editorial policy statements and Instructions to Authors in a current issue of the journal.
    c.   consult the *Publication Manual* of the APA.
    d.   none of the above

APA CODE: 8.14
INDEX NUMBER: 01
answer: b
RR-EXTRA

In theses and dissertations, figures and tables

    a.   should be placed at the end of the paper.
    b.   may be placed at the appropriate point in the text.
    c.   should be placed in an appendix.
    d.   none of the above

APA CODE: 6.03
INDEX NUMBER: 01
answer: b
RR-EXTRA

In typing a dissertation or other final manuscript, it is important to remember that

    a.   the printed copy is final copy and so should be produced on durable paper.
    b.   the left-hand margin should be wide enough to allow for binding.
    c.   university requirements may take precedence over APA specifications.
    d.   all of the above
    e.   none of the above

APA CODE: 6.03
INDEX NUMBER: 02
answer: d
RR-EXTRA

Single-spacing may be used in theses and dissertations for

    a.   references.
    b.   table titles.
    c.   figure captions.
    d.   all of the above
    e.   none of the above

APA CODE: 6.03
INDEX NUMBER: 04
answer: d
RR-EXTRA

Request for Comments

We welcome your comments, suggestions, and feedback about your and your students' experiences with *Mastering APA Style*. Please send this form to the following address:

Director, Publication Development
APA Books
750 First Street, NE
Washington, DC 20002-4242
FAX (202) 336-5630

_____

_____

_____

_____

_____

_____

_____

_____

_____

_____

_____

Signature